M000203787

The
Heart of
Being
Hawaiian

Also by Sally-Jo Keala-o-Ānuenue Bowman

No Footprints in the Sand: A Memoir of Kalaupapa
with Henry Kalalahilimoku Nalaielua

The Heart of Being Hawaiian

by

Sally-Jo Keala-o-Ānuenue Bowman

Illustrations by Tamara Leiokanoe Moan

WATERMARK
PUBLISHING

© 2008 Sally-Jo Keala-o-Ānuenue Bowman

All rights reserved.
No part of this book may be reproduced in any form or by any electronic or
mechanical means, including information retrieval systems, without prior written
permission from the publisher, except for brief passages quoted in reviews.

ISBN 978-0-9815086-0-3

Library of Congress Control Number: 2008927050

Illustrations
Tamara Leiokanoe Moan

Design
Leo Gonzalez

Production
Wendy Wakabayashi

Watermark Publishing
1088 Bishop St., Suite 310
Honolulu, Hawaii 96813
Telephone 1-808-587-7766
Toll-free 1-866-900-BOOK
sales@bookshawaii.net
www.bookshawaii.net

Printed in the United States

He hoʻomanaʻo
In memory of

Mele Elemakule Pā Bowman, 1878-1911

Acknowledgments

I particularly laud my parents, my children and my husband: My mother, Ida May Larson Bowman, for teaching us to write as soon as we could hold a pencil • My father, Francis Moffett Bowman, for telling thousands of stories • My son, Rolf Kaleohanohano Moan, for showing me the way to be a poet • My daughter, Tamara Leiokanoe Moan, for convincing me I am a storyteller • My husband, David Walp, for his financial and emotional support in steadfastly encouraging me to seek my ancestral roots and write about being Hawaiian.

I also thank Kamehameha Schools for providing an education that allowed me to become a professional writer and, even more important, a Hawaiian writer.

Mahalo especially to Joan Lander and Puhipau of Nā Maka o ka ʻĀina, Kekuni Blaisdell, Scotty Bowman, Elizabeth Bond Bowman and Bill Souza, for encouragement, "talking story" and excellent ideas.

I thank the hundreds of people I have interviewed for freely sharing their immense knowledge with me. Those who helped in a major way with the pieces in this collection include Herb Kāne, Nainoa Thompson, Bill Laeha, Richard Paglinawan, Kapono Souza, Jim Bartels, Emmett Aluli, Henry Nalaielua, Noenoe Silva, Leilani Holmes, Bill Rezentes, Betty Jenkins, Leinaʻala Robinson Seeger, Bumpy Kanahele, John Kirkley, Steve Tayama, John Lake, Mākia Malo, Woody Fern, Nyla Fujii, Sam Kaʻai, Clifford Naeʻole, Kalani Meinecke, Māpuana and Kīhei de Silva, Hardy Spoehr, Dan Holmes, John Kaʻimikaua, Chad Baybayan, Jimmy Lewis, Margaret Machado, Ronald Dudoit, Jon Osorio, Charles P. Mahuka, Jr., David Kamiyama, Lovey Slater, Abbie Napeahi, Howard Peʻa, Richard Marks, Leroy and Toby Koyanagi, Chipper Wichman, Maile Meyer, Kamaki Kanahele, Tom Van Culin, Benjamin Young, George Makini, Keoni Agard, Joe Chang, Kaleo Patterson, Lolena Nicholas, Larry Kimura and David Eyre.

And I thank all the editors who let me run with story ideas and then took the time to help me push my writing beyond the merely good, particularly Cheryl Tsutsumi, Bill Harby and John Heckathorn.

Kala mai—forgive me—if I have left someone off this long list. I so appreciate the hundreds of contributions of time, insights and support.

Contents

Foreword

The Heart of Being Hawaiian is a voyage in words for native Hawaiians and for many others who carry Hawaiian values and care for things Hawaiian. It's about a journey. It's about seeking. It's about connecting to something deeply special about Hawai'i and the almost innate, instinctual need to be connected to our special island home. It's an extraordinary, beautiful and necessary voyage for all those seeking a deeper spiritual relationship with this special place.

The ports of call let us visit with practitioners of many Hawaiian disciplines—*hula*, chant, *lua*, *lomilomi*, *ho'oponopono*, language. We meet storytellers, a modern *kahuna*, a child growing *taro*. We learn about *heiau*, the ancient temples, and see children learning with *'olelo Hawai'i*, Hawaiian, as their first language. We are taken to the powerful places of Kalaupapa and Kaho'olawe, and we meet voyagers relearning the arts of building and sailing deep-sea voyaging canoes.

We are also taken on a journey of one woman's quest for her Hawaiian roots. I first met Sally-Jo Bowman in 1992, when she was working on the first of several articles about voyaging in double-hulled canoes. One afternoon she accompanied *Hōkūle'a*, Hawai'i's first voyaging canoe in hundreds of years, on a sail off the Honolulu coastline. Her questions seemed endless and she was always taking notes. Later, when the stories were published, I could see why. All of them were heavy with facts laid out in a concise and sensible way, but, better still, full of perceptive detail from observations she'd made—not only by looking, but by using all her senses. In talking with both crewmembers and canoe builders, she was able to draw out enough to recreate images and experiences we'd had months or years prior.

It occurs to me that, through her research and writing, she has in some ways had parallel experiences to those who have sailed thousands of miles on *Hōkūle'a* and Hawai'i's other voyaging canoes. She begins at home, faces challenges along the way, works hard, learns trust, gains a sense of pride, and returns home standing even stronger and prouder in who she is, a native Hawaiian.

Sally-Jo has a gift. Her words paint a vivid picture of *The Heart of Being Hawaiian*, while so adeptly conveying the intricacies of feelings and sensibilities.

Once Sally-Jo quoted me as saying, "We sail for the honor of us all." In *The Heart of Being Hawaiian*, she writes for the honor of us all.

Nainoa Thompson
Navigator
2008

Introduction

Huaka'i. It means "journey." When I started on the journey that has become this book, I had yet to learn the word *huaka'i.*

When I was nearing the end of the quest for my Hawaiian roots I met Kapono Souza, a young Hawaiian man who had decided in 2001 to model his own *huaka'i* on an ancient practice during the four-month Hawaiian winter. During those Makahiki months of peace and rest, an entourage of chiefs and priests circled their island on foot, stopping at villages for games, entertainments and feasts, and to collect annual tribute from the people. Wanting to understand the ancient rite, Kapono began what became his annual walk around O'ahu. Lacking a retinue, he did his *huaka'i* alone.

"At night," he said, "everything smells different, the *maile lau li'i*, the sea, the rain. I hear the ocean, the wind, the mongoose in the bush. These are the sounds the ancestors heard. They smelled the *maile*, the *pili* grass in Nānākuli. Night is the time when you can pick up on *hō'ailona*, signs, interpreting them in ways that make sense. It's a time of insight." What I learned from Kapono I wrote in "The Long Walk Home" on page 188.

The pieces of my own solo journey appear here as a collection of articles and essays about parts of modern Hawaiian culture. For me, and I hope for you, the group of writings offers insights as a cohesive whole. Only years after the last of them had appeared, in nine magazines and three anthologies, was I able to see that they should be arranged not in order of when I wrote them, but in themes that revealed layers of the Hawaiian heart.

The figurative and indeliberate route of my *huaka'i* twisted and turned as it went along, like the Old Pali Road I traversed many times as a Kailua kid on the grand, infrequent adventure of "going to town." At first, all I knew for sure was my desire to write about a culture I felt I didn't know well enough, even though I was quarter Hawaiian and a graduate of Kamehameha Schools.

In the beginning, not only did I not know the meaning

of "*huaka'i*," I did not even set off on a quest. My intention was to become a full-time freelance magazine writer. But I unconsciously put myself on this particular path in 1984 when I finished a Journalism Master's Degree at the University of Oregon with a lengthy final writing project called "On the Winds of Kanaloa: Rebirth of the Hawaiian People."

At that time I had already lived on the mainland U.S. for 26 years, first at the University of Minnesota following my 1958 graduation from Kamehameha Schools, and then in Oregon. I did come back to Hawai'i every summer during college to work as a cub reporter for the *Honolulu Star-Bulletin*, and then every couple of years to visit my parents for a week or two. It wasn't enough, but I didn't know that then.

When I did the "Winds of Kanaloa" field research in Hawai'i, my first interview was with Adelaide "Frenchy" DeSoto, who had recently badgered the state legislature into creating the Office of Hawaiian Affairs. She had much to say on the subject of the so-called Hawaiian Renaissance, but what affected me most was her huge hug. Had the *honi* been relearned then, she might have stunned me with the nose-to-nose greeting, which, at that time, I had never experienced. Her hug had a similar effect. Having lived away so long, I felt like a foreigner, and I didn't expect such warmth from a woman I had never met. Her *aloha* filled the air. I felt so accepted and loved that my eyes filled with tears.

I'd been a journalist since high school days, always in the employ of some corporate or educational entity. When I finished my long master's tome, my goal was full-time freelance writing. For several years, I fit freelancing around working at a regular job, hustling assignments from local and regional magazines in Oregon, going out on the full-time freelance limb in 1991. When I was home in Hawai'i for a visit in late 1988, I attended a concert by the Makaha Sons, a benefit for some preschool. The school turned out to be Pūnana Leo, the then-new Hawaiian-language immersion preschool. In 1988 I'd never heard of Pūnana Leo—but I recognized it as a story idea, which I suggested to *Aloha* magazine. I got the assignment, my first on a Hawaiian topic. The article, "Pūnana Leo: Saving the Hawaiian Language," appears on page 131.

The whole time I'd been away from Hawai'i, "aboriginal twinges" called to me. I had grown up in Kailua, O'ahu, very near the beach. When I went away, I often dreamed of being in the ocean.

I was a kid in the '40s and '50s, a time when it still was not cool to be Hawaiian. My half-Hawaiian father and his siblings were born in the first decade of the 20th century, the first generation not born in the Kingdom or its predecessors, the several island chiefdoms. They were Americans of the Territory of Hawaii, created in 1900. Under what must have been an uncertain and unsettling political and social climate, at least to adults, their family and lots of others left the Hawaiian language behind, along with many customs and much knowledge.

Kamehameha, my school from seventh through twelfth grade, even though instituted for Hawaiian children, sought to make us thoroughly American. Which I was. Except for those twinges and a gaping hole in my heart.

After the Pūnana Leo story, I consciously—and self-consciously, because I wasn't sure about how I would be received, despite Frenchy DeSoto—pursued article assignments to learn about being Hawaiian as well as to write about specific topics. I learned about *hula, heiau,* the Hawaiian diet. I spent three days on Kahoʻolawe during January *Makahiki* ceremonies, addressed a personal health problem through *lomilomi,* sailed for an afternoon on the voyaging canoe *Hōkūleʻa.* Eventually I came to know dozens of people in the Hawaiian community. They all welcomed me, especially after I learned to approach any Hawaiian by placing myself in my family, school and community. I think it is today's version of what some have told me was the ancient recitation of genealogy between strangers until they came to a point of commonality. Never mind the journalism degrees and writing achievements. I am the younger Pierre Bowman's older sister, Uncle Wright's niece, Scotty's cousin. I am KS '58. I am Kailua, Oʻahu. Now we can talk.

In a few years, with dozens more Hawaiian articles in print, a significant vestige of the heart *puka* nevertheless remained. Then, in Hilo in late 1997, I met Aunty Abbie Napeahi and Uncle Howard Peʻa. For yet another article, I wanted to learn about the Hawaiian conflict resolution process called *hoʻoponopono.* They were practitioners through the Hawaiian social services agency Alu Like. They answered my questions. But they also saw right into the *puka* in my heart. How they gave me their down-to-earth blessing is detailed in the opening essay, "Aloha, Anuhea," starting on page 2. The *hoʻoponopono* piece,

"Setting Things Right," starts on page 146.

For years before I decided to freelance, my professional training in journalism had me keeping my views and orientation out of reporting. But the magazine world is somewhat different, and the Hawaiian world is the opposite. The more projects I took on, the sharper my personal Hawaiian senses became. One of my best editors told me he never wanted to see a piece that didn't have me in it. Someone else told me I was always in my articles even if I never used the word "I." Eventually I wrote occasional essays that weren't based on research but instead were totally about my own experience. Several of these various pieces won Pa'i awards from the Hawai'i Publishers' Association. But my most treasured praise was five words from Noa Emmett Aluli, the Moloka'i doctor who is perhaps the best known Hawaiian activist and with whom I worked on some major assignments. I bumped into Emmett some months after the publication of "Kaho'olawe in Limbo" (see page 150). He hugged me—there it was again! *Aloha* hug! And he said, "The Kaho'olawe piece was great. *Your writing is so Hawaiian.*"

His compliment meant more to me than money, awards or any other accolades. *So Hawaiian.* Those words signaled the beginning of a confidence and gratitude that I was at last finding the Hawaiian: both Hawaiian culture, history and values *and* myself as a Hawaiian.

That was in 1993. Soon, I hit a stride. In 2002 I wrote "Inescapably Hawaiian," the last piece in this collection. In retrospect, it represents *huliau*—another word I learned along the way, which means "turning point" or "time of change." I wrote only two more Hawaiian culture articles after that. The last was the profile of Kapono Souza, "The Long Walk Home."

In the months following its publication in 2004, I felt in my *na'au*—my heart and guts—that I was done writing Hawaiian articles, even though I certainly had not written on every possible topic. But it wasn't until I was arranging the best of my magazine pieces to make the most sense as a book that I saw that I had been working piecemeal on a quilt, and had come to a point where I could see the whole thing.

I am the keeper of a frail antique Hawaiian quilt. My Hawaiian grandmother, Mele Elemakule Pā Bowman, made it around the turn of the 20th century, when the Hawaiian Kingdom had been overthrown and Hawai'i was being annexed by the United States. Her fragile, hand-stitched quilt lies folded in a suitably antique trunk, where I see only a small part of it. The red cotton design portraying leaves of the *'ulu*—breadfruit—has faded, and its white background has yellowed with a century of age. The old cotton batting shows through small *puka* where the fabric has simply disintegrated.

The quilt is too delicate to keep out. And yet, one day a year or so after I wrote about Kapono Souza and his *huaka'i*, I laid that quilt upon my bed where I could see the whole thing. That night I slept under it.

Just recently I have seen that I had been stitching a figurative quilt folded over my lap, words substituting for bits of fabric, my pen working as the needle. With that last story, I metaphorically laid the quilt of words upon my bed and saw my work as a whole. In some places this quilt remains unfinished, but it is complete enough.

The magazine articles and essays are *pau* because I am at that *huliau*, a time of change. But with every end comes a new beginning. The pieces here are the gift of the *huaka'i*, for me, and for you. They are roots, and with the care of a calm and grateful heart, flowers and fruit are sure to follow.

Sally-Jo Bowman
Keala-o-Ānuenue, The Path of the Rainbow
2008

1

Heart of the Matter

❧

Grief, healing, blood ties
and discovering what's important

༄

Aloha, Anuhea

1997

Her name was Anuhea. The last time I saw her, she had given me something as important as life itself. But it took me 40 years to accept it as my own.

In Hilo in May of 1995, I met Hawaiian *kūpuna* Aunty Abbie Napeahi and Uncle Howard Pe'a when I was researching an article on the spiritually based Hawaiian family counseling process *ho'opono-pono*. Aunty Abbie carefully explained the steps of *ho'oponopono*, from finding the core problem to forgiving all parties involved and cutting loose from the pain. And then, part-way through the interview, she gently shifted the focus from *ho'oponopono* to me.

Aunty Abbie asked me to lay before them the problem deepest in my heart, the one giving me the most pain in my life. In my mind I quickly reeled through classic candidates: Money. Marriage. Family. None of them seemed to warrant *ho'oponopono*.

Then I did the bravest thing I've ever done. For the first time, I named out loud the gaping, lifelong hole in my heart: "Although I am Hawaiian by blood, I'm not sure I am a worthy Hawaiian."

I told them my Hawaiian school's mission had been to turn us into *haole*. My *haole* mother and Hawaiian father both had done the same.

My mind reeled off more reasons: I knew no more than a couple hundred isolated words of my language. I didn't even look very Hawaiian. My Hawaiian grandmother had died when my father was a baby, and no one ever passed down to us the knowledge of our guardian spirits, the *'aumākua*. Pain flooded me as if I had ripped a bandage from an open wound.

I did not voice my last, dark secret: I didn't have a proper Hawaiian name, one my family gave me. Without a Hawaiian name, I thought I had no lineage, no place with my ancestors, no heritage: I was nobody. The fact had burst forever into my consciousness when I first enrolled at Kamehameha Schools in the seventh grade. Unlike public school, where my class had only three Hawaiians, all 400 girls at Kamehameha were Hawaiian. Almost all my classmates had both

English and Hawaiian given names.

In 10th grade, in the fall of 1955, Anuhea Nahale-ā brought my problem to the surface. She and I, and about 40 other sophomores, boarded in Dorm K at the top of the Kapālama Heights campus.

About four o'clock one rare afternoon when we were free from the dorm's scheduled after-school tasks like washing and ironing, Anuhea asked me to cut her hair. She'd asked me to do this several times before, though we weren't in the same academic section and didn't know each other very well.

That day she sat in my room with a towel clipped around her neck with a wooden spring clothespin. As I snipped at her unruly waves, she said, "Eh, what's your Hawaiian name?"

I could barely admit I didn't have one.

She said matter-of-factly, "I give you one." She didn't speak again until just before the haircut was over. "Keala-o-Ānuenue," she said. "The Path of the Rainbow."

The name was beautiful, in sound and in concept. I didn't dare ask why she chose it for me. I loved it. But in the back of my mind I thought I mustn't use it because my parents hadn't given it to me. "Keala-o-Ānuenue" felt *kapu* to me. I would be a thief to call myself The Path of the Rainbow. So I didn't use the name. But I couldn't forget it.

After we graduated, I went away to college in Minnesota, where people thought Hawai'i was a foreign country. Occasionally, one of the more worldly people asked me about my Hawaiian name. "Keala-o-Ānuenue. The Path of the Rainbow." And I explained that Anuhea had given it to me, aching in my heart because it wasn't a "real" name. The ache became bigger—an elusive, ghostly void. By the time I was 30, sometimes I wept from the chronic pain, but still I did not know its source. I had moved to Oregon and was visiting Hawai'i more often—a mixed blessing, for in Hawai'i I was far more likely to meet someone who would ask the dreaded question that had become the symbol of my grieving heart. I could lie and say I didn't have a Hawaiian name. But I wanted my name. Yet, each time I spoke it, I always added the disclaimer: I got the name at school.

I mentioned none of the name agony to Aunty Abbie and Uncle Howard. My doubtful worth as a Hawaiian was enough.

Now the room filled with Aunty Abbie's *mana*, her life force, her spiritual power. I felt like I was swimming safely in a deep ocean of no-nonsense love.

"You must stop blaming your parents and your school," she said, touching my arm and looking deep into my *puka* heart with her wise eyes. "Look at what they did give you. They gave you the power to write, the power to do your work. Let go of the blame. And never use it for an excuse again."

Instantly I felt myself do exactly as she said. I began to weep in relief. The time had come for the *puka* to heal.

Uncle Howard asked my Hawaiian name. "Keala-o-Ānuenue," I said, barely able to speak. "Oh, yes, The Path of the Rainbow," he replied, calmly accepting something I hadn't been able to accept for myself. Tears poured down my face. And then Uncle Howard and Aunty Abbie folded me up in their arms and their hearts and told me the name was a special gift—a gift of honor, a name I had grown into, for I had become a writer with the power to touch people's hearts, a writer who writes about Hawaiians, who are the heart of the rainbow.

And then they said, "Welcome home, Keala-o-Ānuenue."

In the weeks that followed, I came to understand that 40 years earlier, on the day of the haircut, Anuhea had given me the answer to the question I had spent my life asking myself: Who am I? All I had to do was grow into the answer, bare my heart, accept the truth of the gift. Now I can speak the simple answer. I am Keala-o-Ānuenue.

I know now in my heart that our Hawaiian names are metaphors bundled in multiple meanings that we grow into. However we receive them, our names are a means by which we know we belong to our homeland, our *ʻāina*.

My name is Keala-o-Ānuenue, The Path of the Rainbow. I thank Anuhea for the name I have become.

◦৵〉

OUT FOR BLOOD

1999

Kailua twilight. Beneath mauve clouds in a pale sky, my niece stands in ceremony in the sand, marrying a Boston Irish man. High tide surges just beyond the *lau hala* mat under their bare feet.

The roar of the surf snatches most of the words, bits of Robert Frost, American Indian wisdom and Hawaiian chant.

I rejoice for my only Hawaiian niece and for her Irish man. But my heart sorrows, too, here on the sand where both she and I grew up, for she is our fourth generation to out-marry.

Ninety-five years ago—1902 in Haili Church in Hilo—her great-grandmother, Mele Elemakule Pā, married the first Bowman, an adventurer from Ohio. And on that day in April, our family stepped onto the long, muddy *ti* leaf slide to ethnic oblivion. I am in no position to chide my niece. I am not merely the pot calling the kettle black. I am a double-boiler pot, for I married *haole* men twice. Some in our family have married part-Chinese, part-Korean, part-Japanese, Filipino, Portuguese. In 95 years, only one besides my grandfather married a full-blood Hawaiian, only a few married other part-Hawaiians. If my niece has a child, the *keiki* will be only 1/16 Hawaiian.

I weep with this thought. But I am of the age of weeping, and she is not. Only the older heart seeks the past and worries about the future.

Our Pā lineage has gone the way of most Hawaiian families. Now we have so little blood quantum, we don't think about land entitlements. But I do think about blood, especially since last year when Office of Hawaiian Affairs *kupuna* Betty Jenkins told me this story:

Her job-hunting son, perhaps in his mid-30s, had recently asked her to compose his résumé. She did a singular job. He came to look it over. The computer design looked great. The information sang his praises well. But he pointed to the last section: Personal Data.

"I don't like this. It says I'm a quarter Hawaiian," he said.

The ghost of racial shame flashed in his mother's mind. But

before she could lecture him about ethnic pride, he added, "I want it to say 'Hawaiian.'"

Our blood is dwindling. But what about our identity? My quest for answers led to Hawaiian sorrow and anger and pride and, most of all, to the open hearts that are at once the greatest strength of Hawaiians and the very reason for our decreasing blood.

We all know the tiresome political and legal facts: The Hawaiian Homelands Act of 1921 established a blood quantum of 50 percent to qualify for homestead awards on 200,000 acres set aside for that purpose. In 1959, the Statehood Admissions Act ceded from federal to state jurisdiction another 1.6 million acres that had been government and crown lands under the monarchy. The ceded lands are mandated for five purposes, one of which is for the benefit of "native Hawaiians" as defined by the Homelands Act. Office of Hawaiian Affairs programs funded by ceded lands monies are subject to that same blood quantum requirement, although OHA supports doing away with it.

The original rub has remained the biggest: administration of the Department of Hawaiian Homelands. From the get-go, little of the 200,000 acres was awarded to Hawaiians, and The List (as in "waiting list") is something Hawaiians speak of as a bureaucratic rendition of purgatory.

Mindful of 77 years of this, Bill Souza, project coordinator for the Native Hawaiian Community-Based Learning Center at Leeward Community College, said to me, "We're getting pain and suffering and whimpering and whining. But no *mana'o*—no meaning. The political issue ties us up in knots and there's no reality to it."

Reality. *Mana'o*. When you eliminate the morass of politics and law, what does blood quantum mean?

"When you have a name like Souza, you're just it," he says. "I just accepted being Portuguese. Never confessed to being Hawaiian."

But about 1983 he volunteered for the advisory board of Alu Like, the Hawaiian job training and social service agency. Later he joined in John Waihe'e's first campaign for governor. "In places like

Kohala and Wai'ōhinu in Ka'ū, Hawaiians greeted John wailing. They composed chants that said 'In this time and place someone Hawaiian comes.' For me, it was chicken skin to be walking with him."

Later Souza joined the Royal Order of Kamehameha— founded in 1865 by Kamehameha V, declared seditious in 1893 by the Provisional Government and reinstituted in 1903 by Prince Kūhiō in a torchlight ceremony at midnight.

Another ceremony put Souza over the top as a Hawaiian: Onipa'a, the 1993 three-day observance of the centennial of the over-throw of the Hawaiian monarchy. At least 20,000 Hawaiians jammed the grounds of 'Iolani Palace, a quantum fact that made much of Honolulu uneasy.

"There were SWAT teams on rooftops," Souza remembers. "But there was no need. I was in an ocean of people re-baptizing them-selves as Hawaiians. It was a passion play in the streets of Honolulu. It was not evil, nasty or militant, but people finding their place on the soil. Nobody in Kāhala got killed, nobody got robbed in Waikīkī, no one was arrested in the name of Hawaiians. Even then I didn't know my blood quantum. But I learned that Hawaiians embrace you if you're even one drop. Are we reading the epitaph of a culture? I think not. In our language classes at Leeward, it's the hapa-haole who want to regain the heritage. Language is giving them an arma-ment, a mantle of pride."

While we talked in a courtyard at LCC, his boss, Lucy Gay, trundled along the walkway.

"Meet Pierre Bowman's sister," Souza said. Pierre was a writer for the Honolulu Star-Bulletin until his death in 1986.

"Oh!" said Gay, and sat down. "I used to be a Medrano, from Kona."

And so began a repeated process, a prelude to giving mana'o. Someone's sister, daughter, cousin. Someone from a certain family somewhere. If we go back far enough, we will be related. It's the latter-day version of chanting genealogy to a stranger to establish relationship before speaking.

Souza described my question. What does blood quantum have to do with being Hawaiian?

Gay is Filipino-Hawaiian-Portuguese, and the only Hawaiian administrator in the community college system. Or one of three or four Filipino administrators.

"It's a dilemma," she says. "Here at the college we have to choose where we place ourselves. What am I? How do I support the Hawaiian cause? If I declare myself to be Filipino, it's evidence of no Hawaiian administrators in the system. Do we want to declare Hawaiian success or be clever and sly like the white man and milk the system?"

Gay is fiercely aware of her multiple heritages, and staunchly Hawaiian. I can't quite tell if it pains her that her half-*haole* son declares, "I'm an American."

Souza led me next to Alika McNicoll, one of the Hawaiian language *kumu*—teachers—on his staff. Alika immediately said, "So you're Wright Bowman's niece."

Alika grew up on Hawaiian Homelands in Nānākuli, fabled enclave of Hawaiians. Now 25, he spent his high school years being cool according to the American television model, driving around at night cussing from his open car window, reggae and rap booming from his car speakers. When he enrolled at LCC, his father advised fulfilling his language requirement with Japanese. Good in the tourist industry, you know.

Instead Alika registered for Hawaiian.

"In that class, I realized, 'Hey, I am Hawaiian.' Who's to say you're not Hawaiian if you're not 50 percent?"

At the University of Hawai'i now, he's part of a group of art students pushing for a class from a Polynesian perspective. His work appeared recently in "Ho'okū'ē: To Resist," a show of 20 native Hawaiian artists at the East-West Center. His piece depicted the current resurgence of Hawaiian language after its ban for much of this century.

Those bygone times came up the next day at my Uncle Wright's Nu'uanu home. His wife, Betty, grew up in Wai'ōhinu in Ka'ū. Although the children were a quarter Hawaiian and spoke both English and Hawaiian, her parents forbade them to play with "the natives." Perhaps those "natives" were the very ones to chant to John Waihe'e 60 years later on his stop at Wai'ōhinu.

But I digress. At Kamehameha School for Girls in the '20s, Aunty Betty was part of the "quarter-Hawaiian gang." The pure Hawaiians ridiculed them by calling them *haole*. When she enrolled at UH in 1931, her English aunts in Mānoa cautioned her: "Never tell anyone you are Hawaiian."

During that time of shame, some falsified documents—in the opposite direction from now, when people want to prove more Hawaiian blood than they have. But for a bogus birth certificate showing his full-blood Hawaiian mother as Chinese-Hawaiian, documentary producer Puhipau of Nā Maka o Ka ʻAina would be eligible for Hawaiian Homelands. But it matters not to him.

"You get on The List to die," he says. "To hell with the list. Just go get on the land."

He knows he's Hawaiian and that's enough.

Enough, too, for OHA trustee Haunani Apoliona. I met her at her office. Immediately she introduced me to her assistant as Pierre Bowman's sister.

She is from a Chinese-Hawaiian family that celebrated being Hawaiian. "Blood quantum was not discussed as a measurement," she told me. "My parents never said, 'This is Hawaiian.' They just lived their values and philosophy. It's what's inside that counts—and environment shapes that. Land needs to be part of the equation for Hawaiians.

"In the big picture, the issue of blood quantum may evolve. In Aotearoa—New Zealand—Maori is Maori. Being Hawaiian is living in harmony with the environment, getting along with each other. Today the challenge is struggling to live these values into the 21st century."

For Jon Osorio, blood quantum is not one of those values. I met him at the UH Department of Hawaiian Studies, where he teaches. He had a new identity quiz for me: Was I a Kamehameha graduate? Yes? Yes. As good as family.

"For some of us," he told me, "Land access and ownership is not the issue. We know our history, we speak our language, we teach our culture.

"From the middle of the 19th century, there were *hapa*—mixed bloods—of all kinds. In the 1860s, Queen Emma was a popular figure, and she was a quarter *haole*. The fact is, Hawaiians never discriminated on the basis of blood quantum."

Osorio echoes many when he says blood quantum "was devised by the federal government to practically assure that the Hawaiian Homelands would be awarded only for a generation or two."

"Ha!" attorney Bruss Keppeler says, after we go through the identity protocol. A Punahou graduate, he tries to recall which

Bowmans went to his school.

"At the turn of the 20th century, we'd been literally deci-mated," he says. "Reduced to a tenth."

In 1920, local *haole* supporters of Prince Kūhiō's Hawaiian Homelands bill wanted a 100-percent blood quantum requirement. Kūhiō wanted none. He offered 1/32. The ultimate compromise was 50 percent.

"It was to make sure the beneficiary class started small and stayed small," Keppeler says. "But ha! Instead, Hawaiians prolifer-ated—in part because of the program. Kūhiō was a sharp old codger. He created ghettos that put Hawaiian boys and girls together. We've exploded to 250,000 now."

But Keppeler, long a leader of the Hawaiian Civic Clubs origi-nated by Kūhiō as a support for his Hawaiian Homelands legislation, is scared. The Bush administration's solicitor general issued an opinion in 1992 that the Hawaiian Homelands program is unconstitutional because it discriminates on the basis of race. Governor Waihe'e had the opinion withdrawn. But that could be temporary.

"This is more of a specter than I'd like to believe," Keppeler says. "Blood quantum would be irrelevant. The opinion would affect everything. Hawaiian Homelands, OHA, ceded lands, any public programs for Hawaiians of any amount of blood, like Alu Like, with funding through the Native American Programs Act. Chicken Little can also raise the question of private trusts giving preference on racial lines. We have some pretty big fish to fry here. We'd better stop argu-ing about blood quantum and save the programs."

He sees blood quantum as a *haole* device to divide and con-quer. It did major damage, but it didn't work. "Now Hawaiians are 19 percent of the general population but 25 percent of public school children. We've got young, big families. That means political clout."

And future leadership. Ka'ohua Lucas in Pālolo Valley clearly is what Keppeler is talking about. Now 38, she works for Nā Pua No'eau, a program for gifted and talented Hawaiian children. She schemes to form a land *hui*—a group—to raise *kalo* and to fish.

Ironically, she says, "My Hawaiian father told us to beat the *haole* at their own game, to learn their ways and not think about being Hawaiian. It was my mother, a *haole* from Texas, who made sure we went to Kamehameha Schools."

Ka'ohua knows full well blood-quantum history. Her two

young sons are 3/16 Hawaiian, children of a second marriage to a fourth-generation *kama'āina haole* Ka'ohua calls "a Hawaiian in a white body." Auli'i, her first child, is 5/16.

"I don't regret not being 50 percent. I don't ever think of how much Hawaiian blood a person has. No matter how much or how little, you're still Hawaiian."

Yet, as I walk out her door into a noontime shimmering in the stillness of Kona heat, she says, "You know what we need? A Hawaiian sperm bank."

Indeed. In another parting shot, Jon Osorio advocated reinstituting polygamy.

A Kamehameha classmate tried to enumerate her blood quantum in sixteenths, lost count, and said, "Oh, whatever." Moments later, she lamented that, of her three married children, none has a Hawaiian mate. The lone bachelor son, she says, is "her only hope."

Blood matters. Maybe not the quantum, but it matters. Why else do I anguish as I watch my niece vow to be the Boston Irish man's wife?

I worry: Can we keep our Hawaiian hearts as our noses grow sharper or smaller, our lips thinner, our skins paler? My hope for our future as Hawaiians is going down the *haole* husband tube.

But after the ceremony I hug the Irish man, John. Really hug him. And he says softly, close to my tearful face, "Maybe I'm just a *manini*—tiny—part Hawaiian now."

And I reply without hesitation, "It will grow."

Later I look up *koko* in the dictionary, a word common now, but seldom heard a generation ago. *Koko*. Blood, the dictionary says. And after a semicolon it says "rainbow-hued."

I start to sort my sheaves of notes, then ruffle through my in-basket of miscellany, in case something important lurks there. In the very bottom I find a quote I copied months ago, long before I had even an inkling of questing for blood.

On a scrap of paper I had scrawled these words from David Kalākaua, king of Hawai'i, 1874-1891: "Remember who you are. Be gracious, but never forget from whence you came, for this is where your heart is. This is the cradle of life."

&

A Statistician's Nightmare

Hawai'i might have 220,000 Hawaiians among its 1.1 million residents. Then again, maybe the figure is 140,000. Or 208,000. Of those, perhaps 4 percent are full bloods, perhaps 35 percent have half or more Hawaiian blood. Then again, maybe not.

"The figures are extremely conflicting," says retired state statistician Robert Schmitt. "The U.S. Census Bureau says to mark the race of your mother or that with which you identify closely. It doesn't say anything about 'part Hawaiian.' The Hawai'i Health Surveillance Program looks at Hawaiian and part-Hawaiian categories, and asks respondents to mark the race of their grandparents. From that they extract numbers of pure and part Hawaiians.

"But nobody really knows. It's statistical chaos. And it's not just Hawaiians. Everybody is chop suey these days. Twenty percent of the population is mixed blood other than part-Hawaiian, like Chinese-Filipino. We're into third- and fourth-generation intermarriages. Racial statistics are so meaningless we should abandon them. They're just hash."

⨖

RAGE, BONES AND HOPE

1995

I first interviewed Charles Mahuka last August, as a success story. He had entered a social service program that pairs Hawaiian parolees and probationers with elders—*kūpuna*—skilled in traditional counseling, and was one of the program's most notable successes. Nobody—neither Mahuka, not anyone who knew him, nor I—would have guessed that within two months, Mahuka would be arrested in the beating and subsequent death of a student in an anger-management class he taught.

In August, when I talked to him, Charlie Mahuka had been on parole for 15 months. He told his story freely, never making any excuse for the years of crime and violence that had preceded his prison term. He credited Leialoha Haleamau, his *kupuna* since his release from prison, with helping him find honorable, nonviolent ways to deal with trouble, with always being available to him. He seemed truly thankful to be home, out of prison, and was clearly working to keep it that way. He seemed centered, spiritual. "My ʻāina is where I belong," he said.

When I heard of his October arrest, my Western-educated mind was shocked. But, like Charlie, I am Hawaiian. I also reacted, involuntarily, in a way I had never experienced before. My body told me how important Charlie Mahuka was. My bones grew so heavy I couldn't sit up. I lay down on the floor, where my skeleton seemed to sink beneath my flesh. Did this have to do with a Hawaiian reverence for bones? What did it mean? And what did Charlie's arrest mean, for him, for the family of the man who died, for his students, for the anger-management and *kūpuna* programs? I lay on the floor, as if anchored to the ʻāina by my bones. And I wondered all these things, certain only that Charlie Mahuka dramatically embodies a particularly Hawaiian triumph and tragedy.

Notoriety came hard and fast for Mahuka. His arrest October 9 on charges of manslaughter filled Honolulu's news for days. The irony of the crime—an anger-management instructor beating a drunk student in the parking lot outside the classroom—caught the attention of the national press, and the news about Mahuka zipped around the nation on the wire services and CNN.

Yet the irony goes way beyond the incident, back into the pain and hope in a life that had apparently turned from a pattern of violence into a path of peace. And the ironies stretch forward, into the Oʻahu Community Corrections Center where Mahuka, at 39, awaits trial on manslaughter charges. Within hours of his arrival at the facility a week after his arrest, center officials asked him to teach a Hawaiian language class for other inmates. And they asked him to help run an anger-management group.

Within two days of his arrest, Mahuka's students—young men given to physical violence—spoke publicly of how he'd taught them better ways to deal with problems, of how to take life one step at a time. They called him humble and soft-spoken, and considered him a role model. Perhaps the best sort of role model, for Mahuka was one of them, living most of his adult life as constant *hakakā*, one fight after another. The fights punctuated nonstop drinking and drugs that had begun when he was a school kid.

Last August, his parole officer, Charles Sizemore, said, "I hear from his former peers who have known him for years that he used to be one mean son of a gun. But they also say he has become a totally different person. It's apparent to me that he's concerned with changing his life, not just with staying out of jail."

The news of Mahuka's October arrest grieved Sizemore. "I would have bet my life savings on Charlie," he says. "He's always been mellow, polite, laid back. I'm shocked. It's sad. He was a man at peace with himself, a real nice guy full of compassion for his fellow man. If this comes to a trial or a conviction, I'll be a witness for his character."

Mahuka had first faced life in Hālawa Correctional Facility in the mid-1980s, when he was serving a 10-year attempted murder sentence for using a spear-gun to shoot a *haole* who had angered him. He'd previously racked up 13 arrests, and had served time earlier for armed robbery. While he was in Hālawa, Mahuka's youngest uncle, and then a *hānai*—adopted—sister died. "I was locked up and couldn't go." He still remembers the depth of his sorrow, based in the visceral Hawaiian tie to family. Under the circumstances, a violent reaction was out. Instead, he began to think. About being Hawaiian. What did it mean?

About six years into that sentence, Mahuka was transferred from Oʻahu to the Big Island's Kūlani Correctional Facility. There a few other Hawaiians asked him to teach them Hawaiian language. He coached them as far as he could, then wrote to Alu Like and the Office of Hawaiian Affairs asking for someone to teach them further. Alu Like responded. When Mahuka was paroled in May 1994 after serving eight years, he went immediately to Alu Like, which had helped him before.

"Auntie Lei started with me," he recalls. "My problem was facing society, being angry, being rejected, being lots of things. She worked with me, comforted me, gave me encouragement."

From a halfway house he moved home, to an aunt's Nānākuli Hawaiian homestead, where dozens of his ʻohana come and go. He joined Alcoholics Anonymous, and met Hyimeen Grilho, the anger-management instructor who later trained him to help lead a new men's group in Waiʻanae, E ʻImi Kākou Ke Kahua Ma Ke Ola, "Let Us Seek the Foundation to Life."

Mahuka's redemptive life then, and the tragic events of October, point up a major problem among Hawaiians—they comprise nearly 40 percent of Hawaiʻi's prison population, but account for less than six percent of the general population over the age of 18. The dismal statistics grow worse: Two-thirds of those released on parole end up back in prison, most often because of alcohol and drug problems.

In 1990 Alu Like tried to combat this recidivism with the Kūpuna Outreach Facilitator Program. Now, among the program's clients, the repeat offense rate has dropped from 60 percent to three percent.

Unfortunately last October, Charlie Mahuka, who seemed one of the program's biggest successes, joined the three percent. But, says program administrator David Kamiyama, who knows Mahuka personally, "Alu Like's services are always open to him. He made so much progress in his time on parole. He made the transition back to his family, he stayed away from drinking and drugs. He was very well liked, a quiet guy who wanted to share, a guy who really became spiritual. We don't condone what he did, but it's not right to abandon him now. We'll go to court for him."

Meanwhile, Auntie Lei visits Mahuka twice a month in prison, continuing their *kūkākūkā*, the discussions of the past year and a half. *Kūkākūkā* is one of the techniques of the *kūpuna*, members of the grandparent generation.

Like Alu Like's other five *kūpuna* on Oʻahu, Molokaʻi and the Big Island, Auntie Lei is trained in both Hawaiian and Western approaches to counseling. The *kūpuna*—venerated by Hawaiians—root their work in the ancient Hawaiian concepts and practices of *lōkahi*, harmony, and *hoʻoponopono*, "to set right."

"In our Offender/Ex-Offender Project we saw that Western-style counseling wasn't working," says Kamiyama. "Counselors go in saying, 'How can I help?' The *kūpuna* begin with genealogy, until there's a bond. They don't specifically target alcohol and drug abuse, but it comes out in their holistic, spiritual approach."

When you meet *kūpuna* Uncle Howard Peʻa and Auntie Abbie Napeahi, they seem more like grandparents than counselors, grandparents who love you no matter what but won't let you get away with anything. What might at first seem like small talk is crucial: Where is your family from? Who's your father, your uncle, your *ʻohana?* In moments they find family threads that link you to them. To Hawaiians, that's not an intellectual curiosity, but the entire basis of trust, an unbreakable bond of blood.

From the first, they lean forward, closing the space that Western counselors maintain. They touch you, a gentle hand on your arm, perhaps. And they look right into your eyes, reading you as if you have no skin. Even if you bug out on *kūpuna* counseling, even if you can keep up a wall of denial, sooner or later, in the back of your mind, you'll be answering to them. And the only answer is the truth.

Their process is deceptively simple.

"*Hoʻoponopono* is looking at yourself," says Auntie Abbie. "The past, you cannot do nothing about it. Take it out and throw away the experience, and put in its place something positive."

She and Uncle Howard liken past problems to layers of an onion, to be peeled away one by one. Spouse. Job. Childhood. Bad habits. The task is *kūkulu kumuhana*—to lay out clearly so everyone understands. The problems are *hihia*—entanglements.

"We're thorough," says Auntie Abbie. "The entanglements are like fish caught in a net. This is where the client gets scared. And where we can find if he's telling the truth or lying."

She probes, gently, peeling away the layers, to the most underlying problem at the center.

"Are you sure that is the problem?" Her voice is warm, encouraging but patient. Auntie Abbie is 77, and she's had a lot of practice waiting.

"You gotta let it go," Auntie Abbie says. "You gotta agree to release it. And you cannot bring it back and use it as an excuse."

Mihi, kala and *'oki*—to repent, untie and end—combine for complete forgiveness, of others and yourself. They form the last step, though the process may take time. "When you make it here," Auntie Abbie says, "You go away with power." Power to choose a new life. Power to live with self-respect.

Most of those who saw Charlie Mahuka go through this process do not believe he failed, not entirely. No matter how tragic or ironic his arrest, those in the program use the term "setback" for what happened to him, not the word "failure." They may have a point: The Charlie Mahuka who was arrested for this crime is simply not the same as the Charlie Mahuka who went to prison 10 years ago.

But not all of the *kūpuna* program's successes are that ambiguous. Daryl Kim Seu found in the program the power to change his life. "I know now that I'm responsible for Daryl," he says. "I'm not into blame anymore."

It wasn't always so.

At 18, Daryl Kim Seu had graduated from Kamehameha Schools. Two years later, he'd earned an associate's degree in liberal arts at Leeward Community College. By age 20 Kim Seu made his first big choice for his future. He began dealing drugs.

"I started with marijuana," he remembers. "And then it escalated to cocaine. Eventually I ended up with crystal meth."

In some ways, Kim Seu's case is not typical—he's well educated, comes from a stable family, even held down a good job most of the time he was taking and pushing drugs. In another way, he was classic—insisting his drug habits were someone else's problem, going back to drugs within two weeks of his first exit from jail.

For more than a decade, Kim Seu lived two lives. By day he really enjoyed his job as a customer service representative for a TV cable company. He was gregarious, personable—in short, a perfect guy to deal with the public. The cable company even put him in a TV commercial. Nights, in his words, were constant drinking, drugging and partying. But his drug idyll finally came to an end—at work he called in sick once too often.

His supervisor offered him company-paid counseling if he needed help with fighting his drug habit. "They never outright said, 'Do you have a drug problem?'" Kim Seu says. "They did say I was such a good employee, they'd like to help. I said no."

Years went by. And then, one evening, in a private office, a vice president uttered private words. "We have evidence you've been dealing drugs on company premises."

"I said, 'What?'" Kim Seu remembers. "I was in big-time denial. It was their problem."

The company gave him a choice: quit or be fired.

"They'd had a private investigator tailing me for two weeks," Kim Seu says. "I blew up. I said, 'You can't fire me, I'm union.'"

But he knew, in truth, the resignation offer was the best he could do: $5,000 severance pay, vacation pay, unemployment compensation eligibility and a promise of a confidential personnel file.

In the long run, the deal was no blessing. "I had money and a lot of free time," Kim Seu says. "My drug habit escalated. And one night I was at a house where I shouldn't have been. The cops broke the door down."

It was August 1991, 16 years since his first drug deals. The nine charges the district attorney filed could get him 35 years in prison. He'd be more than 70 years old when he got out.

In jail awaiting trial, Kim Seu wrote to his mother, pleading with her to bail him out. After three months, he was released on "supervisory leave" that required him to be in his parents' house from 10 p.m. to 6 a.m. and to wear an electronic identification band on his ankle.

"I was good for the first two weeks," Kim Seu says. "And then I got back to my old friends. I cut that band off my ankle and I said, 'Mom, I need to do my drug.' A warrant came out for my arrest. I was on the run for four months, until March of '92, and again the doors came flying down and I was handcuffed. This time I stayed in jail eight months. They talked to my father, and he said, 'Keep him in.' So I went to school in jail, I went to classes, and I worked in the prison store making 25 cents an hour."

And then Kim Seu the drug dealer cut a deal with the prosecutor. He pleaded guilty to promotion and possession, and the district attorney dropped seven other charges.

"The judge said, 'I can put you in jail for 20 years. But you graduated from Kamehameha, went to college, held a job. I'm giving you five years' probation. If you get re-arrested, you're in jail for 10 years straight.'" It was November 1992.

Kim Seu was already a hopeless statistic. And still he skated on thin ice. He flirted with drugs again. Four months later, he surrendered, not to another door bashed in by cops, but to a door opened at a residential drug and alcohol treatment center.

He completed the two-month regimen, then was invited by the staff to stay another six months as temporary house manager.

But then, Kim Seu, still on probation, was out of work. He showed up at Alu Like's Offender/Ex-Offender Project, which provides job training and placement for men and women coming out of prison. The project itself had a vacancy for a secretary.

"I took it, to get back into a work mode," Kim Seu says. At Alu Like he also met *kupuna* counselor Nona Davilla. Kim Seu was about to become a positive statistic.

He recently joined the staff of a new Alu Like program aimed at keeping kids from dropping out of Wai'anae and Nānākuli high schools. And he's enrolled as a social work major at the University of Hawai'i.

"Even though I went to a Hawaiian school, I never knew what a *kupuna* was until I met Auntie Nona," Kim Seu says. "She's got—I don't know what—but so much love emanates from her. You go in her office and whatever is bothering you is gone. I still see her now and then, and I give her the biggest hug I can. I don't have the compulsion to use drugs or alcohol. I have a whole new group of friends. Is this a spiritual awakening? Time to do something with my life? I get chicken skin just talking about it."

Kim Seu is more typical than Charles Mahuka. In five years, the *kūpuna* program has served more than 700 clients. To Hawai'i taxpayers it means about 400 guys they aren't warehousing in prison at an average cost of $25,000 a year. It's a big chunk of change—more than $9 million annually. *Kūpuna* funding—about $172,000 for 1995-96, mostly in salaries—comes from the federal government through the Hawai'i Department of Health's Alcohol and Drug Division.

Division chief Elaine Wilson says, "The statistical outcomes are excellent. It's a good example of how to empower people and their families to get on with their lives."

Daryl Kim Seu regained that power, and he believes Charlie Mahuka did too. The two men attended the same AA meeting for about six months in 1994, until Kim Seu moved from Wai'anae. They talked most recently in September. Mahuka's arrest shocked Kim Seu.

"He had this warmth, this *ha'aha'a*—humility," Kim Seu says.

Kim Seu was not the least surprised to hear that Mahuka's parole officer volunteered as a character witness. "I will be too," says Kim Seu.

"I just can't see how the incident took place," he continues. "But there are no guarantees in life. You never know what's going to happen."

In his fashion, Charlie Mahuka is getting on with his life. The same day prison officials asked him to help with anger-management training he asked Auntie Lei to get him the course materials he'd used before.

"He told me he hoped the anger-management program in Wai'anae wouldn't be shut down for something he alone did, that he should be the one to take the pain. He told me he can do whatever the courts require." Auntie Lei's voice grows softer, perhaps regretful. "He tried so hard to do the right thing."

Tried so hard. We all try. Try our best, and fall short. I wrote this article once before Charlie was arrested—and several times since, as I wrestled with my conflicting feelings about the story: my sorrow that this had happened and my curiosity about why. My desire for my fellow Hawaiian to be a success at changing his life permanently for the better. And my struggle to reconcile my Western-style skepticism with my faith that through the *kūpuna* program, Charlie Mahuka really had changed.

I thought more than once about abandoning the project, but I stuck with it.

I think of all those who stick by Charlie Mahuka: Auntie Lei, David Kamiyama and Charles Sizemore, the parole officer. Daryl Kim Seu, Charlie's family, the prison officials inviting him to teach fellow inmates. Who is this Charlie Mahuka, this man with whom I shared barely more than an hour but whose tragic arrest had the power to affect me to my bones?

I think back to last summer, when Uncle Howard and Auntie Abbie took me through *ho'oponopono*. They told me a person does not choose his true work, but is chosen by *akua*, a higher power. Could it be that Charlie Mahuka is being chosen? That his work inside the prison is not finished?

And when I ponder all these things, my bones begin to rest.

Father of Waters

1998

At dawn on a Sunday, I swam in a surfless sea. I had swum in these Kailua waters since before I could walk. We lived four house lots beyond the high tide mark. When I was growing up, the beach, with its warm coral sand and sparkling, frothy waves, was just a fact of life.

On this particular morning, I recalled all the years of seaside living, and realized that the ocean was not a scrap of exotic geography to me, but the context for life itself. I had just strewn my brother's ashes in these quiet morning waters, and I lingered in a peace I had never before defined.

When we were little, my mother took us to the beach every morning, and some afternoons. We splashed at low tide, and once I filled Baby Pierre's swim trunks with wet sand as he sat digging. When he got up, his drawers dropped around his ankles like a sand bomb. My mother thwunked me on my fanny when her darling Pierre began to cry, and the wet sand from her hand stung me. But seeing Pierre lose his pants was so funny, it was worth a spank.

One morning, instead of walking to the beach, my mother took us past two houses to the main road to watch President Roosevelt ride by in a jeep. She tugged on me as the convoy approached.

"Wave!" she said, and tugged again. "Wave! He's President Roosevelt!" She put her hand over her heart.

This was Hawai'i, 1944. Roosevelt was reviewing the troops at the Naval Air Station not five miles from our home. Three years earlier, the first Japanese bombs had hit the air base, dropped from planes on their way over the mountains to Pearl Harbor. At the time, I didn't know this, but if I had I wouldn't have cared.

I jerked my arm up and flapped my fingers twice. The president waved back, right at me. Then he was gone.

I coughed in the jeep fumes and said, "So can we go to the beach now?"

Usually, as the tide came in and the waves grew, some grown-ups went in the water to body surf. My daddy was good at it, and when the waves weren't too big, he would take me with him.

"Now, don't take her way out," my mother scolded. "She's too little." My mother was from North Dakota. She didn't go way out herself.

"Yeah, yeah," my daddy winked. And he took me beyond the breakers, lifting me under my arms so I could jump the waves with him. Sometimes my mother would signal, motioning us to come back to shore.

"She wants us to go in," I said.

"Yeah, yeah."

He taught me how to watch a swell, to tell by its exact shape whether it would be good to catch. If it was no good and not breaking yet, we jumped it, floating easily upward.

If the wave was starting to break, we'd drive through it head-to-sea, so that the force of the white curl would not smack us. If the wave looked good, my daddy held me just below the ribs and cast me off it at the precise moment the break began. After a few yards, the wave boiled full around my shoulders and I flailed to keep from being rolled under.

But often I did tumble in briny clouds of churning sand. Instinctively, I held my breath, closed my eyes, pushed my feet against the bottom and blew out as I broke the surface.

I learned to look around as soon as my head was above water, to find my bearings. The shore was constant, solid, a terrestrial North Star. Opposite was the water, dynamic and dangerous, ever-moving.

"Face the breakers or you'll get hit," my daddy said. I could have run to the beach for safety, but he took my hand and we faced the sea.

The deep green beyond the breakers was a club in which my daddy and I were the only members. Swimming in the deep green was like scrambling into a tree house and pulling up the ladder before my mother could enter. In the water, we were bonded by more than blood, and it was only here that we gossiped and told secrets.

His confidences were from a time I considered to be the olden days, when his father and stepmother, Elizabeth, were still alive.

"Once the old man locked me in the car trunk all the way from the volcano to Kona," he told me, his face to the sea. "There wasn't enough room in the seats, and he thought I was a trouble-maker. It was that damn Lizzie who caused it all."

My contributions were from the immediate past. "I didn't eat my toast crusts this morning. I threw them in the garbage and Mama didn't see." He made a goofy, upside-down smile.

My daddy's skin was the color of weak coffee. His Hawaiian mother had died when he was a year old. I heard years later that when she lay dead in the front room of the old house in Hilo, Hawaiians came wailing and keening in the ancient, eerie way, despite her *haole* husband's objections.

In the anguish and upset and trying to provide for her seven young children, no one paid the baby much attention, except his five-year-old sister, Nina. And she cried the loudest when their father shunted the baby to an orphanage for a year. Later, their father packed most of the kids off to board at Kamehameha Schools.

When he finished Kamehameha in 1931, my father moved in "temporarily" with Nina and her husband. He would have stayed longer, but he met my mother on a blind date in 1939 and they married the next year. Just before I was born, they bought a place in Kailua, a small beach house not 100 yards from the green and untamed waters.

Sometimes on a Sunday, my daddy woke me just before sun-rise and we'd shiver our way to the beach as fast as we could walk, hunching our shoulders under thin towels. Then the sun would break the watery horizon, turning the sea luminescent. At that hour, the ocean was always gentle, as if it still slumbered, dreaming of daddies and little girls coming to visit. We waded out to the deep green, where the water, warmer than the air, rose over our shoulders.

Small swells washed over us, glowing gold through green as sunbeams filtered through them in a slow, oceanic *hula*. The rhythm of the waves was like the repetitive sway of dancers as they reached and bent, telling the story of the chant to the beat of a fish-skin drum.

Like the *hula*, the sea held *kaona*, hidden meanings. My daddy and I didn't talk of "meanings," but I felt graceful and weightless, and I dove a few times, bathing in the dance.

One of these mornings, when we floated in the glowing green, my daddy told me of the *'aumākua*, the personal spirit guardians of Hawaiians. *'Aumākua*, he said, often take the form of animals. Ours, he was certain, were creatures of the sea. They watched us always.

But even in our magic, secret green place, that was all my daddy told me about the bond of our people with the sea. He didn't know of the ancient migration voyages from Tahiti and the Marquesas, nor of Kanaloa, the god of the ocean. He didn't even know the names of his Hawaiian grandparents, his *haole* father having so abruptly severed the family ties. He simply lived what he couldn't explain, his heart's ancient tie with the sea.

Once he set out to accompany my mother and us kids to see my mother's family in North Dakota. But when our steamer docked in San Francisco, the thought of being away from the sea, of being thousands of miles and days of travel away from it, was too much. He waved goodbye to the three of us at the train station.

"I want to go with you!" I cried to my daddy. But Pierre and I went to North Dakota with my mother, and it was months before I returned to my ocean.

In time, I could see that the water was imprinted on my brother, too. As Pierre grew, my daddy taught him to surf. But then came a time when my daddy would rather drink than go to the green water with us. I couldn't understand why.

He became another person entirely. He sat slack in his living room chair, slurring his speech, repeating himself, spilling his highball on his soiled undershirt. Sometimes he came home late at night, loud and stinking, never seeing that my mother had left his share of supper on the stove. Sometimes he didn't come home for days. I hated him. I missed him.

The weaker drink made him, the stronger my mother tried to be. She became the family safety officer, with rules for the beach laid out in detail, owing to the water's clear and present danger. No swimming alone. No one under 14 to be in the water without an adult present. No board surfing. No one to swim after 4 p.m. No one to swim at all if the surf is rough. No swimming in the rain.

Her rules did not forbid walking on the beach. Sometimes Pierre and I returned to the ocean at twilight, when long shadows marked the sand with palm trees and catamaran masts. The light danced obliquely on the water's surface, and the smell of salt wafted heavily on the trade winds. The tide was on its way out again, leaving scalloped rows of tiny shells and bits of seaweed. Incoming tides sometimes brought hand-blown glass fishing floats from Japan that bobbed like big jellyfish on the waves. We walked at water's edge, splashing ankle-deep. Sometimes the 'aumākua would beckon us too strongly.

"What happened?" our mother screamed when we got home, salt water dripping from our clothes and sand clinging to our wet feet.

"We went swimming."

"In your clothes? After 4 o'clock? You mustn't!"

But we did. And we did again.

Pierre and I formed an unspoken pact to protect ourselves from the strong, long arm of our mother and the unpredictable drunken outbursts of our father. The water became our haven, and we became its creatures. Sometimes it seemed that Pierre had always been my only companion in the green waters.

Yet every year, once in summer and once right after New Year's, my father went "on the wagon." In a month of no drinking, we'd go to our ocean, as if we had never parted.

Once, more than once, I told him I wanted to be an artist or a writer. He told me more things from the olden days, about how mean Lizzie had been, but how Nina and his other sister sneaked treats to him when he was being punished. He talked of playing football at Kamehameha, coached by Nina's husband, the legendary Doggie Wise. He talked of living with them all those years. And once he said he thought Nina was a fool for divorcing. Yet Nina remained to him as Pierre was to me, the sibling with an unbreakable bond.

When I was just short of 16, Nina took to staying with us whenever she came to O'ahu from the Big Island. She was born on the same date as my mother, and she was, even in midlife, my father's whispering, giggling confidante. Both facts rankled my mother.

One evening Nina said, "I have a schemey idea." She always said "schemey idea." It could be anything—buy shave ice, pick guavas, give the dog a bath. This time she said, "Let's go to the beach."

It was probably 7:30, but midnight-dark. "Oh, no," my mother said. "It's too late."

Nina took it in stride. "OK. We won't be gone long."

She and my father, Pierre and I picked our barefoot way along the coral road that led to the beach. The loose sand felt cool, and we could see bits of waves spitting in the starlight. I was thinking of how it felt to jump in at twilight with all our clothes on when Nina said, "Let's go swimming!"

"We'll all catch hell," my father said.

"Come on, I brought towels. We'll just take our clothes off and run in."

The water was at once the same as always, and altogether different. It was as if I had grown up and my lifetime friend had become my true lover. The breaking surf teased me in the dark to the place I knew was the green, where I couldn't quite touch bottom. The water folded around me, holding me warm in the cool night air, kissing me gently and slowly, combing its wet and reverent fingers through my floating hair. Tiny, tantalizing shivers, shivers I had never felt before, ran up my back. I opened my mouth a little, letting the seawater run in, tasting the salt and feeling the insides of my cheeks with my tongue.

I rose and fell as the swells rolled under me toward shore, and in the hypnotic minutes of the water's night rhythm, I lost the bearings of time. In the dark that was only the sea, I was consumed by a feeling I could call surrender, if ever I had resisted.

Eventually, my mother gave in. Before I left for college, she acknowledged that, although we were hopeless, Pierre and I weren't going to drown.

Fourteen years later, at 61, my father learned at last that alcohol had betrayed him. As he lay in a Honolulu hospital, he schemed for release so he could be near the water of life. One afternoon, as I leaned over the high hospital bed to kiss his cheek, he whispered so softly I wasn't sure I heard, "I think I'm dying." But he talked the doctors into letting him go home.

In the seaside room of our old house, he lay sober in his own bed, where the waves and the *'aumākua* still called at night. His second night there, he died trying to say something to Pierre and me. The words would not come out, but his mouth started a smile and his eyes opened wide. In my last look into those droopish brown eyes that were so like mine, I saw no weakness or fear, but a happiness I had seen only in the green waters. I knew he had just gone home.

My mother bore no objection to us taking his ashes to the ocean, just as he had taken us so many times. And when she died some years later, her instructions were to scatter her ashes in the waters she had warned us from.

After my father died, Nina couldn't bear to come to the beach. But when she passed on, her grandsons took her ashes to the Kailua waters, too.

Too soon it was Pierre's turn. At 42, he lay like our father before him, in the same seaside room, cancer slowly doing its work. The sea breeze rustled the coconut fronds outside, and geckos chirped from the eaves. At night these sounds subsided, and we heard only the tide washing its sandy rhythm, and the *'aumākua* calling.

Once I sat cross-legged on the big bed next to Pierre and asked him, if he had one wish, what would it be?

He knew without thinking. "To go to the water."

On a September Sunday morning, Pierre's wife, their two children and I rose in the dark. A few friends gathered, and we carried to the beach a *pū'olo*, a parcel wrapped in *ti* leaves. The sky was getting light as we arrived. The sea was calm. We waded through the shallows to the deepness of the green, where veins of gold shone in the swells. *To go to the water*, he had said.

We took handfuls of the coarse, gritty ashes from the bundle, and swirled them just beneath the surface, where they spread in the watery glow, indistinguishable from the sand of the ocean floor.

I thought of how the sea with its tides brought things and took them away, and revealed secrets and then covered them again, in its unfailing rhythm. In the green I faced seaward, my nose just above the water, my arms moving just enough to keep me upright. At eye level, the water shimmered, and below its surface it caressed me gently, moving again in the *hula*. I swam quietly with my family—Pierre, my daddy, Nina and even my dry-land mother. And the *'aumākua* and Kanaloa, god of the sea.

One of them, or some of them, or all of them whispered: *I am with you always.*

I was home in the warm suspension of the green waters.

2
Faces

❦

Hard heads, *kāhuna*,
bull squeakers and finding a
few more disparate Hawaiians

❧

CONVICTION

1998

A hundred hundred times I have viewed Mount Olomana from the Pali Highway, the familiar fortress wall of an ancient volcano. Yet it wasn't until last summer that I discovered at the far end of Olomana's wall, on the Waimānalo side, a natural rock spire near Puʻuhonua o Waimānalo, where the most faithful of Bumpy Kanahele's followers have fashioned a village instead of falling flat on their faces in the Koʻolau mud.

I went to find the faithful, and Kanahele himself. But the pinnacle stunned me the most. A spire visible from a dead-end street; I took it as a symbol. My next two weeks would crawl with metaphors and ironies, and I would come to love a one-time small-time Hawaiian crook, a Buddhahead *lōlō* from Kalihi, and a Confederate from Alabama who'd been a businessman in Alaska and Hawaiʻi. This is against the rules, and my editor will have to scold me. But I can't help it if journalism school didn't take.

Acquaintances had suggested Dennis "Bumpy" Kanahele was 1) Dangerous. "Whoa! He rides around in a pick-up full of guns." 2) Nuts. "Ho! Those guys tried to make a fund-raiser with bungee jumping off Makapuʻu Lighthouse." 3) Underground. "I haven't heard anything about Bumpy lately. He must be up to something." 4) Subversive. "He's been hanging out in the law library."

All the rest I "knew" about Kanahele was headlines:

"Nation of Hawaiʻi warns U.S., state judges."

"Nation leader Kanahele jailed."

"Kanahele bail denied while he awaits trial."

Was any of it true? Is Kanahele an ex-con has-been? Or is he a 40-plus, mellowed radical sliding into *kupuna*-hood? Is his "Nation of Hawaiʻi" in pieces like a busted conch shell, or are the families on the "Waimānalo kibbutz" living out Kanahele's conviction—however you interpret "conviction"? Has the federal mistrial-turned-plea-bargain actually shut him up, or has it merely elevated him as a folk hero among sovereignty fighters?

Kanahele wasn't hard to find. He's in the phone book.

But along with him, I found Steve Tayama and John Kirkley, whose Japanese and *haole* lives have converged with Kanahele's in a *pas de trois*, a dance of conviction that just may, someday in some way, play to some kind of a packed house.

I first met Kanahele in the pre-fab house that is both village office and Nation of Hawai'i headquarters. Barebones furniture. Phone. That's it. When Kanahele got popped in the clink in August 1995, the Nation went on hold.

But on the wall are posted the United Nations Declaration of Human Rights and the 1998 Ancient Hawaiian Moon Calendar Related to Fishing and Farming, thumb-tacked underpinnings of the Nation and the village.

Outside, roosters, doves and mynah birds crow and coo and call their morning messages. Family laundry hangs under small party tents in limp, damp hope.

Kanahele's interview agenda—as any Hawaiian's—is to discover who I am. Not what. Who. Hawaiian, from where? Kailua, O'ahu. But where in 1897? Hilo. And the name? Pā.

He fetches a stack of legal-size photocopies. On a Hilo list is a signature in a fine, upright hand: J.K. Pa, age 32. I have never seen this document. At the top is printed "PETITION AGAINST ANNEXATION." The date is Sept. 11, 1897. And the signature is my great-grandfather's brother, John Kalili Pā.

By this document of 21,259 names Kanahele and I are forever linked, for his great-grandparents' signatures parade down the right-hand column of the petitions from Nāpō'opo'o: Kamaka Pakiko and her husband, J.W. Pakiko. Kamaka's name is flanked by those of her daughter and her mother.

Kanahele only discovered these roots of demonstration in 1998, ironically the centennial year of the annexation the petition protested. He'd been a natural genealogical rebel from the beginning.

Kanahele cut his baby rebel teeth at, of all places, Thomas Jefferson Elementary School "across the zoo," where his schoolbook heroes were Lincoln and Ben Franklin—"'cause the kite"—Gandhi and Martin Luther King. And John Kennedy "'cause PT-109, war hero, you know."

Yet, because of visiting his father, Bumper, in O'ahu Prison for 11 years for safecracking, he says, "I hate cops. I could never handle authority. I see one sign 'Do Not Enter,' I like go check 'em out."

Teenage "beach larceny" landed him in both the Job Corps and Ko'olau Boys Home. He dropped out of Kailua High School, opting instead for drugs and paint-sniffing.

"It wasn't no secret," he says. "I was hard-head, stealing and dealing."

In 1976 *kupuna* Aunty Pīlahi Pākī, a composer and a supporter of the early Hawaiian activists, who was distantly related to Kanahele, gathered Kanahele and two other young Hawaiians. "She wanted to go to Ala Wai Yacht Harbor," Kanahele says. "Where the ocean no more ears." More to the point, she would be out of earshot of people. Kanahele already had observed at close range the Hawaiian land demonstrations at Kalama Valley and Sand Island. Now Aunty Pīlahi wanted to talk about Hawaiian issues, dangerous issues, like the fledgling Protect Kaho'olawe 'Ohana's guerilla tactics against the U.S. Navy, and sovereignty, though that word itself wasn't in anyone's vocabulary yet.

Kanahele had never met her before. "She took my hand and said, 'You are *pu'uhonua*,'" he says. "'Huh?' I said. She told me *pu'uhonua* is a feeling of ecstasy. Not the jollies, but an emotional and spiritual state. And Pu'uhonua would be my name."

And that night, Kanahele said, "Aunty, everyone of us get this feeling that something is wrong. If it could be fixed … that would be *pu'uhonua*."

The fixing is a long time in the coming. But—after three stints in prison, and setting a record for wearing a court-ordered electronic ball and chain on his ankle—Kanahele sees his own evolution.

In the summer of 1987, he and his extended family occupied Makapu'u Lighthouse property. The property, they argued, had been ceded lands to which their family had title.

"I 'acquired' keys to the gates and got documents in order," Kanahele says. "That's how long ago we started to lay paper trails."

The group grew to about 50, including some 20 kids, among them some of Kanahele's nieces, who now live in the Waimānalo village. In 5 a.m. dark in the occupation's seventh week, the scene, in Kanahele's words, "turned hardball big time."

According to contemporary newspaper accounts, the raid was precipitated by reports that the group was stockpiling weapons and drugs. The Honolulu Police Department sent in 28 officers from the Special Services Team and 10 patrolmen, along with two dozen law enforcement officers from the state Department of Land and Natural Resources. They arrested somewhere between 31 and 36 adults (news accounts vary) and about a dozen juveniles. Most were charged with trespass and released on $10 bail.

Kanahele and two other men were charged with felony possession of firearms.

Kanahele, of course, has his own version of events: The SWAT team showed up, "all in black, even with painted faces. I had a carbine at the side of my leg. My family was all behind me. I thought, 'Ah, f---, if I lift up this gun, we all get shot.' I dropped the carbine, walked right up to them and yelled, 'You f---ers get off our land.'

"I'm looking at my cousin get whacked. I hit the ground, guns pointing at my head, and I see my 11-year-old son running to me. He gets clothes-hangered. My niece 'Ilima goes to help Cousin and gets nailed. Seeing your kids go down makes you piss off. Later I had the kids write down what happened." [Contemporary news accounts do include claims that juveniles were roughed up by police.]

The court, of course, refused a landownership defense, and Kanahele was convicted of trespass and terroristic threatening with a weapon—not the carbine he laid down, but a shotgun he claims he never had.

"For me, I did a lot of crimes and got away with them. The one time I'm innocent, I serve time."

Kanahele still believes the ceded lands belong to Hawaiians. But, he says, "We had the wrong approach and we were too early."

It was passion with no plan, knowing only "A for Activist when you need A to Z."

He was still on "A" when he and his band of followers occupied Waimānalo's Kaupō and Makapu'u Beach Parks starting in 1993. But they progressed through the alphabet to "P" for Publicity and Protest by virtue of a high-profile, tourist-popular roadside location and the ability to call out hordes of other protestors who had spent the intervening years demonstrating about the same issues from Kaua'i to the Big Island.

After 15 months, the state cut a deal in 1994. To get the demonstrators off the beach, the Department of Land and Natural

Resources negotiated a 55-year lease for 45 acres of *mauka* land.

The group moved, but Kanahele returned to his family's Waimānalo Hawaiian Homestead, where he still lives.

With the *mauka* village as its core, he formed the Nation of Hawai'i, which elected him head of state at its 1994 convention and adopted a constitution. Soon the Nation's citizens racked up traffic citations by the dozens for using Hawaiian Sovereign Nation license plates.

In July 1995, the Nation of Hawai'i provoked another game of hardball when it served U.S. officials with public notices accusing them of war crimes against the Hawaiian people. The notices specified the recipients would be arrested, imprisoned and brought before an international criminal tribunal from which there would be no appeal. The Nation served copies on Hawai'i offices of the U.S. Attorney, U.S. Marshal, the FBI and the IRS, as well as on Hawai'i's federal district judges.

Senior U.S. District Judge Samuel King publicly declared the notice a threat, and pointed out that it is a crime to threaten federal judges.

Islanders can hardly help remembering what followed: In early August, Kanahele was arrested for harboring tax fugitive Nathan Brown and obstructing federal marshals when they tried to arrest Brown twice. The original events had happened about 18 months earlier.

Kanahele was held without bail for four months, only to have proceedings end in a mistrial in October 1995. He was released on bail pending a new trial, the electronic monitor on his ankle and orders in his pocket not to set foot in Waimānalo.

Almost two years later, Kanahele pled guilty to one felony charge and the U.S. prosecutor dismissed two others. Last February, U.S. District Judge Helen Gillmor, who had heard his original case, sentenced him to four months in prison and four months under electronic surveillance. With credit for time served, he spent only two more weeks in prison. It was a crucial fortnight.

During his first spell in Hālawa Medium Security Facility in 1995, his talk about U.S. Public Law 103-150, the "Apology Bill," fell on deaf incarcerated Hawaiian ears.

But in the interim, the "braddas" had seen beaucoup TV news coverage of sovereignty, including the controversial Kanahele.

"I just gave them the Apology Bill," Kanahele says. "Some of them were lifers and double lifers. I told them, 'You know what, you've done a lot of shit that was wrong and we're not making excuses, but if you knew your history, you'd understand it could have been different.'"

Dozens of people have told him that his going to prison slowed down everything in the sovereignty movement. But Kanahele sees it as a necessary rest period.

"Man couldn't tell Bumpy what for do," he says. "I figure, Ākua said, 'You so hard-head, get one government hold you down, lock down your 'okole.'"

The first month in Hālawa, he was angry. But slowly he simmered down. He had time to think.

"We had tried fighting," he says now. "I tried sacrificing myself. It wasn't the time and the way. Now we can pick and choose the time. We ain't ready for what type of government we want. We can't just go 'Rah-Rah-Rah' without a general consensus. We go with one thousand names and the government says, 'Yeah, right.' We'll never compromise. But there's levels to go, and I got time.

"When I got picked up in '95, I was no match for those guys. From that time on, it was study, study, study. We indulged ourselves in learning, because when you know A to Z, then you can find a letter when you need it."

Kanahele's ball and chain came off in July. Probation will be over in February. Everyone agrees he's changed, even himself. He draws flow charts depicting the social, political, economic and cultural aspects of a nation.

He's on the board of the Waimānalo Neighborhood Council and the Waimānalo Health Center. In August, 120 members of the Nation of Hawai'i—Kanahele included—provided security services for Honolulu's annexation ceremonies. They also served five meals to some 5,000 participants, and provided them with water.

"Now I'm working within the system to change the system," Kanahele says. "We're forming a nonprofit organization, Aloha First. I've learned to cope. It's almost like self-defense. Take the force and utilize it. Why try to crawl up a 1,500-foot mountain water pipeline when you can go with the flow?"

❧

Steve Tayama has known Kanahele through the changes.

"Bump's too much of a diplomat for me now," Tayama says. "He was a little crook, a warrior type, young and bold. Then, like Kamehameha I, he saw the power of the Americans and he's willing to be a diplomat. He's not so much changed as grown. If I were the leader, some would be dead, probably me."

Tayama has lived at Puʻuhonua o Waimānalo from the beginning, across the driveway from the office, where he can keep an eye on comings and goings. The first day I came to the village unannounced he—diplomatically—ascertained my mission. Within two minutes he pointed out that he is not Hawaiian, but Japanese. And radical.

"An ordinary kid coming out of high school in Hawaiʻi now faces $1,200 a month in rent while he's making six dollars an hour. He says to himself, 'I going do something crooked.' He knows it's crooked. He has to change his whole moral fiber to survive. It sucks. The village is the beginning of a solution."

Tayama gravitated to Hawaiians early, especially as a teenager in Kalihi.

"At my house there were no hugs and kisses," he laments. "Hawaiians had hugs and kisses, and food and music. I'd go to Hawaiian things and cry."

But his senior year, teachers at Farrington High School considered him a "gangster from Kalihi," a wise-ass with seven D-minuses. The school gave him a diploma in 1964, he says, to get rid of him.

Neither the school nor Kalihi prepared him for the next four years, which he spent at Travis Air Force Base in California "unloading dead and burned bodies" from Vietnam. Berkeley erupted in antiwar protests, and, for the first time in his life, Steve Tayama was called "Jap."

"I was a redneck lōlō Buddhahead," he says. "I thought I was white, or at least equal. We were pumped up about killing gooks in Vietnam. And then I realized, 'Hey, I'm a gook.' I could get killed in my own barracks by my own people."

After he got out of the Air Force, Tayama enrolled in Napa Junior College, got on the honor roll, and was recruited by UC-Santa Cruz to bolster minority enrollment. Two professors introduced him to Marx, Lenin and Trotsky, and cautioned him not to get stuck on race when the struggle was about class.

Then "Nixon broke the trust for me," Tayama says. "When he was pardoned, it broke my spirit for America."

By 1978, Tayama had a 3.7 grade-point average and a specialized degree in Racism and Ethnicity in America. He'd already demonstrated against the shah of Iran and UC's investments in apartheid South Africa, and for coal miners, Chinatown's Filipinos, and Puerto Rican independence.

"From 1973 I could see that independence for Hawai'i was the best way," Tayama says.

Back in Hawai'i, he joined the Protect Kaho'olawe 'Ohana. In the late '80s, he got arrested protesting Big Island geothermal development, and joined what he calls the "politically homeless"—homelessness as political statement. Eventually, he heard somebody say, "Hey, this guy Bumpy, he get class."

When Kanahele called for help at Kaupō and Makapu'u Beach, Tayama showed up. He's been with Kanahele ever since.

"The village is a beginning of a solution," Tayama says. "We started here in the mud and the mosquitoes, lower than any immigrants. Now we have houses. My roof doesn't leak, and my house doesn't have bugs. And it cost a thousand dollars to build. We're trying to create something that's real."

Reality set in late for John Kirkley. Now 54, he was 40 in 1984 when a final week of 35-below in the dark of Fairbanks put him over the weather edge. He'd been visiting Hawai'i for some years. This time he moved permanently to Maui. He got a real estate license, and bought an Upcountry place for himself.

"I was living in a million-dollar house," he recalls. "Why wasn't I happy? Finally it came to me: The only thing that makes sense is truth, and the only thing I can change is myself."

To hear Kirkley tell it, about that time, the public burgeoning of the topic of sovereignty led him to discover that his property was ceded land. When he decided the title was no good, he quit paying on the mortgage. Then, in his words, "The bank foreclosed, the court threw me off the land and took my money.

"And here I am, in this village since 1995. No land, no money, still in search of the truth."

I asked him if he was happy, though I was sure what his answer would be.

"Yes," he said in his soft Alabama way. "People think we're a bunch of radical idiots up here. You can't go by what's printed in the paper or on TV. It's all propaganda. Bumpy, he's a hero. He stood up for the rights of Hawaiians.

"As Americans we have outsmarted ourselves. We know more than we feel. We're all in our heads, and your head lies to you. But your heart doesn't. Hawaiians are heart. The problem with American society is that our heroes are baseball players when they should be Buddha or Jesus Christ.

"This village is a real place. The phonies washed out a long time ago. The progression of truth is that it is first denied, then put off, and finally becomes self-evident. This is a lifetime commitment. The Nation will happen.

"Yes, we're radical. You can't be on the front line without being radical. What Bumpy has gone through is an exhaustion of remedies. But after going to jail, we've had to back off. You can't progress from jail."

You wouldn't think a stringbean white guy from Alabama would team up with a big brown crook from Waimānalo and a local Buddhahead. But Kirkley's forebears fought on the losing side of the Civil War. For him and Kanahele and Tayama, a common sense of injustice to the underdog runs strong.

Passion runs strong, too, but, after collective decades of experience, they're bridling it to choose battles instead of pick fights.

The last day I spoke with them happened to be the day Kanahele went off in mid-morning to meet with Governor Cayetano. It was also the day the U.S. Ninth Circuit Court of Appeals ruled that the state of Hawai'i can allow only ethnic Hawaiians to vote for trustees for the Office of Hawaiian Affairs. The 1996 challenge, brought by non-Hawaiian Big Island rancher Harold F. Rice, contended such OHA elections violate the U.S. Constitution's ban on racial discrimination in voting. The prospect of opening OHA elections to the general electorate has hung like a specter in the Hawaiian community. OHA trustees called the ruling "wonderful" and "exciting."

"Unreal," Kirkley said.

"No," Kanahele replied. "Real."

The days of wasting time in traffic court for using Hawaiian

Sovereign Nation license plates are over. Instead, Kanahele preaches his Gospel According to the Apology Bill, which—to him—both outlines the sorry history of the overthrow of the Hawaiian monarchy and virtually provides for the exit of the United States and Hawai'i's renewed independence.

The trio's vision for an independent Hawai'i is an economic model, a tax-free nation along the line of Leichtenstein.

They're big on a scenario—details to come—whereby all of Hawai'i's current citizens—aboriginal Hawaiians, multigenerational immigrants, or even outright recent *malihini*—would retain the benefits of their present status, but could gain citizenship in an independent Hawai'i, or even hold dual citizenship.

Fantasy, skeptics say. Foolishness and fantasy. Toothpaste back in the tube. Pie in the tropical sky.

But there's this Hawaiian precedent: Kaho'olawe. Who expected success in 1976 when a few ragtag radical Hawaiians demanded that the U.S. Navy give back the island? In time, the Protect Kaho'olawe 'Ohana "shoot from the hip" leaders transformed themselves into *akamai* negotiators—and they got what they wanted.

Could it be that, some decades from now, the Nation of Hawai'i will serve Hawai'i's citizens pie-in-the-sky on a tropical plate? As Bumpy says, "I get time."

Kirkley offers a homily: "They say the 40s are the old age of youth and the 50s are the youth of old age."

And there they are, Kanahele at 44, studying, negotiating, educating. And Tayama and Kirkley in their 50s, gardens outside their neighboring Pu'uhonua plywood houses, their radical edges honed like old tempered steel.

I asked Kanahele if all the hard-head years are past. "Oh, no," he smiled. "Not *pau* yet."

Pu'uhonua o Waimānalo perches on the hillside below the fluted vertical cliffs of the Ko'olau Mountains, some 20 up-by-the-bootstraps plywood houses along a gravel driveway, young coconut and *'ulu* trees pale green between them, neat gardens in back yards. Blue and yellow plastic swings and slides dot a sloping lawn near well-tended dryland *taro*. Up *mauka*, villagers are putting in *loʻi* for wetland *taro*.

About 90 people live here now, down from the 200 who moved here in June 1994 when the State of Hawaiʻi evicted them from Kaupō and Makapuʻu Beach Parks after a 15-month occupation.

Those who left "weren't looking for rules and regulations," says village president Gina Maikaʻi. About 20 percent of the current population, including John Kirkley, applied to be part of the village after it opened.

Many of the 30 village children attend a Hawaiian-language immersion school in Kāneʻohe.

The houses appear makeshift. But, built by community families and self-financed, they are a vast improvement on beach tents and a camp kitchen.

"The state cleared just the playground area, but nothing will grow under eucalyptus so we all cleared the rest of these five acres," says Maikaʻi, whose two brothers and sister sit on the village council. "It was wet, muggy and full of mosquitoes. When it rained, we were stuck in or stuck out. The state thought we would fail. But no way. We're here to stay."

Contrary to public perception, most adult residents are employed, which is why progress on the *loʻi* goes slowly—they only have evening or weekend time to spare. Residents resent people calling this "Bumpy's Village."

"He doesn't like it either," Maikaʻi says. "It comes from people who's never been here. We named it Puʻuhonua because it's a sanctuary. We weren't even thinking of it being Bumpy's name. Now we've nicknamed it 'Mauka.'"

Though the village is now in its fifth year, the lease with the state is still pending, which hamstrings improvements such as a better water system

Maikaʻi, confident the lease is coming, presides over a weekly village meeting and otherwise is "like a social worker. I'm only 37, but people come and say, 'Aunty, I can't,' and I help them. But you know, you can only cut and clean and dig and build so long. A lot of us paddle, and we go camping and play golf. To me, things are in place and we're waiting."

To Kanahele, the village, "the foundation and strength of the whole movement," refutes the tiresome stereotype that Hawaiians are lazy. Puʻuhonua o Waimānalo and its little plywood houses is the first sprout of the seed of the Nation of Hawaiʻi, an idea in the flesh, not unlike the Hawaiian idea of *kino lau*, a tangible lifeform of a god.

In Kanahele's words, "This is blank pages of history being written now."

From the red dirt of the *mauka* village I can see, miles away, the turquoise waters where Kanahele and his followers occupied the beach a few years ago.

I think of his family names on the Petition Against Annexation, and of the signature of J.K. Pā, my great-granduncle. A certain teary pride wells up inside me.

But the time for major weeping is not yet.

"We're not just front-line activists," Kanahele says. "When the Nation of Hawaiʻi comes again, hold onto your hearts, because we are going to cry with the feeling of *puʻuhonua*."

Update: The 22 plywood houses at Puʻuhonua o Waimānalo look a little more careworn these days, but the yards and play areas for the 30 children are neatly kept. A third of the 40 adult residents have been here from the first days. Bumpy Kanahele remains a strong presence. John Kirkley and Steve Tayama still live at the puʻuhonua. *Kirkley is treasurer and board member for the Aloha First non-profit organization that oversees the village. Tayama runs security from his home at the village entrance and conducts educational talks for visiting groups.*

PERFECT BALANCE

2004

On a humid Sunday at Mauna 'Ala, Hawai'i's Royal Mausoleum, Hawaiians gather to honor their last ruling monarch, Queen Lili'uokalani. Near her family crypt in Honolulu stands John Keola Lake in full ceremonial regalia, chanting. His rich, resonant voice does not seem to break for breath. His powerful presence makes the silver-haired Lake seem seven feet tall. Lake's appearance matches his reputation. Now 66, he is among Hawaii's most visible native Hawaiians, a master of *hula*, chant, Hawaiian language and Hawaiian history, which he has taught for almost four decades. He also is *kahuna nui* (high priest) of Pu'ukoholā Heiau on the Big Island. He's in constant demand to conduct ceremonies and present workshops in Hawai'i and elsewhere. Thousands of students he's touched as *kumu*—teacher—revere him.

Lake is quite mortal, though. It's a shock to discover at his *hula kahiko* class that he is actually 5'10". He wears shorts and a dark T-shirt. He's used his tall *ipu* so much in 20 years of keeping the cadence for dancers that he reinforced its cracked bottom with layers of duct tape.

"'*Ekahi! 'Elua! 'Ekolu! 'Ehā!*" he calls out as his *haumana* warm up. One! Two! Three! Four!

"Five, six, seven, *huli!*" They turn 180 degrees. "Use your thighs, your hips, not your ankles!" By now, sweat stains appear on Lake's T-shirt. "*Mākaukau!*" Make ready! He begins a *kala'au*, a stick dance, the students working in pairs like fencers.

"*Ho'o ka mana!*" Lake begins chanting. Light my fire!

The students strike their sticks tentatively.

"Whack 'em!" Lake calls. "This is a battle cry! You folks are hitting like you're playing cue ball!" He giggles at his own joke, and his students laugh, too.

Lake grew up on Maui, Catholic/Episcopalian and bilingual. Both sets of grandparents were fluent in Hawaiian, and his maternal grandmother raised him dancing *hula* and chanting. He did not segue, however, automatically toward Hawaiian language when he graduated from St. Anthony High School in 1955. Lake spent a year at the University of Hawai'i studying political science before transferring to the Jesuit University of San Francisco.

"My roommate was from Bolivia," he recalls. "I said, 'I teach you English, you teach me Spanish. You'll get by in English, and I'll use Spanish as a minor.'"

Lake later earned a master's in education, then, in Spain, the equivalent of another master's in Spanish linguistics. After two years teaching junior high school history and Spanish in San Francisco, he was recruited by Honolulu's all-boys St. Louis High School in 1962 to teach Spanish, English, world history and American history.

One day, the head of language curriculum casually said, "It's too bad that we don't teach Hawaiian language." Lake became part of a pilot project that expanded to other schools and later formed the 'Ahahui 'Olelo Hawai'i, Association of Hawaiian Speakers. Shortly, Lake was involved with at least another dozen new organizations devoted to language and culture.

The biggest surprise came right after football season in 1965. St. Louis enrolled a great many native Hawaiians, including most of the team. All 45 players came to Lake and said, "Teach us *hula*."

In the '60s, very few men danced in public. No men danced seriously for fear of being considered sissies.

"You've got to be kidding!" Lake said.

"No. Teach us. We'll come after football practice."

"OK. Get 45 girls.'"

The boys recruited the girls from other Catholic schools, and Lake had to teach.

"Me and my big mouth," he says now, clearly cherishing the memory of a class that grew to 376 students performing dance, chant and song. They became so good that he took some of them on tour, from California to Maine, to Canada, Mexico and Tahiti, and throughout Hawai'i.

During this time, he studied with a number of major Hawaiian masters of chant and dance. He kept teaching Spanish and world history at St. Louis, but added Hawaiian language and history. He helped organize an interschool "talk story" day of Hawaiian language that included *Jeopardy!* in Hawaiian. At night, he moonlighted, singing and dancing at a hotel and at Paradise Park.

He helped gain recognition for teachers of Hawaiian history and arts, a move that propelled the state in 1974 to mandate that Hawaiian history be taught in the public schools. He helped create or became associated with the State Foundation on Culture and the Arts, the annual Kamehameha Day *hula* competition in June, and the Hawaii Music Foundation. He also founded a private academy of Hawaiian traditions, Hālau Mele.

In the mid-1970s, Hawai'i received its first invitation to participate in the South Pacific Arts Festival.

"Before then," Lake says, "everyone else in the Pacific thought there was not any more Hawaiian culture."

As president of the State Council on Hawaiian Heritage, Lake helped prepare a group of 50 dancers and cultural experts to participate. When they arrived in New Zealand in 1976—with elders who were all women—they had a rude surprise. The Hawaiians had forgotten that women are forbidden to speak at a Maori *marae*.

Besides that embarrassment, the Maori asked the Hawaiians, "Where are your *marae*?" The answer: the *heiau*, especially Pu'ukoholā on the Big Island. The Hawaiians had to admit that they hadn't used their temples in many generations. "It was a cultural reawakening," Lake says.

In Tahiti, eight years later, in reinstituting the *'awa* ceremony involving strict protocol in making and sharing a drink made from *'awa* root, the Hawaiians accidentally broke another *kapu*. When they served women first, the Tahitians got up and left. "Another learning experience," Lake says.

Lake was extra cautious the next year when his cousin, Sam Ka'ai, who had worked with the staff at the Big Island's Pu'ukoholā Heiau National Historic Site on a plan to commemorate its bicentennial, approached him. At a historical turning point in 1791, the *heiau* became Kamehameha I's temple of state when he sacrificed within it his primary rival, his cousin High Chief Keoua Kuahu'ula.

Two centuries later, bitterness still consumed loyalties on both sides. Planning a commemoration would be touchy. Ka'ai asked Lake to handle all the protocol.

Lake hesitated. "I had to find out if it was *pono* for me to even stand there. Then, I had to consult my bosses at my Catholic school. And there was the *heiau* itself. I love not the mystery but the history, and the history is full of the fallacies of Western historians."

In the *mele inoa* and *mele kanikau*, the name chants and lamentations, for Keoua, Lake found ancestors. He discovered that his family also descended from Kamehameha's *heiau kahu*, keepers of the temple.

"Now, I could stand there and kill myself," he quips. "I was connected to Kamehameha and to Keoua Kuahu'ula."

For two and a half years Lake researched chants. "They are marvelous," he says. "They had been discarded, and we had not learned them. I came to understand their beauty and that God is present, no matter what we call him."

August 17, 1991, marked 200 years to the day of Keoua's death, which unified the Big Island under Kamehameha and set in motion events that would unite all the Islands in the next few years.

Lake, Ka'ai and other Hawaiians insisted that the commemorative event not be a pageant; it had to go far beyond a historical re-enactment. "It was called *Ho'oku'ikāhi*—reconciliation," Lake says. "We cannot correct or forget the past, but forgiveness can happen."

Six hundred people participated. Thirty-two hundred were invited guests. Another 6,000 came as observers. Lake included his sons. The younger, Iwi, still in high school, declared that he would wear a *malo* only if his father paid him to do it.

August 17 began auspiciously at 3 a.m. with a ritual cleansing in the sea. "As soon as we stepped in the water," Lake says, "eight turtles came up."

As he and his group of men and women chanted into deeper water, he instructed them to leave their *pilikia*, their troubles, in the sea. Three sharks circled them. When they emerged from the water, a flock of owls flew overhead.

"*Kumu!*" one of the men cried out. "You saw what happened?"

"*'Ae!*" Yes! "We got it right!"

The ceremonies went on throughout the day, Lake receiving the *ho'okupu*, offerings. Descendants of Keoua arrived by canoe, as had the chief of old. This time, the descendants of Kamehameha welcomed the travelers ashore. Although Keoua's confiscated feather cape has long reposed in a museum, they ceremonially returned a replica.

By sunset, Lake had been chanting for more than 12 hours with neither microphone nor script. With 44 men in the sacred interior of the *heiau*, Lake was trusting that he would know when and how to end the ceremonies. He looked uphill.

"I saw a darkness like a shadow, a streak coming over the *heiau* to the sea. The sun was just setting, and the waves were glittering in the light."

He cried out, "Get out the *pahu!*" The huge sharkskin drum was brought. "We are closing!"

He began an ancient chant: "There is a darkness that appears in the mountains. There is a darkness that appears in the sea. In the sea, there is darkness. In the sea, there is brightness … The star of the day is being humbled, and the moon ascends. Only the crabs know what it means."

Lake recounts, "We lit all the torches on the *heiau* walls and chanted until the full moon was up. And then it was *pau*."

In an *'awa* ceremony afterward—a time of truth-telling—the men spoke of being part of the first ceremonies at this temple in seven generations.

"They talked of the rebirth of being Hawaiian, of an intense sense of pride, of the richness and value of what Hawai'i was and is. The best gift was from my son. He embraced me and said, 'You don't have to pay me for wearing a *malo*. I am Hawaiian.'"

In the years since, Hawaiians have gathered annually at Puʻukoholā, with Lake as *kahuna nui*.

"We are reclaiming our temples of learning," Lake says. The *heiau* is not for meditation. It's our meeting place for discussions of political, social, economic and religious matters. It has a wealth of functions and focal points."

Lake, now in what logically might be retirement years, is busier than ever. He's an associate professor, *kumu*-in-residence and head of the Hawaiian Traditions program at Chaminade University of Honolulu; *kumu* of Hālau Mele; senior adviser for the Center for Hawaiian Studies at the University of Hawaiʻi at Mānoa; *kahuna nui* of Puʻukoholā; and presenter or conductor of ceremonies at countless Hawaiian events outside Hawaiʻi.

He knows he has to learn to say "no." So far, it's not in his vocabulary—in English, Spanish or Hawaiian.

A man of strength, grace and good humor, Lake jokes with students through tough lessons, coaches them kindly through endless repetitions even when their chants sound like sick frogs and their dance steps are a beat behind. As their *kumu*, he has faith that they will improve and flourish.

Lake's slightly irreverent interpretation of his full Hawaiian name reflects all this. Keolamakaʻāinanakalāhuiokalaniokamehame-haʻekolu literally means "The life of the common people, nation of chiefs of Kamehameha III." An ancestor received the name in 1843, when Kamehameha III was king. For Lake in the 21st century, it means "working with the multitudes."

Any public figure is not without detractors. Some *kumu* think that Lake embodies an irreconcilable clash between Christianity and pagan gods and that he misuses Puʻukoholā. Others claim that he allows too many modern interpretations into *hula kahiko* and various ceremonies. Some grouse that he is a self-promoter.

Regardless, Lake has received countless awards, and his students uniformly characterize him as a gift.

"He is an educator extraordinaire," says Clifford Naeʻole, cultural director at the Ritz-Carlton, Kapalua on Maui. "I take every opportunity to be with him and learn from all he has to offer.

He makes allies, not enemies. He is one of the best examples of walking in two cultures and is respected by the entire community. If there is *pono*, perfect balance, he is a fine example."

Tellers of Tales

1997

Once upon a time, Mākia Malo was invited to tell stories at the Bishop Museum's Family Day—his first public performance. Blind by age 30 as a result of Hansen's disease, Malo had lived from 1947 to 1972—age 12 to 37—at Kalaupapa Settlement on Moloka'i.

At Family Day, Malo recalls, "This guy, Floating Eagle Feather—he was a Papago Indian—he was storytelling. You follow somebody good like that, nobody remember you. So I figure I wouldn't have to work so hard. So, I'm sitting on this bench, and a couple with two small kids, they tell me they have seen Kalaupapa from the top (from a cliff overlooking the settlement). I was going to tell Hawaiian legends, but I start talking story about Kalaupapa, and pretty soon a dozen people had gathered around me. I heard them laughing. When it was over, I hopped the bus and went home.

"A month later I told the organizer, Jeff Gere from the Honolulu Parks and Recreation department, I'd had a fabulous time at Bishop Museum. 'I had 12 people!' I said. 'No,' Jeff said, 'you had 70.'"

That was 10 years ago. Now 62, Malo is among Hawai'i's premier professional Hawaiian storytellers. His "traditionalist" or "talk story" style brings to life his own adventures and experiences.

Nyla Ching-Fujii, on the other hand, is a "revisionist" story-teller, relying mostly on written sources from many cultures. Fujii—of Hawaiian, Japanese, Chinese and Korean heritage—also is an actress and children's librarian.

Interestingly, when she was five, she didn't speak at all. And then, her kindergarten teacher, Mrs. Otsuka, read *The Little Red Hen* to her.

"She takes the flour in a little red wheelbarrow that goes 'tin-tin-tin' down the road," Fujii says, as if 45 years have not elapsed since Mrs. Otsuka's reading. "'Tin-tin-tin.' I was so taken with the story, I told it myself. And I have never stopped."

At Kaimukī High School (Class of 1965), instead of gaining athletic recognition, Fujii "lettered in storytelling." Her bachelor's degree in speech from the University of Hawai'i is a hybrid of communication and performing arts.

Fujii sometimes envies Malo "his own history, magnificent with authenticity. I've had an uneventful life. People like me have to make do with polishing the craft."

Yet she spins a vision of times past in her own life, of growing up in Kapahulu, when Hawaiian was the "language of secrets," when "Waikīkī ended at the Moana Hotel, and there were ranches and lettuce farms in the area—but no sidewalks. The Fiftieth State Circus came to Kapi'olani Park, and my brother went spearfishing off Sans Souci Beach in the mornings before school. There were piggeries and Hind Clark Dairy in Kāhala. Imagine the smells in Kāhala!"

Her naughty eyes twinkle thinking of the malodorous perfume wafting through the high-hat district of opulent residences, giving credence to the theory that storytellers remain one age for life. Her grown daughter believes Fujii is permanently fixed at age five.

Fujii turns serious. "The power of story is not just communication, but communion, one soul to another. You can't get it through a TV screen. In storytelling, the audience is an active participant."

She warms to the topic. "Storytelling is not talking, but the art of listening. I'm listening to you through your eyes, your posture. Both sides—teller and listener—take on the essence of each other, in exchange of what Hawaiians call *hā*, the breath of life."

Fujii talks of "growing a story," a memory-jogging method of forming images of the past. In the telling, the memories coalesce into a story, such as friend and fellow storyteller Woody Fern's "Jackie" tale.

When Fern was an industrial management student at the University of Hawai'i, he took a storytelling class because he needed an elective, the time was convenient and it would be an easy A.

But wait. That's another story. We're talking about Jackie.

Fall semester starts at UH. Woody gives a former Punahou classmate a ride every morning. Jackie is *haole*, blonde *haole*, taking Hawaiian language. Monday she begs Woody to give her a Hawaiian name. "Please, please, please."

Tuesday she bugs him. "C'mon, Woody, it would mean the world to me."

Wednesday Woody says, "OK. I give you a name. 'Ōpala.'"

Jackie is thrilled. "'Ōpala." Short. Sweet. At last she has a Hawaiian name. Given by a real Hawaiian.

The next morning, it's raining. The dirt parking lot is already turning to Mānoa mud.

When Woody comes back after classes, his car seems to have sunk into the mud. He looks more carefully at his left front tire. It is flat. He walks around the car. All four tires are flat.

And Woody Fern laughs, loud and raucous, from deep in his *kolohe*—naughty—Hawaiian soul. Jackie has discovered the truth. "'Ōpala" means "garbage."

The Jackie episode is more than 30 years past, but the story still brings Woody—and his audience—a genuine belly laugh, especially when local listeners know the meaning of "'ōpala."

Fern, a former Hawaiian Airlines executive and now a sporting goods representative because "you can't survive here just on storytelling," says, "Nyla talked me out of a master's degree in speech at UH. She said I'd only find out why people lisp."

In truth, Fern is a natural storyteller. "What makes me be able to do it?" he says. "Nyla thinks I look at the world cockeyed."

Maybe he does. "There is a reason the Lord gave me big ears," he says. "I listen a lot." And that's the source of many of his stories, most of which are rooted in his own family—Hawaiian on both sides—or in tales he's heard of the *ali'i*.

His grandmother, who lived to be 93, was "a haughty old thing, very attractive." Grandma's *koa* rocker now stands in his living room, the old joints going "tick-tick, tick-tick" as a guest comfortably rocks in the chair.

Fern's grandmother told him the following story many times. He tells it now, and it's one of his best.

Just after the turn of the century, Harriet Hi'ilani Jones, from a Big Island ranch, boarded at Kamehameha School for Girls. The campus then was near where the Bishop Museum is now. Each Saturday afternoon, seniors with good grades and perfect deportment were permitted to take the streetcar downtown to shop and have an ice cream soda.

One Saturday, the streetcar had a new conductor, a young Hawaiian on his first job, dressed in a brand new dark blue uniform. The next Saturday, he was on duty again. Harriet was last to step into the car. The young conductor tipped his hat.

"Hello," he said. "My name is John. What's yours?"

Harriet, taken aback, held her head high, looked him in the eye, and without a word, took a seat among her classmates.

The girls begged for the details. Harriet replied that the conductor was pompous, forward and rude.

The next week she was prepared. John smiled at each girl. Again, Harriet was last. And again, John introduced himself. But this time, Harriet thought to herself the worst ranch word she knew: jackass.

And then prim, proper Harriet blurted, "You donkey!"

The girls giggled. John steeled himself silently.

Harriet graduated in the spring, married later and had a family. John went from the streetcar into business and politics. Whenever their paths crossed, infrequently, each gave a slight nod of faint recognition.

About 1940, Nani, Harriet's high school-age daughter, and John's youngest son began keeping company. In time, they got engaged.

Some months before the wedding date, Harriet heard someone call her name outside her house. Through the screen door she saw a man dressed in a suit. He tipped his hat, and did what politicians of the day did at rallies—began to sing and dance. Harriet drew closer to the door. When she recognized the man, she called, "You donkey!"

And then she invited John in to discuss the wedding over tea.

After that, John stopped by now and then. Each time they repeated the ritual: the call, the song and *hula*, and "You donkey!"

John Fern was Woody's paternal grandfather. He died in 1956. For 20 more years, until she too passed away, Woody's maternal grandmother, Harriet Hiʻilani Jones Peterson, told the story. And every time she did, tears came to her eyes.

Woody remembers the house where John Fern came calling, on the corner of Koa and Uluniu streets in Waikīkī. The lemon tree that grew outside the bedroom window then is still there.

❧

Such details bind us to our past and our ancestors, vital elements in understanding who we are, which Fern believes is a key to life.

The way in which stories grow with each telling feeds another of Fern's tenets: "If you don't learn something every day, you might as well roll over and die."

Many times Mākia Malo thought about rolling over and dying. When he was sent to Kalaupapa at age 12, diagnosed with Hansen's disease, three of his eight siblings already were there. Although the sulfone treatment that finally brought the disease under control had recently been introduced, Kalaupapa still spelled doom.

"We lived for the past," Malo remembers, "because we had no future. But most of my stories don't share the burden of Kalaupapa."

Yet somehow he conveys the sorrow that is behind the funny episodes he relates—"Kids my age who died in their 20s, they're all buried at Kalaupapa. The more I tell the stories, the more I think I'm living my life for them."

One of them is his younger brother, Pili, who went to Kalaupapa before Malo. When Pili left home, Malo thought he'd lost his best enemy.

When Mākia also was ordered to the settlement, he was assigned to share a room with Pili in the cottage also occupied by his oldest brother, Bill, and his sister, Pearl.

Pili was 10. "So *mōkākī*—a slob," Malo remembers. "Stuff all over the floor. Pearl told him to clean it up, and he threw his bedspread over the whole thing. Then it was a big bunch of lumps."

As brothers always do, Malo and Pili fought. "I hook him," Malo says. "Then he rap me on the face, on the head." But Malo also realized Pili was his best friend. Years later in 1964, after Malo totally lost his sight and was living at Hale Mōhalu, the Hansen's disease residential program on Oʻahu, Pili "came and spent all his time with me."

Some of Malo's best stories are adventures with Pili. His tales of Kalaupapa, and Oʻahu before then, resonate with a boy's naughtiness, embarrassment and a fear of bogeymen.

Malo is open to questions, and audiences of kids pull no punches. They ask about his guide dog, Inca Blue, and want to know why Malo's hands and nose are misshapen.

The first time he had to answer such questions he was in

individual mobility training in Waipahu. He was wearing long pants, an *aloha* shirt and his usual dark glasses.

"I'm tap-tap-tapping—you have to keep a rhythm," he says. "As I'm concentrating, I hear these sounds behind me. My mind says it's kids. Then a kid says, 'Man, man, what that stick for?' I think, 'Go away. Scram.' And I walk faster, concentrating on the cane.

"Then I realize the kid is walking faster yet, in front of me, along the fence. I stop. I explain, 'This is to help me walk.' And the kid says, 'But you get glasses.'"

Years later, at a storytelling program at 'Ewa Beach Elementary School, "Even before I started the program, a kid asked me how come I wear dark glasses. I said, 'It's like your mama wears lipstick to look nice—you know, shaka with shades.'"

In private, Malo becomes philosophical, introspective.

"Like kids," he says, "I build ghosts. As a kid myself, I had a poor self-image." When he first started telling stories in public, he lacked the confidence to negotiate payment for his storytelling. "I was just sharing Kalaupapa's history. Then Ann (his wife since 1989) said, 'You're a professional. You should act like it.' I struggled, I buried my head under the pillow so I didn't hear her telling anyone they have to pay for storytelling. I still didn't feel any self-worth."

Perhaps it's Malo's version of what Fern says about the need to know who you are.

Who am I? Malo first came face-to-face with the question in 1964. In July, one eye was surgically removed, and he was prescribed medication to stave off continuing damage. By August, recuperating at Hale Mōhalu, the other eye worsened.

"I couldn't see but I thought it would only be temporary," he recalls. "When the nurse brought my food, I'd wait until she left. Then I'd lock the door and close the drapes, and struggle with my fork.

"When the doctor came, he'd ask how I was. 'Top shape, doc. Top shape.'

"Then one day I asked the nurse to put my pills in a little paper cup instead of an envelope. She immediately said, 'What's the matter, boy? You blind?'

"The doctor came. He said, 'How long?' I said, 'Six weeks.' They moved me to the side of Hale Mōhalu for the blind.

"About a year later, my sister, Pearl, wrote from Kalaupapa that she would buy my hunting guns for her husband. When I signed over the ownership papers, I cried. It was the last foothold in my life before."

That turning point directed Malo not only to mobility training, but eventually to the University of Hawai'i, where he earned a degree in Hawaiian Studies in 1978. After the 1987 Bishop Museum episode, he was hired as a storyteller for O'ahu's Summer Fun program, and was part of the first Talking Island Festival of storytelling (now called the Bankoh Talk Story Festival) two years later. Since then, he's told stories in Spain, New Zealand and Canada and at the National Storytelling Festival in Tennessee.

For all his travels, the supreme satisfaction for Malo comes from "touching one life at a time." Some years ago, he recalls, a Hawaiian high school senior told her counselor the University of Hawai'i was beyond her abilities. Then she heard Malo tell stories, tell about himself. And she went back to the counselor, asked for a UH application, and said, "If *kūpuna* can do it, I can try."

Malo had touched a life. "But this works two ways," he says. "These things touch me, too."

So Fujii is right. The power of story is communion, one soul to another.

Sums up Fern, "Life is a story. Maybe there is no fiction. I just know that stories grow. And if I have this distinctive voice and way of speaking, I should use my God-given gift."

༄

Remembering Mr. Bowman

1999

In the open-air basement woodshop of my Uncle Wright's modest Nuʻuanu home, saws and sanders, drills and planers whine and hum and buzz. Acrid blue smoke curls as he makes a cut on a table saw and admits, "Dull blade." The stench mingles with the fragrance of *tiare* blooming just outside.

Rockers and arms and back slats for *koa* chairs are stacked here and there. Paddle blades line the wall. As on most mornings, Uncle Wright is working. Uncle Wright is 91 now, and the loves of his life are here, beautiful woods in his basement and upstairs his wife of 60 years, Elizabeth Kaleiluluʻu Whittington Bowman.

This last statement might be too philosophical for him. As Aunty Betty puts it, "He keeps working because he found out sitting around watching TV makes him feel lousy."

No one in Hawaiʻi can speak of canoe building without mentioning Wright Bowman and his late son Wright Bowman, Jr. More than 20 years ago, Honpa Hongwanji Mission named Uncle Wright one of Hawaiʻi's "Living Treasures."

The original meaning of "Bowman" is easy to guess, but Hawaiians today might rather call Wright Bowman "*kahuna kālai waʻa*," or master builder of canoes.

Uncle Wright first laid hands on a canoe nearly 80 years ago, but the vessels are only part of his calling as a master of woodcraft.

He jokingly refers to himself as a "wood butcher," but the woodgrain of *koa*, *kou* and *milo* seems to shimmer with life under the mere touch of his fingers. His legendary *koa* rocking chairs—he's got orders backed up for years—are perfectly suited to the human *ʻokole*, and so perfectly balanced they rock a full minute on their own after you get up.

Like many, Uncle Wright's apprentice, Ryan Satsuda, calls him "Mr. Bowman."

"I'm learning a lot more than woodworking," Satsuda says. A few years ago, he remembers, Hui Nalu Canoe Club ordered a scale model of a racing canoe. Satsuda was at the Bowman home when the club representative came to pick it up.

"Mr. Bowman said to me, 'You watch. The woman will come with a check, and then I'll tell her it's free. They raised the money, so I'll give it.'" Satsuda pauses. "That's what I mean. I'm learning how to be a better human being."

Perhaps Mr. Bowman learned that kind of generosity when he was a kid of about 12.

In those days—1919 or so—the Bowmans lived in Hilo but spent a month each summer at their Hōnaunau house next to the City of Refuge, now Puʻuhonua o Hōnaunau National Historical Park.

"An old Hawaiian named Nahau was the park keeper," Uncle Wright remembers. "He built canoes in the park. I watched how he did it. All the kids, we cleaned up the park for him, planted coconut trees and watered them. In exchange, he let us paddle. We pile inside, catch small waves, race. Good fun.

"Right after the war—World War I—a couple from New York came with an old car and camped. Nahau felt sorry for them, brought them fish, papaya. After they went back to New York, Nahau got a letter from a lawyer saying that from now on he would receive a check from them for $200 a month. Imagine. Just for being nice."

Talent to match generosity may have been foretold by Donald and Mele Bowman's names for their fifth child. "Wright"—surname of a family friend—appears in the English dictionary: "Worker, especially constructive worker." His middle name, "Elemakule," which means "old man," was a ship's carpenter, whom he learned only recently was his great-great grandfather.

Uncle Wright took naturally to carpentry at Kamehameha Schools, where he boarded from first grade. His eighth-grade report card noted: "Carpentry, exceptional."

He remembers winning five dollars—big money—in a contest to build something practical of wood. His prize entry was a rabbit house, its door hinged with leather salvaged from old shoes.

When he was 11, in 1919, he worked for a Honolulu planing mill mixing glue and sweeping up. He was paid three silver dollars a week. One of the workers inspired the boy because he dressed in white shirt, necktie and coat. This man worked in an office, where he wore a white apron and made beautiful things. He was a pattern maker. A few years later, Uncle Wright and his older brother Donald enrolled at the General Electric School in Lynn, Massachusetts, where Wright did become a pattern maker.

The highly skilled work lasted through World War II, but then the development of welding eliminated the need for patterns for cast metal.

Wright returned to his birth island, to Aunty Betty's childhood home district of Ka'ū, where he made furniture and curios to sell to tourists, and he patched outrigger canoes.

In 1950 Kamehameha Schools asked him to teach woodshop. In the next 23 years, thousands of students funneled through his classes.

Because of it, he says, "I can't go anywhere now without someone calling, 'Eh! Mr. Bowman!' They come up to me, people almost 60 years old, and tell me they still have their pig board or their turtle plant stand, or the shoe shine kit they made."

At the prep school, where he taught sixth graders, "The problem was the boys and girls together. They fight. I hated that. So I had a nail-pounding contest. The boys selected a representative and so did the girls. We'd settle who was best.

"I put a block of wood in a vise and started a spike. Ho, the girl pounded her nail all the way in. But the boys were still so cocky. They thought their guy could pound it faster.

"But he lost. The hammer kept coming off the nail. He couldn't even strike it.

"You know, I never told this until now. I greased the head of the boy's nail." Mr. Bowman looks sheepish. "But the contest kept them quiet a long time."

One of those long-ago students—Ed Kame'enui, now a professor of education—recalls, "Most of the teachers were strict and aloof. He stood out—he was approachable, kind, and he had enormous integrity. Kids connected with him immediately."

It was in the Kamehameha teaching years, in 1970, that Uncle

Wright built his first outrigger, a basement project for Waimānalo Canoe Club. When Bishop Estate trustee Papa Lyman heard about the basement, he suggested Uncle Wright build on campus. He and Wright Jr. worked there for years after he retired from teaching in 1973.

When the Polynesian Voyaging Society was constructing *Hōkūle'a* about the time Uncle Wright retired, Herb Kāne consulted Uncle Wright on how to make curved *'iako*.

"He suggested lamination," Kāne remembers. "Then he went to the Kamehameha shop and created jigs to do it. He was always good at solving a problem. He looked at it logically and devised a procedure. It always worked.

"Later I asked him for help with the spars and booms, him and Wrighto. They were at *Hōkūle'a*'s launching in 1975. They had put their *mana* into her."

I asked my uncle about how he learned to build canoes, expecting a complicated answer about long apprenticeships.

"I just watched," he says. "There are certain specs, but there's no drawing. It's all in my eye. All you need is a center line and a stick to get the sides even."

Some lucky paddling clubs have canoes built or patched by Uncle Wright. Hundreds of people own *koa* rocking chairs or dining tables signed with the wood-burned stamp "WB." Thousands—myself included—own his *koa* paddles. Some of the thousands made the paddles themselves under Mr. Bowman's watchful and foolproof eye.

Anyone who's attended a service at Kamehameha Schools' Bishop Chapel or browsed in the Heritage House next to it is surrounded by Uncle Wright's craftsmanship and *mana*.

Kamehameha alum and current graduate student in art at UH Ka'ili Chun—too young to have been his student in high school—now works with him in his basement, learning to make *'ōhi'a* spears and stands to incorporate into her modern sculpture.

She's wearing shorts and T-shirt. Her arms are covered in sawdust. But I can tell by her posture, her eyes, her hands on the wood, that to go to Uncle Wright's basement is to go to a Hawaiian woodworker's mecca.

"Mr. Bowman is the master," she says. "He's the man."

He is The Man, the last of my father's six half-Hawaiian full siblings. Uncle Wright told me once, when I was only about 40 and too young to really understand, "The only important things in life are health and love."

Some years later, when I had the privilege to sail a few hours on *Hōkūleʻa*, it came to me that his words apply not just to individuals, but to all of us, together. Long ago, he watched Nahau patch old canoes, learning by observing. Since then, many of us have looked to him, hoping to learn canoe building or woodcraft. We save the tangible evidence of our efforts—the shoe shine kits, the turtle plant stands, the canoe paddles—in our houses. And the most important lessons, the *mana*, the model for how to live life, we save in our hearts.

Update: Wright Elemakule Bowman worked in his shop until a just a few months before he died in 2003 at the age of 96. His memorial service was held at Bishop Chapel on the Kamehameha Schools campus where he had spent more than 40 years as student, teacher or canoe builder. The title of the eulogy was "Let Us Now Praise Famous Men."

◡◞

RELUCTANT KAHUNA

2000

"*Kahuna*," says Sam Kaʻai, "is not a titled position. They're recognized by what they do. Supposed to be keepers of secrets." His words sound like a lecture, but his eyes twinkle. "All you have to do is kiss me, and I'll tell you the secrets. I must not be a *kahuna*."

The first time I heard of Sam Kaʻai was just before midnight in January 1993 during Onipaʻa, the centennial commemoration of the overthrow of the Hawaiian monarchy. I had arrived at the lawn near the Kamehameha statue across from ʻIolani Palace with a friend, both of us dressed in black, as directed. Kerosene torches burned orange and smoky in the cool night air.

We had signed up for a two-hour stint in a 24-hour vigil beating the *pahu*, a tall sharkskin drum. We'd never kept this sort of vigil. And never beaten such a drum. Perhaps our 50-something faces betrayed these sorry facts.

A teenage kid emerged from under a canopy.

"Beat it like this," he thumped the heels of both hands on the drumhead, pushing away. "Do it exactly together, just so."

I thought he would add something about honoring the Queen. But instead he admonished, "Do it well. Do it properly. Sam Kaʻai made this drum."

The drum was as close as I came to Sam Kaʻai then, although I learned later that he conducted a public *ʻawa* ceremony on the palace grounds that historic weekend, the first in generations.

But months later, I was invited to sit in on an ancient warfare presentation in a Hawaiian Studies class at Windward Community College. The guest: Sam Kaʻai.

With a *kīhei*, a cloak, flung over the shoulder of a brown shirt, the fabled Sam Kaʻai sliced the air with a shark-toothed *lei niho manō* he'd made himself. The weapon fit perfectly around his right hand like brass knuckles, the row of ripper teeth jutting over his fist.

Kaʻai seized a polished *pololū*, a long spear, and pinioned an imaginary enemy. Grabbed a *pāhoa*, a short dagger, and stabbed him in the *ʻōpū*. Hooked out his eyeballs with two fingers.

His blunt teeth strung themselves across his face in a smile above his graying beard. It reminded me of the enigmatic grin of the red-feathered image of Kamehameha's god of war, Kūkaʻilimoku. Kaʻai's eyes bored through every squirming student. And me.

Some say that Sam Kaʻai is kēnā—born to command.

That day he was in commander mode. Now, at 62, he says he worries that he will "arrive at the campfire of the ancestors" and they will laugh at him and say, "Here comes our special damn fool."

"I had that feeling as a child," he says softly, pondering how dyslexia has colored his life. "I was a child who was supposed to have less than most, who looked out at the world and saw different things."

Sometimes the early self-doubt dyslexia spawned still creeps up on Kaʻai.

But I didn't know that in 1994, when I was writing an article about lua, the Hawaiian martial art, and I needed an expert on ancient weapons. Of course I looked him up.

I arrived at his house on Maui just after lunchtime. The carport was stacked with ʻōhiʻa, kou and kauila wood waiting to be transformed into museum-quality spears and daggers. Inside, his collection of Polynesian artifacts reduced the open floor space to about four feet square.

This time Kaʻai was unarmed. But in three split-seconds, he gave me a personal taste of ancient hand-to-hand combat. First he sliced a muted sidehand crack to my collar bone. Then twisted my thumb and little finger in would-be debilitation. As his finale, he tripped me behind the ankle with his tattooed leg, and would have had my ʻōkole on his floor had he not deftly caught me on the descent.

After that, he talked the rest of the afternoon. At the end, I could think only of finding two Advil, maybe three. Kaʻai had overburdened my poor female head with too many weapons and too much warfare. The attendant god Kū, the ultimate male symbol and the archetype of the god with the ambiguous smile, seemed to thump a drum inside my skull. In the short rests in the rhythm, Hina, the female deity who tempers it all, glimmered like phosphorescence on the night tide.

Later, when Kū had subsided and Hina had soothed my headache, I realized that Kaʻai had visions of young chiefs, and heard the voices of those long dead.

☙

Kaʻai grew up in what is still one of Hawaiʻi's farthest outposts, Kaupō, way beyond Hāna, in a rugged land requiring self-sufficiency.

In 1938, three days after Kaʻai's birth, he was given as a *hānai* son to a childless aunt and uncle. The family grew *taro*, sweet potatoes, cabbage, tomatoes. Orchards of papaya and avocado mainly fed the pigs.

"Nobody there noticed World War II, except there were barbed wire fences on all the beaches," he says. "In that kind of environment, my Hawaiian tastes began."

At Kaupō, and in the valley of Honokōhau on the other end of Maui, he learned the old ways from *kūpuna*, especially his Tutu Man, his granduncle Lihau Kaula Kaʻaihui, before he went off to high school on Oʻahu.

There, the dyslexic eyes, and the questioning spirit that is the bane of mundane teachers, led him to A's in art—and even two art scholarships—but too many F's in academics at "Tokyo High," which he insists is a more apt name than McKinley. "[McKinley], that cheapskate that went take over my people. Who's going to praise the name of a guy who stole the nation? Tokyo High sound more better."

At graduation in 1957, he got a certificate of completion instead of a diploma.

Yet he can deliver impromptu discourses on the Knights Templar, the Crusades, the Coptic Church, the Huguenots and Uther Pendragon. Pressed, he admits to wallowing in the Lincoln Library, the old-time one-volume encyclopedia. One of his few regrets is losing the family copy in his 1985 divorce.

Looking back, the divorce was a classic crossroads, the Big Intersection. But even now it's a raw subject and Kaʻai himself will not speak of it. For him, it marked the end of carving fee-for-service classy wooden signs for Lahaina businesses or crucifixes for Catholic churches. From then on he devoted himself to making items of ancient Hawaiian material culture.

"Through our hands come the ways of the old," he says. "Into what we make goes our *mana*."

He'd rounded one Hawaiian turning point in 1976 when he carved the male and female stern images for *Hōkūleʻa*'s first voyage to Tahiti. In 1980 and 1985, he sailed to Tahiti as part of the crew.

Then, in 1988, Ka'ai became the first nonacademic scholar to receive a Fulbright grant to study with the Maori in New Zealand. His voice still retains a tinge of British Maori influence.

In 1991, he co-chaired the bicentennial ceremonies at Pu'ukoholā Heiau that have now become an annual focal point for Hawaiians. More recently, he formed Ka Meheu 'Ohu o Ka Honu, a nonprofit organization to revitalize ceremony, ritual, protocol and culture.

We met again in 1999 at the Ritz-Carlton Kapalua, where he opened the annual Easter weekend Celebration of the Arts the first evening under a full moon, *Māhealani*. This time, his only weapon was a conch horn.

"Too-TOOT! Too-TOOT! Too-TOOT, too-TOOT!"

The double calls of his *pū* jumped a perfect octave. Anyone else who's tried it sounds like a cow.

He sat on a small *lau hala* mat, *kīhei* over the shoulder of that same brown shirt he calls his "habit." Island visitors and Hawaiian families also sat cross-legged on the floor, half-circling themselves around him in a wide berth I interpreted as respect.

"*Kawaihae a makalae*," he said, so softly the audience strained to hear. "Whispers from the shore."

He rambled in the traditional talk-story way, his words forming elusive images that came and went like cloud wisps drifting across *Māhealani*. I listened intently, knowing it was up to me to fit the fragments together, like 3-D puzzle pieces, until they made sense. This is how ideas work with Hawaiians, not neat left-brain units marching in parallel formations, but bubbles weaving in circles that wander and bulge elliptical, overlapping like invisible tracks left after a *hula*.

"'*Aloa hā*," Ka'ai said. "It's not, '*Aloha!* Sheraton Maui!' '*Ā*' is light, '*loa*' without end, '*hā*' life's breath. *Aloha* is about an affectionate feeling having no boundary, no limitation, no question. It's about doing something for somebody so hard that you are poverty struck. But in the end, you can bring the treasure, perhaps '*iliahi*, sandalwood, the light of life without end, to the campfire of your ancestors. That is *aloha*. The Greeks call it *agape*."

Afterward, the former Mr. Blood and Guts invited me to

share lemon herb tea in the Ritz-Carlton's elegant lobby. This time, Kaʻai didn't give me a headache, but entranced my brain with visions of Hawaiians fishing up islands, with notions of warriors routinely calling on the spirits of the dead, with the reality of more than 3,000 ancient dead right under the lawn between the hotel and the sea. They were all stories of the sort told nightly in the *Hale Mua*, the men's house, the ancient "house to move forward," the house that is coming back with young men Kaʻai calls "The Young Chiefs."

Recently, Kaʻai's own house has become an adjunct to the *Hale Mua*, an informal learning center where his Young Chiefs show up weekly to study language and history, to learn ceremony and protocol from this ʻelemakua, elder adviser, who has inspired them to go beyond the study of *lua* they began years ago. The rest of the week they are firefighters, accountants, public-maintenance workers, teachers. But when they meet at the *Hale Mua*, they are Kaʻai's living vision of tomorrow's Hawaiians, healthy leaders aiming purposefully at the future because their roots are in their proper past.

That night my enchanted dreams conjured up a *Hale Mua*.

The next morning, Good Friday, the lobby was shoulder-to-shoulder with people conversing in Hawaiian. Outside, Hawaiians in regalia, many staying at the hotel, formed into a procession.

"Too-TOOT! Too-TOOT, too-TOOT!" Kaʻai's *pū* silenced everyone—except a tourist whispering, "Ooh, this is a cultural event!"

In the breezeways, visitors carved canoe paddler petroglyphs in balsam foam sprayed black. Outside, in the medicinal garden, others learned to string shell *lei* from the Niʻihau contingent.

In a swimming pool shaped like an *ipu* laid on its side, Hawaiian kids invented a new game: Dive from the side, but before breaking the water hurtle yourself over the volleyball net. Until then I'd never seen a chlorine-clean Ti-D-Bowl-blue swimming pool full of laughing, splashing brownies.

Kids were the only Hawaiians in the water. No grown-up had time for pool or beach—too many official lectures and discussions. Too many impromptu meetings. I sat next to Kaʻai to watch *And Then There Were None*. The film counts down the full-blood Hawaiian population figures decade by decade. In the year 2044 there will be none.

Next to me in the dark, Kaʻai wept.

But not for long. Moments later, I caught him in the hall, rubber slippers rooted to the marble floor, lecturing a young man on the need to dive into politics.

"Politics is the negotiation of bloodless war. The art of it is to choose *aloha*, peace," he counseled. "For all we have to replace it is blood war."

For two full days I followed Ka'ai like gum stuck to his slippers, watching and listening. By then, I longed for a swim. But he said, "Come. We go."

He led me to Room 2536. Within were nearly 20 young chiefs. On a *lau hala* mat over the carpet sat Ka'ai's own *koa 'awa* bowl. Only one other woman was present in this Ritz-Carlton hotel room, which was temporarily turned into a *Hale Mua*, the men's house to go forward.

"Dwell not on pain," Ka'ai tells them in these private meetings. "You are obligated to make joy, no matter how sweet or bitter the drink. You need to learn the song. Someday you will be *kūpuna*. There will be no one else to ask, and the face in front of you will be your own shadow, your *mo'opuna*, your grandchildren. I want you to remember these stories. If you tell them, I will live forever. But if you are distracted by a Big Mac attack, then the Lord Makani, the Lord of the Wind, will blow me away like yesterday's dry leaves, and I will be *kawaihae*, just a whisper."

A young warrior is learning to make *'awa*. Two knights of the round bowl fill it halfway with water. The novitiate plunks in handfuls of shredded damp *'awa* root, swishing it until the water turns muddy, then clarifying it with a *hau* bark strainer that looks like a grassy mop. He has trouble wringing it, so Ka'ai demonstrates, one fist over the other, just so.

Cups of *'awa* pass to one person at a time, by protocol. But in this informal setting, the air is jovial. The elder guest of honor downs his cup, then couches his speech carefully, for *'awa* is sacred and requires the truth.

His story has to do with his wife, who at this moment is taking a nap because he's tired her out. The Young Chiefs laugh. But wait, there's more. One young warrior had advised him to eat 12 oysters, one for each lovemaking. *Auwe*, says the elder. The technique failed. Ohhhhh, the crowd sighs. Then he says the last two oysters didn't work.

We women try not to laugh the loudest.

When all the men have been served, each throwing the coconut shell cup back to the server, Ka'ai himself serves me.

The 'awa is not bitter as he had warned me, but it does taste like dirt. By the third swallow, my tongue feels numb.

When the guest of honor prepares to leave, I take the cue. It's time for me to exit. The door closes behind me. In the hall, my head seems clear, but my body is Jell-O.

My mind is full of ideas of truth-telling in the presence of 'awa, of ideas about mana, of culture dying with the seventh generation unless the eighth generation wises up before it's too late.

The next evening, Ka'ai parks himself at the end of a front-row table at the celebration lū'au, ignoring the "reserved" sign. The fragrance of frangipani—he won't let me say "plumeria"—fills the place.

Clifford Nae'ole, the hotel's cultural specialist, who has engineered much of the celebration, confers on Ka'ai "Native Hawaiian Hunting and Gathering Rights" at the buffet. Ka'ai approves the array of traditional foods, but observes that the buffet also includes "foreign dishes for all."

While we wait our turn, Ka'ai babbles to a couple across the table, wannabe Hawaiians, retired, from California. Oh, but we've had a place here for 25 years. Mrs. California, in lace-yoked mu'umu'u, has armored herself wrist to elbow in gold Hawaiian bracelets.

Ka'ai plucks the dry 'opelu out of the centerpiece, planning to have the serving kids throw the stiff fish on the grill to warm it up.

"It's the season of Kū," he remarks, "The end of Makahiki is when the 'ōhi'a 'ai—the mountain apple—blossoms. The coming and going of the whale is part of the season, the coming and going of the gods."

Mrs. California is all ears. She introduces herself and her husband. Sam politely gives our names. She says, "Mr. Ka'ai, may I call you Sam?"

He grins his best Kūka'ilimoku smile. "Sam I am," he says. "Green eggs and ham."

Easter morning, although he left me at the lū'au at 9 p.m.,

Ka'ai looks green around the proverbial gills. It seems, No. 1, the young chiefs had issues to discuss in the *Hale Mua* until past midnight. No. 2, he had lingered too long in front of the *lū'au*'s outrigger canoe ice sculpture that cooled the *wana*, *'opihi* and oysters on the half shell. Except for the dried *'opelu* and *poi*, everything he ate was raw. When he finally got to bed, he laid awake for hours paying for the overindulgence. We step into the mirrored elevator on the fourth floor. "Let us descend from our heavenly perch," he says.

I take the cap off my pen. "Don't write that down," he barks. He's guessing correctly that my notebook—now nearly 200 pages long—contains both his pearls of wisdom and his drivel. "That's the book that makes me naked," he says.

Outside, Ka'ai leads me beyond the *kapu* signs to the grassy seaside dunes where the 3,000 Hawaiians lie buried.

In the wake of these ghosts, the Ritz-Carlton invented this annual weekend that combines Hawaiian arts and entertainment with panels, film screenings and meetings.

The hotel catapulted into notoriety before its concrete foundations were even poured. In 1987, site-prep excavations turned up bones. Hawaiian bones, 12 centuries of burials deep in the sand where the hotel was to sit next to the beach at Honolua Bay. The count stopped at 1,016. Archaeologists said the total would exceed 3,000.

Iwi, bones, are perhaps the most sacred relics to Hawaiians, and these became a *cause célèbre*. In the end, builders set the hotel back about 500 feet. Now visitors take shuttles or hoof it on an asphalt path to the beach, past signs warning them from the dunes where Hawaiians reinterred the ancestors.

It's a quiet cemetery of unmarked graves now, but in 1988 the dunes teemed with Hawaiian protesters.

"Under state law, 1,016 personages were removed from this area, with the intention that the site could be rendered 'neutral' so the hotel could be built," Ka'ai says. "At about 800 we protested."

For reburial in 1989, Hawaiians wrapped the disinterred individually in *kapa*. For the last 16, women made black *kapa* in a single ritualistic day at a Moloka'i *heiau*, the first wet stage of the bark cloth carried in a calabash made by Sam Ka'ai.

Abutting the west boundary of the rolling burial dunes is more mowed grass—a golf course fairway.

"Over there is the green," Ka'ai gestures across a rocky, deep-water cove. "Shoot over the water. Calm day like this, some guys go dive for balls."

At the edge of the cliff he turns toward the east, his back to golf. "And from this place here," he says, "prayers were called to the dawn."

From this sort of place, he is likely to shift spontaneously into poetic power drive. Things like this come out: "For the order of change, the Lord Makani is always ready. He blows in the dark times of the night. Time is moving season by season. What will you keep? Have you picked the flower too early? The fruit too young? Are you the seed from a tree destroyed? Or the living tree?"

He speaks of *ka'au*, a measure of 40. "*Kanahā* means 40. But *ka'au*, it is a mystical word for the full measure."

Desperate with a sense that Hawaiians must learn their ancestral ways before it's too late, he commands, in his Don Quixote way, "Either come with your retinue, or join another as a servant."

I have no retinue, so I give him a gentle servant's kiss in the soft spot between the cheekbone and the beard. But Ka'ai spills no more secrets. He only humphs, "People want to quote mystic pearls of wisdom from me," he says. "It's just Spam in a can."

Maybe it will take a *ka'au* of kisses. The way his eyes twinkle, I bet he'll take my other 39 smooches and then reluctantly tell the one secret he's trying to keep.

It's not so bad, Mr. Green Eggs and Ham. Dr. Seuss was a *kahuna*, too.

3
In Footsteps

❦

A mansion, a Victorian spinster,
a wounded island and retracing
old journeys

﹌

House of Stories

2003

Across from the Hawai'i State Capitol in downtown Honolulu, past the shimmering blue haze of Beretania Street's six lanes of traffic, a white mansion stands in a shady oasis behind a wrought-iron fence. Many know Washington Place as the governor's residence; some remember that Hawai'i's last monarch, Queen Lili'uokalani, once lived in it. And now that it will be open to the public as a historic interpretive center, visitors can immerse themselves in the tales that make Washington Place, above all, a house of stories.

One such story comes from a transition time, 1917. At 78, Queen Lili'uokalani was near life's end, nearly 25 years after her Kingdom of Hawai'i government was overthrown in a *coup d'état* led by foreign businessmen. The aging queen rested often on her big four-poster bed jammed against the French window in the downstairs bedroom—a perfect spot to play peek a-boo with a little neighbor girl who frequently sneaked into the yard. Their giggles brought the queen's nurses and ladies-in-waiting running. When the queen heard them coming, she would motion to her young accomplice to hide beneath the windowsill. When the attendants departed, the little girl popped up again.

Today, you can picture the scene as you visit that very room. Last fall, the queen's bedroom was opened to the public after extensive renovation. Guided tours of the main floor are now being offered, and work is scheduled to begin soon on new galleries in the upstairs area that for the last 83 years served as the living quarters of Hawai'i's state and territorial governors. But no more. When the state's new governor, Linda Lingle, took office in December, she moved into a new house at the back of the property, freeing the second-floor living quarters for conversion into public galleries to share the stories of Washington Place.

✂

The story of the house itself began in 1837, when Beretania Street was a dusty path through a parched, treeless plain sprinkled with a few chiefs' residences and the churches and houses of the growing *haole* population. Enter a mysterious sea captain from New England, John Dominis.

"Dominis had arrived in New England in 1819, a polished, aristocratic gentleman who spoke perfect English, but no one knew where he came from," says Jim Bartels, who oversaw the renovation of the home as Washington Place director under former Governor Ben Cayetano. "Even his son never knew where he came from, and if his wife knew, she never told."

Dominis married the belle of a prominent Boston family, Mary Lambert Jones. The captain first appeared in Honolulu as early as 1823, and in 1837 he moved to Honolulu permanently with his wife and young son, John Owen. According to Bartels, Mary Dominis took one look at Honolulu and demanded 1) a mansion and 2) trees. In 1847, she got both at Washington Place.

In the interim, Capt. Dominis sailed the seas in command of merchant ships. In 1842, he filed with the U.S. Patent Office for a patent on a complicated instrument to measure canvas for sails, signing the application "John Dominis of the Sandwich Islands."

In 1846, he set sail for China, intending to return with elegant furniture for the new house, but he was never heard from again, presumably lost at sea. The enigmatic captain never lived in the mansion he spent five years building, but Mary and young John moved in, taking in boarders to make ends meet.

A decade later, Mary Dominis was among the first in Honolulu to have a Christmas tree. At her holiday party, Santa Claus bestowed a gift on each of about a hundred children—much to the disapproval of the strict missionaries who had grown increasingly influential in Island life. "They believed, correctly, that Christmas was based on a pagan ceremony," Bartels says. "You know, the winter solstice and all that. They considered it right up there with idolatry, and singing and dancing for pleasure. And they disliked the idea of giving children gifts for which they had not worked and sacrificed. They thought it taught bad habits and worked against the all-important idea of thrift." In this light, Bartels says, "Mrs. Dominis' Christmas parties were a brave political and social gesture in those early years."

In 1862, Mary's son John married Lydia Kamaka'eha Pākī—the future Queen Lili'uokalani—in a small ceremony at the home of her *hānai*—adopted—sister, Princess Bernice Pauahi, who was also married to a prominent American, Charles Reed Bishop. "By most accounts, John's mother waited at home," Bartels says. When Lydia moved into her mother-in-law's mansion, she wrote decades later, she was considered an "intruder," a fact she was "forced to realize from the beginning."

At the time, Lydia Pākī was just one of a number of high chiefs, far less prominent than her husband, who had become governor of O'ahu in 1864. In 1877, the tables turned when her brother, King Kalākaua, named her heir apparent. To her dislike, he also gussied up her name. "Her Hawaiian name meant 'Sore Eyes,'" Bartels says. "Like many Hawaiian names, it marked an important situation when she was born—a relative suffered a painful eye problem. King Kalākaua didn't want her to become Queen Sore Eyes the First, so he tinkered with the name, until it meant "The Smarting of the Royal One,' which was actually the same thing."

When Kalākaua died in January 1891, Lili'uokalani inherited a host of political troubles along with the throne. Two years later, a small group of resident American and other foreign businessmen engineered her overthrow and created a Provisional Government, which they converted into the Republic of Hawai'i in 1894.

After a failed counter-revolution in 1895, Republic officials came knocking on the Washington Place door with a warrant for the queen's arrest. She wrote later that her private papers were "swept into a bag and carried off by the chief justice in person," and then militiamen ransacked Washington Place "from garret to cellar ... no trifle left unturned ... Every drawer or desk, table or bureau was wrenched out, turned up-side down, the contents pulled over on the floors ..."

"During the first days of her imprisonment, officials led her to believe she might be shot," Bartels says. They forced her to abdicate the throne, signing the document as "Liliuokalani Dominis," which had never been her legal name. They tried her before a military court, convicted her of "misprision of treason" (knowing about treason but not reporting it), fined her $500 and sentenced her to five years in prison at hard labor.

They actually imprisoned her in a second-floor bedroom of 'Iolani Palace, releasing her eight months later to Washington Place—on parole. When they lifted parole in December 1896, she went to Washington, D.C., to plead the Kingdom's case. At that point, Bartels says, "She began to reinvent herself. She knew she was too significant to just vanish."

For a decade, she continued to labor for the reinstatement of the Kingdom. She held regular public audiences at Washington Place. Later, when automobiles came in, she bought two and hired a chauffeur. He drove her to Moanalua Field to witness the flight of the first airplane in Hawai'i, a canvas-and-wood construction similar to the Wright Brothers' machine. When Buddhist immigrants established a temple in Honolulu, some local Christians considered it akin to devil worship, but Lili'uokalani, a staunch Christian herself, visited the new edifice. She also established the Lili'uokalani Trust, which now provides social services to thousands of Hawaiian children. After the Queen's death in 1917, Lili'uokalani Trust sold Washington Place to the Territory of Hawai'i with the stipulation that it be used as the governor's residence and a memorial to the queen.

When Hawai'i became the United States' westernmost shore, it fell to Territorial governors to welcome Asian dignitaries on their way to Washington, D.C. A garden at the back of the house was sacrificed to add a state dining room, where food became the ingredient for new stories.

Once, in the 1930s, the food service staff deliberately planned a steak menu for a visiting Hindu potentate. When the guests sent their plates of sacred cow back to the kitchen, the staff scrambled eggs for the guests and ate the steak themselves. By the 1960s, however, the staff had presumably become more politically sensitive, and they invented the first porkless *lū'au* for Jordan's Muslim King Hussein.

At another state dinner, U.S. Vice President Lyndon Johnson noticed that the serving staff had come up short on steaks. "Incredibly," says Bartels, "they had miscounted. Johnson saw the problem. With characteristic decisiveness, he just grabbed a steak, cut it in half, and plopped it on the plate next to his."

That was in the days of Bill Quinn, the last appointed

Territorial governor, who was then elected the first state governor in 1959. In 1960, Bill and Nancy Quinn hosted the young monarch of Thailand, King Bhumibol Adulyadej, and his wife, Queen Sirikit, for four days. Of course, Quinn knew that the king was a devout Buddhist, but the governor, an amateur musician, also discovered that the king played the clarinet. Quinn chose the entertainers for the state dinner accordingly—*hula* master ʻIolani Luahine, followed by Kenny Alford and his Dixiecats. He told Alford to have a new silver clarinet mouthpiece in his pocket.

Following dinner, the party repaired to the patio. After the Dixiecats had played a couple of songs, Quinn said to the king, "Your Majesty, I understand you play a mean clarinet. I wonder if you would join the band?" Queen Sirikit suggested Quinn first sing a number, and then the king borrowed a clarinet and jammed with the Dixiecats. At the end of the hour, the 50 guests gave him a standing ovation.

When the royal couple left Hawaiʻi, Quinn said later, "I had a tear in my eye, and he did, too." Afterward, the American ambassador to Thailand told Quinn, "You know, Governor, in Thailand they still approach the king on their knees, and there's nobody that he has any closeness with except possibly a relative or two. You're the best friend he's ever had."

Bartels thinks the Quinns win the prize for having the most fun at Washington Place. But recent governor Ben Cayetano and his wife Vicky get credit for turning the grand old mansion into a more public place, while still housing Hawaiʻi's heads of state on the property. The new governor will still hold state functions at Washington Place, but mostly it will serve as a public museum.

The new living arrangements are a boon to history-minded visitors, and they should also offer a bit more privacy to Hawaiʻi's chief executive. Vicky Cayetano likes to tell the story of an impromptu encounter that happened several years ago during a public open house. She was standing at the front entrance greeting people and posing with them for pictures. Just as she was shaking hands with a woman and her young daughter, her husband—having forgotten about the occasion—barreled down the grand front staircase wearing a T-shirt, shorts and rubber slippers.

"Mommy, look!" the little girl said. "It's the governor!"

As Cayetano retreated up the stairs, the mother said, "Oh, it couldn't be the governor. He would never dress like that."

BIRD IN HAND

1996

Hilo. There is a saying among sailors, *"Follow a Pacific shower and it will lead you to Hilo,"* Isabella Bird wrote.

'Tis still true. This February day, winter rain drums on tarps covering the Farmer's Market located in sight of the spot near Coconut Island where Isabella alighted from a whaleboat to stay two days before venturing on to Kīlauea. Hilo, she noted, is *the paradise of Hawaii ... such a lively place for such a mere village ...*

'Tis still true. This morning, customers crowd the market's makeshift aisles, fingering and pondering: limes, oranges, lemons. Lettuces, radishes, purple sweet potatoes. Roses, variegated anthuriums, yellow *kāhili* ginger. Everything costs a dollar—except a dozen roses, which go for eight bucks. Men and women cradle long-stemmed flowers, or babies, in their arms and dangle plastic grocery bags of potatoes and papayas from their fingers, timing their dash from the market to their car to coincide with a gap in the rain.

My photographer companion, Brad—yes, Isabella, I know, I should call him "Mr. Lewis"—comes here often. "The beauty of the rain in Hilo," he tells me, "is that it keeps Hilo real. People don't come all the way to Hawai'i to sit in their hotel rooms and watch it rain."

We breakfast on *'ahi* and eggs for three bucks. I think about buying *kūlolo* roadside at Kimo's Lau Lau Stand. Mr. Lewis thinks the post office lawn is where, in Isabella's time, the city fathers passed their mornings playing croquet.

Volcano of Kilauea, Jan. 31, 1873. The track, on the whole, is a perpetual upward scramble ... nearly 4,000 feet in thirty miles. Only strong, surefooted, well-shod horses can undertake this journey ... Often, I only knew that my companions were ahead by the sparks struck from their horses' shoes ... We reached the crater house at eight, clouds of red vapour mixed with flame were curling ceaselessly out of a huge invisible pit of blackness.

❧

Brad, I mean Mr. Lewis, zips along the track, scrambling smoothly upward toward Kīlauea at the wheel of a Thunderbird. Surely Isabella would have chosen a Thunderbird over a horse, had the option been available. After all, it took her only a few miserable hours of galloping to forsake sidesaddle for riding astride.

At Kīlauea, something akin to Isabella's crater house still stands—a rustic, weathered 1877 hotel that is now the Volcano Art Center. Isabella slept not a hundred feet from here, in this building's grass-and-bamboo predecessor.

This morning is wet and murky, as many mornings here are. So far, nothing has changed. I warm myself at the art center's rock fireplace, along with a Mainland visitor who is as resourceful as Isabella: She is wearing her large but damp hotel bath towel as a shawl.

Isabella's guide, Upa, was a Hawaiian *who boasts a little English ... and was got up in the native style with garlands of flowers round his hat and throat.* Our guide is Jim Kauahikaua, a Hawai'i Volcanoes Observatory geologist who boasts a little Hawaiian and who is "got up" in the geologist style of camouflage pants and Teva sandals.

Upa and his party climbed down into Kīlauea, the lava *so hot a shower of rain hissed as it fell upon it ... I fell through several times, and always into holes full of sulphurous steam ... Halema'uma'u appeared as a fiery sea whose waves are never weary.*

I look across the crater, knowing the tilt meters recently showed the possibility of a summit eruption. I squint until I imagine fountains of fire. I open my eyes and see plumes of sulphur steam. The promise of Pele.

Today we trundle out onto Kīlauea's 1790 flow in Kauahikaua's government-issue four-wheel drive. He talks about geology. And then he speaks of Pele legends. I perk up. For Isabella, *Pele was undoubtedly one of the grandest of heathen mythical creations.* For our Hawaiian geologist, stories of Pele are clues.

"You can read legends and figure out which flow they pertain to, look at features and identify them in the legends," Kauahikaua says. He discards from the legends what he calls the "moralistic aspects," and is left with information. "We record information differently now," he muses, "but is it better?"

I sort out the moralistic bits from Isabella's letters—her references to the "heathens" and her commentary on the Christian influence—and in the remaining narrative, as in the legends, lie verifiable facts.

For our departure, Mr. Lewis and I are right with Isabella: *The drip, drip, of vertical, earnest, tepid, tropical rain accompanies us nearly to Hilo.*

At Rainbow Falls, we pad 100 feet along a paved walkway from the parking lot to the vantage point over the Wailuku River, instead of spending all afternoon slaloming by horse around rocks and holes, as Isabella did. Tourists snap pictures with throw-away cameras and pan with Camcorders. Above us, buds are forming on enormous old mango trees. Did Isabella know them as saplings?

Isabella loved Onomea, *600 feet high … exquisite ferns and trailers which mantle the cliffs down to the water's edge … women in rose and green holokus … a whole cluster of grass houses under lau halas and bananas … The distracting beauty of this coast is what are called gulches … we came through eleven, fording all but two. The descent into some of them is quite alarming. You go down almost standing in your stirrups … grasping [your horse's] mane to prevent the saddle [from] slipping.*

Today, Mr. Lewis grasps the steering wheel to prevent the auto from a head-on collision on a narrow, old bridge. "Old" is 1922, built nearly 50 years after Isabella stood in her stirrups to cross the gulch streams, which still tumble and rush past banks jungled with palms and mangoes and ferns. And here we discover another bond with Isabella: our first mosquito. She also found, in the lowlands, *ants that assemble in legions as if by magic and monstrous cockroaches really the size of mice.* I take a perverse comfort in the familiarity of these pests.

In Waipi'o Valley, Isabella wrote, *I am in a native house in which not a word of English is spoken … this beautiful valley was once very populous, and even forty years ago … there were 1,300 people here. Now probably there are not more than 200.*

Today in Waipi'o, the Hawaiian language is gone. *Taro* struggles in a few *lo'i*. But the streams still braid themselves from the falls to the sea, and the rose-crimson mountain apples and golden balls of guava that Isabella wrote of still hang ripe for the picking. We come to horse tracks in the mud. Isabella? We follow, and find day travelers on an hour's trail ride.

After Waipi'o, Mr. Lewis and I belt ourselves into our six-cylinder steed. In moments, it seems, we pop over a rise.

Mauna Kea's pristine snow mantle gleams sharply against a perfectly blue and cloudless sky. Like Mauna Loa and Kīlauea, this mountain has changed since Isabella's time, but not by act of God—or of Pele, if you prefer. Even at this distance, the round heads of astronomers' observatories appear as pimples on the White Mountain's profile.

Like Isabella, we head for the mountain from Waimea. But not before breakfast. Through the window of the Paniolo Country Inn, I see pickups pulling horse trailers. Is this as close as we'll get to horses? Mr. Lewis, who has purchased a *Hawai'i Tribune Herald*, says, "Your horse is now reading the sports page."

We hit the road, a reasonable lane through Parker Ranch land. Gone are the sheep of Isabella's time. *The afternoon fog, which serves instead of rain, rolled up in dense masses.* The fog appears, on cue, for we have Bird in hand. The red dirt washboard road grows ever less distinct, and we slow to Isabella's pace. We stop for photos: the Kohala Mountains behind us, the mass of Mauna Kea ahead. And that is all. No cows, no horses, no cowboys. Just rolling green with a lone *koa* tree bent to the wind on the horizon.

And then, suddenly, a *pueo*, a Hawaiian owl, hovers not 30 feet from us. He lights on a grassy knoll, his round, white face quizzical on his swiveling neck. We spot wild turkeys and a China pheasant rooster with two hens. At 8,500 feet, my ears pop. The radio gives a small craft advisory and flash flood warnings for all islands. Too late. Washouts from yesterday cross our path. Wahoo! This is nature at its wildest—just like Isabella experienced!

By mid-afternoon, we wind up Mauna Kea's observatory road. And then around the fateful bend, those horizon pimples pop. Mr. Lewis exclaims, "Science Central!"

Skiers emerge from a red Isuzu Amigo, buckle their stiff boots into their high-tech skis, bail over a guard-rail and disappear into blowing fog. The wind gusts and buffets the car while we eat tortilla chips, waiting for the fog to blow away. I get out and discover I can barely walk, I'm so dizzy from the altitude—almost 14,000 feet.

After riding steadily for six hours, our horses, snorting and panting, and plunging up to their knees in fine volcanic ash, and halting, trembling and exhausted, every few feet, carried us up the great tufa cone which crowns the summit of this vast fire-flushed, fire-created mountain … This summit is a group of six red tufa cones … the clouds … lay in glistening masses all round the mountain about halfway up, shutting out the smiling Earth …

No kidding. In the fog, the cones appear and disappear, as if by some trick of smoke and mirrors. When the sun breaks through, Mr. Lewis is eating a bite of banana. By the time he swallows, the cones have disappeared again. He sets up a camera with a lens the size of a telescope. A five-second blast of sun hits the cones. And then all we can see is immediately next to us: 10-foot-wide letters made in a snow bank with cherry shave ice:
HAWAII
Aloha
2/26/96
The fog turns to snow. We abandon our plan to camp near the visitor center. Instead, I call my Aunty Betty in Kohala to beg for a bunk for the night. Isabella toughed it out in a hut at a sheep sta-

tion, though she woke at three from the hopeless cold. Are Brad and I wandering wimps? The Milquetoasts of Mauna Kea?

At Aunty Betty's house, my cousin Lani has a good suggestion: "Make the story 'Where Isabella Didn't Go: Mauna Lani Resort.'"

The next morning, Mr. Lewis and I scan the skies and decide to try climbing Mauna Loa from the Saddle Road. Isabella ascended from the Kīlauea side, but hey, this is better than nothing. Besides, we can make a stop at the U.S. weather station at about 11,000 feet.

Isabella began on horseback at 7:00 a.m. with a Mr. Gandle and *two natives who knew not a word of English*, after a night in a cabin at 'Ainapō with swarms of fleas. Ahead was 7,000 vertical feet of lava. *I put on all my warm clothes … which gave me the squat, padded look of a puffin or Esquimaux. At timberline began the vastness of this mountain. The whole south of this large island, down to and below the water's edge, is composed of its slopes. Its height is nearly three miles, its base is 180 miles in circumference, so that Wales might be packed away within it, leaving room to spare … For twenty-four hours the lower world, "works and ways of busy men," were entirely shut out, and we were alone with this trackless and inanimate region of horror.*

In our first view, Mauna Loa's purple, snow-frosted summit appears as a sky-island floating on a frothing sea of clouds. The one-lane roller coaster road to the weather observatory is marked down the middle by a wavering white stripe, not to divide the pavement but to use as a guide in fog. In the oceans of 'a'ā lava, 'ōhelo bushes cling in crevices protected from the wind. I hear the whinny of horses. I'm so sure, I look for riders to come over a rise. In a moment I realize I'm hearing wind-ghosts.

We begin hiking from the observatory. An Isabellian description of the sound of 'a'ā clinkers crunching underfoot eludes me.

Our steps sound just like chewing dry Cheerios. When I stop, I hear Mr. Lewis' shutter cheeping like a small lost bird.

We pick our way from cairn to cairn 50 yards at a time, over ropes of *pāhoehoe*, up coils of black lava that cascade in steps. I stop often, breathing hard in the thin air. We are alone in vastness. The horizon on all sides is the mountain—blue-black, yellow ocher and sienna patched with the white of snow. There is no vista here, no coastline to be seen, no other peaks. Mauna Loa is the world.

We lunch in a cave, a cinder-floored lava tube with a skylight entrance. Someone has left bottled water. Half-melted candles perch on a lava shelf. The ceiling is frescoed in calcified white. My thermometer says 40 degrees. Refrigerator temperature.

Our guide took us a little wrong once … "Wrong" on Mauna Loa means being arrested by an impassable a-a stream. Mr. Lewis takes us "a little wrong" right after the last smoked oyster and tidbit of cheese. I step immediately up to mid-shin into a snow-bridged *'a'ā* hole. "Holy *'a'ā*!" he declares. We survey the expanse of snow-covered *'a'ā* ahead. We confer, mentioning prospective broken ankles and a helicopter rescue. In 30 seconds, we turn downhill.

Oh, Isabella, forgive us for giving up on Moku'āweoweo, the summit crater. It's still another 1,500 lung-busting feet up, and, unlike in your day, it's not erupting. Call us quitters. Call us sissies. Call us smart.

In a condo kitchen in Kailua-Kona, Mr. Lewis sautees *'ahi* while I sip chardonnay on the *lānai*. Have we totally taken leave of our heroine? Maybe not, for just beyond the hotel grounds the eternal sea pounds the same black lava shore, coconut palms dance in silhouettes against the twilight and geckos cluck in the trees.

At Kealakekua, Isabella stayed at a boarding house near Christ Church, a small Episcopal chapel still perched *mauka* of the road. But after a few days of the languid life and stifling heat of Kona, she had a relapse of itchy feet. The cure was her last Big Island adventure. And ours: Hualālai.

While at the boarding house, Isabella met a Mr. Greenwell, who ran a store and had orange and coffee plantations, though *he has a disagreeably embittered sarcastic tone and has a bad temper …*

Today we meet our guide at Mr. Greenwell's stone-and-mortar store, now the Kona Historical Society Museum in Kealakekua. Sherwood Greenwell is the merchant-farmer's grandson and president of the historical society. This younger Greenwell, now a man of years himself, is as charming as his forebear was severe. Sherwood and his cousin-in-law, society historian Jean Greenwell, speak of Isabella as if she is a friend who visited just last year. Sherwood stashes bento boxes and a cooler of beverages in the rear of his four-wheel drive, and up we go, climbing steadily from 1,500 feet through cattle country into grass and shrubby *pūkiawe* at 5,200 feet. In Isabella's time, before cattle, this area was densely forested in *'ōhi'a, koa* and tree ferns.

Above timberline, she found *no permanent track, and on the occasions when I have ridden up here alone, the directions given me have been to steer for an ox bone, and from that to a dwarf ohia …*

The slopes of this ranch land are laced with jeep trails that are barely better than nothing. Sherwood may well be steering from an ox bone to a bonsai *'ōhi'a*. By lunchtime he has turned and backtracked so many times that all I can tell for sure is that Hualālai's 9,000-foot summit is over yonder, because I can see it.

At Kealapū'ali, I sit on a fallen eucalyptus balancing the bento box on my knees. We joke about getting home, given Sherwood's circuitous navigation. He says, "Maybe it's not a good idea to eat both your rice balls now."

Isabella stayed with Hawaiians in this wild country, at a sheep station, in a wool shed and in a "wigwam" of grass, eating boiled jerked beef or mutton, sour *poi* and pilot biscuits soaked in coffee. She was reduced to a single chemise for underclothing. It seems she washed her only spare garment and hung it out the window to dry, but, as she would put it, alas, some hogs or calves destroyed it.

At Kealapū'ali, the air is customarily still, and the trees grow straight. The silence, Sherwood says, drives some people mad. Hualālai's slopes feel gentle, perhaps hospitable, compared with the other worlds of Mauna Kea and Mauna Loa. This mountain beckons rather than challenges. Come live on my slopes and in my forests.

We dine at the ruins of a dairy that occupied this place in the 1880s after the sheep business was doomed by lamb-killing wild dogs and pigs. I step gingerly into the remnants of the main house, hoping not to fall through the rotting floorboards. It's hard to be sure whether this is one of the places Isabella stayed. All that's left of her other Hualālai stops is a wool press at a sheep station some eight miles away.

"I want so much for her to have stayed here," Jean Greenwell says. Me too. I want to step in her actual footsteps, not just imitate her itinerary.

In mid-afternoon we turn downslope, though Isabella twice ascended to Hualālai's summit. For me, it's enough for now.

I left Hualalai yesterday morning, and dined with my kind host and hostess in the wigwam. It was the last taste of the wild Hawaiian life I have learned to love so well, the last meal on a mat, the last exercise of skill in eating "two-fingered" poi … It is best to leave the islands now. I love them better every day, and dreams of the Fatherland are growing fainter in this perfumed air and under this glittering sky.

It is best to leave Isabella's trail now. I love it better every day, and dreams of doing this properly—of riding these mountains on horseback, of sleeping in huts and dining on jerked beef and black coffee—grow ever larger in this perfumed air and under this glittering sky.

After her travels in Hawai'i, Isabella Bird was never able to settle down to ordinary existence again. She went on to the Rocky Mountains, to Japan, to Malaya. Persia, Kurdistan, Manchuria.

And after my travels with Mr. Lewis? I shall never come to the Big Island again without wanting to travel its shores and slopes with Bird in hand.

じ

A Night at Washington Place

2001

Sunday, 5 p.m. Beretania Street is devoid of traffic. I squint into the sinking sun from the front *lānai* of Washington Place, easily conjuring a horse-drawn carriage in the dusty street, or a touring car coming to Queen Lili'uokalani's home.

My Hawaiian family speaks of its connections with the *ali'i*, of *kuleana* lands and royal patents that we must have held onto well into the 20th century. It's easy to imagine my Hawaiian grandmother, Mele Elemakule Pā, as a teenager during the overthrow and its aftermath, standing with her parents in Hilo, loyal to the queen. I know for sure my *haole* grandfather met Lili'uokalani a little later, in his dashing days as a bachelor, newly arrived in 1900 in Hawai'i at age 22, seeking yet more adventure after Rough Riding with Teddy Roosevelt on Cuba's San Juan Hill.

Shortly after he landed in Honolulu, a friend of my grandfather's arranged a royal audience at Washington Place and coached him in courtly decorum. Bowing, young Donald Scott Bowman kissed the queen's hand. Fifty years later, he remembered her saying, "Young man, I like you. You may call on me again. And when you do, don't kiss my hand, kiss my cheek."

In the queen's parlor, I stand before the low, Renaissance Revival armchair where she received visitors in the last two decades of her life.

I ponder the curtsey—left foot back, bend the right knee? Washington Place director Jim Bartels tells me that, in the early 1900s, the queen held audiences at least weekly. Long lines of people shuffled up the Chinese granite steps, including any new interesting visitors—a welcome diversion in a city that, in 1900, had fewer than 40,000 residents.

Rats. My queen-kissing granddad was a dime a dozen.

⚬

I'm here in this grand, square, white house by the grace of Gov. and Mrs. Ben Cayetano, the driving force behind converting Honolulu's oldest occupied mansion from a governor's residence into a public historical facility.

The deal is this: The Cayetanos are away at the Governors' Conference. I am allowed alone in any of the public rooms, though Bartels must lurk discreetly around the corner, in case I try to trampoline on the queen's bed. I may use any other furniture, and turn lights off and on.

I may waltz with the queen until midnight. I'm wearing the closest thing I have to a ball gown (a long *mu'umu'u*), and although I have no glass slippers, at least I do have footwear, which I was not required to leave at the door. I feel like Cinderella.

Last January, the Cayetanos announced their idea that the whole mansion ought to be a more public space. But it's tough, when you live with your family on the second floor, to have troops of people marching through the house every day. Besides, the queen's heirs sold Washington Place to the Territory of Hawai'i in 1922. It's supposed to be the governor's residence as well as a memorial to Lili'uokalani.

The Cayetanos thought they could do better on the memorial part—but they wanted to honor the residential purpose, too. And then there was the convenience factor, since Washington Place is located across the street from the State Capitol.

Cayetano came up with a solution. Let the governor, whoever he or she is, continue holding state functions in Washington Place. But create new living quarters in an annex on the back acre of the property, which the Territory acquired in 1946. The arrangement resembles "the bungalow" on the 'Iolani Palace grounds—torn down long ago from its location where 'Iolani Barracks is now—more homey quarters where King Kalākaua and his predecessors preferred to spend much of their private time, rather than in the formal Palace itself.

Currently, governors and their families live upstairs in Washington Place, in an apartment cobbled together from original bedrooms. Moving the living quarters out to the proposed annex would free this space for use as galleries. It would still take the governor only 20 seconds to walk from the state dining room to his bedroom in the new annex, and maybe a couple of minutes to "commute" to the State Capitol across Beretania Street.

As for beefing up the queenly memorial, the first lady proposed hiring as director Jim Bartels. Having served 28 years as curator of ʻIolani Palace, he knows the queen as well as any 21st-century person can.

Of course the plan will cost money. The funding goal for the nonprofit Washington Place Foundation is $3 million, plus a $1 million endowment. With $1 million of that already raised privately for the new residential quarters and $200,000 appropriated by the state to renovate the mansion and develop exhibits, the Cayetanos expect Washington Place to open to the public next fall.

Docents will guide visitors through the first-floor rooms. But the best stuff will be upstairs, where visitors can linger over changing gallery exhibits Bartels is designing from hundreds of little-known artifacts and thousands of forgotten historical details.

On my Cinderella night at Washington Place, he offers a few of the stories he's gathered.

"In 1919, two years after the Queen's death, Democratic Territorial Governor Charles McCarthy kept after the Legislature to acquire Washington Place as the governor's mansion. But when he finally moved in, he didn't change a thing. He didn't even move the furniture," Bartels says.

"We found out he came to Hawaiʻi from New York in the 1880s and was a Royalist. After the overthrow, he was at the top of the Provisional Government's 'most wanted list.' Making Washington Place into the governor's mansion was his way of showing *aloha* by preserving the queen's home."

While Royalist McCarthy was becoming *persona non grata* in 1893, young Prince David Kawānanakoa was interning as a clerk at the government building, Aliʻiolani Hale. So abrupt was the overthrow of the kingdom government that the patriot Prince, the queen's second heir to the throne, actually handwrote some of the earliest proclamations of the Provisional Government before realizing their import.

The queen herself might not have been on the throne in 1893 had romance taken a different turn when she was young. One story has it that, about 1860, William Charles Lunalilo, who would be elected King when Kamehameha V died in 1873 without naming a successor, once wanted to elope with her. They were aboard an interisland steamer and he tried—unsuccessfully—to get the captain to marry them.

Or maybe it wasn't the captain. Another story says it was a Catholic priest who happened to be on board. It will be Bartels' job to sort the true details from the hogwash. If you believe all you hear, the Hawaiian royal family had love lives as complicated as any group of contemporary royals. One of the stories—maybe true, maybe not—has Lunalilo, one day before the ship episode, giving a grand ball. At the ball, he was supposed to announce his engagement to Lydia Pākī, the future Liliʻuokalani, and the engagement of her brother, Kalākaua, to Princess Victoria Kamāmalu, sister of Kamehameha V and the reigning Kamehameha IV. But Kamāmalu scoops the evening by announcing that she is engaged to Lunalilo.

The ball and the engagements could be fibs, but the fact is, Victoria married no one and neither did Lunalilo. Kalākaua later married a widow, Kapiʻolani. Lydia wed John Dominis.

That's how the future queen first arrived at Washington Place, then the domicile of the Dominis family, a mansion that Liliʻuokalani found fully furnished with a mother-in-law in residence.

The story of the house—and the elder Mrs. Dominis—begins a bit earlier, shortly before Liliʻuokalani's birth as Lydia Kamakaʻeha Pākī in 1838.

In 1837, New England sea captain John Dominis moved to Hawaiʻi with his wife and young son, John Owen. Honolulu was dry and dusty, treeless except for seven shoreline coconut palms. Mary Lambert Dominis demanded 1) a mansion and 2) trees.

The captain soon had his eye on the property that is now Washington Place, where the *haole* city and the Hawaiian countryside met. Many neighbors were rollicking *aliʻi* of great consequence. But not above scandal.

In 1840, for instance, Dominis' potential neighbor on the Waikīkī side, Kamanawa II, became the first *aliʻi* hanged for murder.

"The point was," Bartels says, "to show that no one, even so high an *aliʻi*, was higher than the missionary law." The particular law that started the trouble prohibited an adulterer from remarrying ("that is," says Bartels, "from having a love life"), unless the wronged party either remarried or died.

Kamanawa II compounded his crime of adultery when he tried to live up to the letter of the remarriage law by poisoning his wife, Kamoku'iki.

Kamanawa and Kamoku'iki were Lili'uokalani's paternal grandparents. She was but a toddler of two at the time, but her older brother, the future King Kalākaua, is believed to have seen part of the execution.

Just short of four years old, he and his older brother, James Kaliokalani, were students at the Royal School, located where the State Capitol now stands. Schoolmaster Amos Starr Cooke reluctantly granted Kamanawa's request that the two grandsons visit him while he was imprisoned at the fort awaiting execution. With no buildings between the school and the fort wall where the hanging took place, "The gallows could be seen from the school room door and window," Cooke wrote. The execution hour, 2 p.m. October 20, coincided with the regular dismissal time at the school.

Says Cooke, "The children were very anxious to see, and did see some." In other words, it's likely the future king saw his own grandfather hung.

This much is certain: Kalākaua later acquired the hanging rope. It was found among his effects when he died 51 years later.

The area of the future Washington Place was not perhaps the most promising neighborhood, but that didn't keep Dominis from building a classical Greek Revival-style house on his lot. The work proceeded in fits and starts, according to available funds. In 1846 Dominis made a trip to China to buy furniture, and was never heard from again, presumed lost at sea, along with numerous VIPs on board.

He had two daughters, who had been left on the East Coast for school. Both died. His widow was left rattling around in her mansion with their teenage son, John Owen. She opened her home as a genteel boarding house. With suitable quarters at a premium, prominent respectable foreigners gladly rented from her.

During the 15 years she spent happily ensconced with her son and her boarders in her thoroughly American mansion, Mrs. Dominis introduced Honolulu to new holiday traditions the missionaries had steadfastly tried to avert: the Christmas tree and Santa Claus.

But then, in 1862, a nuptial event rocked life at Washington Place. John Owen Dominis married Lydia Pākī.

"My husband took me at once to the estate known as Washington Place," the bride wrote later. "He really was an only child. As Mrs. Dominis felt that no one should step between her and her child, naturally I, as her son's wife, was considered an intruder; and I was forced to realize this from the beginning."

Bartels calls it a "challenging household situation." Yes, he says, "There was a closeness of John and his mother." It would go on until Mrs. Dominis died in 1889.

For the first 15 years—until King Kalākaua named his sister as heir apparent in 1877—John Dominis was the more important spouse. His connections to government stemmed from teaching at the Royal School. He served as governor of Oʻahu under the Kingdom's last four monarchs, from 1864 to 1888—and again in 1891. He also governed Maui from 1878 to 1886.

Not surprisingly, important visitors passed through the lives of the prominent couple—and perhaps some secrets lurk even among these chance meetings. For example, in 1869, the Duke of Edinburgh, Queen Victoria's eldest son and commander of the ship-of-war *Galatea*, visited the Hawaiian Kingdom. At the request of Kamehameha V, Liliʻuokalani (then, of course, Lydia Dominis) gave a grand *lūʻau* in his honor at her Waikīkī residence. When the duke sailed from Hawaiʻi, the two exchanged musical compositions and he gave her a heavy, solid gold bracelet resembling a ship's cable with an anchor appended.

She saw him again only once, when she and Queen Kapiʻolani attended Queen Victoria's 50th Jubilee in London in 1887, where he was her escort at a dinner at Buckingham Palace.

Bartels points out that photographs taken throughout subsequent years show Liliʻuokalani constantly wearing the duke's gift. "When she's not wearing her full-on queen stuff, she's wearing that cumbersome bracelet. It must have meant something."

❧

Back in the present. It's 8:30 p.m. The house is becoming familiar, comfortable, smaller by the minute. Its musty, humid heat is getting to me. Sweat trickles inside my "ball gown" and I wonder if the queen had the same problem. I picture her mopping her face with a linen hanky and flinging all the French doors wide open.

Bartels suggests we repair to the only air-conditioned area, the state dining room, created in 1922 from what was the back *lānai*. He roots around in the kitchen—a disarray of stainless steel that is being de-asbestosed and updated—and comes up with black coffee and guava juice.

In the dining room, which is chilly, I lay my notebook on the embroidered tablecloth and write down a story that Bartels relates.

It's about the time when Lili‘uokalani was past 40, and barren. She picked out a suitable partner with whom John could have a child. When the baby was born, Lili‘uokalani loved him extravagantly.

In her own handwriting, Lili‘uokalani confirms that John did father a child by one of her retainers. Born in 1883, this son was called John Dominis Aimoku, carrying his mother's legal surname as required by law. Princess Lili‘uokalani did support him—and later legally adopted him and changed his name to John Aimoku Dominis.

Her political life was as complex as her personal. Though she was heir apparent, she sometimes was at odds with her brother, the king, as he struggled with sugar planters and *haole* businessmen, who wanted more control over kingdom policy.

While she was at Victoria's 1887 Jubilee in England, word came to her that the *haole* men had succeeded in forcing a new constitution on the king. The "Bayonet Constitution" stripped him of considerable executive power and vastly changed voter qualifications, expanding the electorate to include noncitizens of American or European origin.

The forced constitution created unrest. In late 1890, the king made a trip to California to try to improve his health, leaving Lili‘uokalani in charge as regent.

Then, in January 1891, Kalākaua died in San Francisco.

"All of a sudden, Lili‘uokalani is in the palace with the bitterest enemies of her family," Bartels says. "And they're saying, 'Sit in your seat and do as we tell you.' But she is the 58th generation of governing *ali'i* and her people come to her. She's caught between political expedience and ancient obligation. She doesn't simply abrogate the Bayonet Constitution, but plays a waiting game. But I think she underestimated the desperation of her enemies and how frightened they were."

While the political intrigue played out, husband John Owen Dominis died just two months after Lili'uokalani became queen. About that time, some 70 people in the *haole* community shipped some *koa* to New York. In 1892, the wood came back as a Fisher baby grand piano, their gift to the new monarch. A copy of the illuminated calligraphy presentation document still hangs framed on the parlor wall near the piano.

MADAM: We desire to approach YOUR MAJESTY With the most profound feelings of loyalty and the truest friendship for you as our beloved Queen and a Hawaiian Lady, and venture most respectfully to ask YOUR MAJESTY'S acceptance of this musical instrument as a token of our loyal homage … PRAYING that YOUR MAJESTY may long reign over a happy, prosperous and contented people …
We are,
with most respectful greetings,
YOUR MAJESTY's most dutiful subjects
SIGNED ON BEHALF OF THE DONORS,
F. J. Hackfeld
John Philips
John H. Soper
Comittee (sic).

The document is dated May 12, 1892. Bartels believes the gift was made in good faith, but eight months later, some of the very men who gave her the piano engineered the queen's overthrow.

Lili'uokalani lived almost a quarter century after that, "reinventing herself so she could continue to serve her people," as Bartels sees it. "At least until 1910, she was constantly put down. Her strategy was to never defend herself, apologize or explain. Her book, *Hawai'i's Story by Hawai'i's Queen*, was the only defense."

She could have lived at her Waikīkī home, or at the one in Kalihi. But she put herself in Washington Place, living essentially in a fishbowl. She held public audiences. For visiting children, she hid candy in her pockets. She kept a talking parrot and an enormous Galápagos tortoise, who often wandered into the street and got flipped on his back.

Her *hānai* grandchildren played in the house. Their parents, John Aimoku and Sybil McInerny Dominis, had moved into Washington Place with the Queen after their 1910 wedding, repeating the mother-in-law situation.

Lili'uokalani loved the children. Once, so another story goes, she sat down to read her Bible at her usual time, and discovered that the *mo'opuna*—grandchildren—and their friends were embarking on a game of "Hide and Seek."

"Play quietly while I read," she instructed.

John Jr. was hiding. The others hunted to no avail. Where could he be? Eventually he peeped out from his secret place—under the queen's skirts.

Soon after this children's game, on November 11, 1917, Lili'uokalani passed away. During the following week, the queen lay in state at Kawaiaha'o Church.

My Uncle Wright was among the thousands who came to say farewell. He was barely 10, a boarder at Kamehameha School for Boys. The campus then was where the Bishop Museum is now.

"We went at nighttime on the streetcar," he still remembers clearly. "The queen lay in state on a little platform. I saw ladies all in black with *kāhili*. I thought of my mother's funeral in Hilo, with all the old ladies right in the parlor with her body, chanting and wailing. Spooky, you know.

"So, in the line I shut my eyes and held onto the shirt of the kid in front of me. When I felt him bow, I bowed. But I never did look."

⁂

"Aloha 'Oe," the most famous of the 170 songs the queen composed, was sung numerous times during her funeral. But it's a love song, not a dirge. She said so herself.

I must have sung it at least a hundred times while I was a Kamehameha student. I know it in the key of G.

The queen's piano sits kitty-corner in the parlor, century-old *koa* case gleaming thickly in the yellow lamplight. I ask Bartels if I may play it.

Yes. He opens the lid and puts up the music stand. The royal coat of arms is on the inside of the key cover as well as inside the box, along with the queen's "L" monogram.

I sit down on the bench, my feet feeling for the pedals. The ivory of the three central octaves is yellow with use.

I touch the keys, my right thumb on D and my left hand spreading over the G major chord. The first few notes of my "Aloha 'Oe" tell me the action is stiff, the sound not as resonant as it once must have been, the whole instrument arthritic in a climate notoriously unkind to pianos.

Bartels tells me the queen viewed the piano unsentimentally, as a tool that she "jammed in the hallway." But it's hard for me not to remember whose piano it was, and when I do, my fingers stumble.

I finish "Aloha 'Oe." I play "Ke Aloha O Ka Haku," the Queen's Prayer. Then "Kaulana Nā Pua," the song composed by the queen's friend Ellen Prendergast for the Royal Hawaiian Band members who refused to sign the loyalty oath required by the Provisional Government. Mrs. Prendergast called it "Mele 'Ai Pōhaku," the "Stone-Eating Song." The musicians would rather eat stones than bow to the traitors.

I end my concert with a modern song, "He Hawai'i 'Au," cascading down through C, G and F, then back to C. The song's last line is this Cinderella's message to the queen:

I understand—I am Hawaiian.

It's nearly midnight, the almost-full moon overhead in a clear sky. Bartels walks me out the back to my Mazda.

"Thanks for letting me play the piano," I say. "I thought the queen would especially like 'Kaulana Nā Pua.'"

He hugs me, in that enveloping Hawaiian way. And he whispers, "I think she did."

෨

The Way Back

1992

The conch sounds at 5 a.m. By starlight I slide from my warm sleeping bag. At the beach the silhouetted *moʻo Lono* silently offers a sip of consecrated water. I step beyond this Hawaiian priest into the dark waters of Kahoʻolawe, a tiny, uninhabited island in the rain-shadow of Maui's Haleakalā.

The houses and temples of Kahoʻolawe are ruined, the once-verdant slopes denuded by goats, the soil swirled away by relentless wind and torrential rain, the hardpan surface cratered by 50 years of U.S. Navy live-fire practice bombs. But like Hawaiʻi's aboriginal people, who have endured the cultural battering of two centuries of Western influence, Kahoʻolawe clings to life. I am here as a guest of Protect Kahoʻolawe ʻOhana, a group that has spent two decades healing the island. Though they were branded "radical natives" when they landed on Kahoʻolawe against Navy regulations, five years later their work resulted in the island being added to the National Register of Historic Places. In 1990 the bombing was stopped. As stewards of the island, members of the ʻOhana—which means "extended family"—have inventoried archaeological sites, built water-catchment systems, and started revegetation projects. Now, in this windy January, the ʻOhana is bringing the ancient annual thanksgiving celebration to a close.

I am a Hawaiian—but, like Kahoʻolawe, tenuously connected to my past. My native grandmother died when my father was a baby, and I grew up knowing little of my culture. Now, submerged in Kahoʻolawe's waters, I follow instructions for the first ceremony: Until the sun rises and the conch sounds again, silently praise Lono, the sustainer of life. Pray for misty rain to nurture Kahoʻolawe with green.

For years I have gone to the sea to meditate at sunrise. I'm suddenly sure that I received the practice from unnamed ancestors who also sought in ritual some sense and order to life. Just then the conch blower, floating far off in the Pacific, lifts his shell horn against the rosy sky.

All morning, people wrap offerings to Lono in *ti* leaves: banana and sweet potato; *taro*, redfish and black coconut. At noon a dozen couples line up along the beach wearing white *malo* and *kīkepa*, the loincloth and sarong. Chanting slowly, they bear their bundles to the *imu*, the hot and earthy-smelling cooking pit.

At day's end, two more processions wind to the ruins of the women's and men's temples. In bare feet the Hawaiians feel their way over the lava path, white raiment and Lono banners fluttering. This time the offerings are laid on raised platforms.

The next day we hike the full length of the island, 11 miles under a parching sun. The Navy has cautioned us against picking up anything, because the island is still scattered with unexploded bombs. At mid-island those in the ceremony change into white again and pad barefoot a half-mile off the trail to a promontory where ancient priest-navigators once schooled postulants to read the stars and the currents to sail 2,500 miles back to Tahiti, where the Hawaiians came from a millennium ago. From here I have a clear view of the channel Ke-ala-i-kahiki, the-way-to-Tahiti. The ritual begins. In the gusts we hear only snatches of the chants. Then the final conch blows.

By late afternoon we're blistered, sunburned and dehydrated, but we must reach the western tip of the island before sundown. An hour later we arrive at our destination.

As the celebrants prepare for the final ritual, a regal and massive gray-haired Hawaiian I have not seen before appears. On the sand a hundred feet behind him a four-foot-long scale-model *koa* canoe sits balanced on her outrigger, her *kapa* cloth sail a white triangle in the waning light. For the last time, pairs of Hawaiians make their offerings to the *mo'o Lono*. Carefully the priests pack the canoe.

At the ocean's edge the chief strikes the waves with a broom of *ti* leaves. When the surf calms, four of the strongest swimmers guide the canoe toward the channel. The sky fades, and from the shore we can see only the tiny sail, still upright. At last light the canoe catches the current of Ke-ala-i-kahiki, the connection to our ancient homeland.

In the starry night, cold winds blow from both the sea and the land. My skin crinkles with salt. My sleeping bag is damp, but I crawl in and lay my head on a hump of sand. Around me lie other Hawaiians; under me Kaho'olawe feels alive. I can see the campfire, its flames the shape of the canoe sail, the color of the sunset sky.

4
Ancestral Paths

War, peace, the staff of life
and finding that the ways of
the ancients are still alive

ROOTS

1995

Leroy Koyanagi lives with his brother in a *taro* patch on the windward slopes of the West Maui Mountains.

Koyanagi is a lean young man of 22, Hawaiian-Japanese, a ninth-grade dropout. He says he was a *"pilau* kid"—until he found what he calls "my brother, *taro."*

Though *pilau* means "rotten" or "stinking," Koyanagi uses the Hawaiian word as a blanket covering his youthful sins of rebellion and irresponsibility. He refused to help his parents with the little *taro* they farmed on leased land. Koyanagi's grandparents had farmed part of it a generation earlier, but the *loʻi*—the flooded paddies of the crop that was the mainstay of the ancient Hawaiian diet—had become overgrown. Koyanagi quit Baldwin High School because he thought it sufficient that he could read, write and do math. Then he batted around from job to job—dishwasher, carwash attendant, construction laborer. By the time he was 17 and the father of a little girl named Ariel, he could see "my future coming ahead."

His labors had led to Maui's Aloha Poi Company. In the company's commercial *taro* patches, Koyanagi was brushed daily by the large elephant-ear leaves. He liked the work. In time it occurred to him to also farm his own family's abandoned *loʻi* nearby.

Taro and Hawaiians arrived in Hawaii together on voyaging canoes from the South Pacific more than a millennium ago. The word *"taro"* eventually softened to *"kalo"* as Hawaiians replaced the "T" and "R" of other Polynesian languages with "K" and "L." Yet with a few words, such as *tapa* and *taro*, Hawaiians often retain the ancient form. Today Koyanagi and his *taro* are the descendants of humans and plants that have nourished each other for 50 generations or more.

Taro, common in areas as far-flung as Africa, China and Central America as well as Polynesia, provides not only outstanding carbohydrate in the bulbous root called its corm, but also is a rich source of vitamins and minerals in its leaves and stalks. In today's Hawaiian cuisine, *taro* products appear most commonly as *poi, laulau,* squid or chicken *lūʻau,* and *taro* chips. *Taro* is the foundation for the modern Island health regimen known as the Hawaiian Diet, Molokaʻi Diet or Waiʻanae Diet.

Koyanagi and his wife, Toby, are fond of steamed *taro* sautéed with corned beef. Sometimes they pound their own *poi* on an antique *koa* board with pounders made for their family in papa, mama and baby sizes.

In three years Koyanagi has cleared and planted more than half the leased five acres. He topples 15-foot-high cane grass with his truck, then sets his two cows to munching. Later he burns the stubble and wrests thick stumps from the soil with a pick. Like an archaeologist, beneath the overgrowth and rubble he finds the remains of the ancient stone walls of *taro* patches, dozens of small *loʻi* shaped to fit the land, placed on the slope so water will flow eternally from one to another. By day he cultivates *taro* for Aloha Poi, 6:30 a.m. to 2:30 p.m. Then, a half-hour rest, and into his own *loʻi* until dark or later.

He bends low, barefoot and nearly knee-deep in mud, pulling weeds from a young patch, harvesting corms one by one from a year-old planting, setting *huli*—the cut tops of corms with a short length of stalk—to re-root and send out new leaves in the fertile mud of a recently fallow *loʻi.* Some days a cousin or a friend comes by to help with the *lehua eleʻele, moi* and a dozen other *taro* varieties Koyanagi grows.

Koyanagi's back grows brown in the sun, or cold in winter rains. Water gurgles through PVC pipe, a replacement for ancient bamboo connecting *loʻi.* Peking ducks quack, their orange beaks searching beneath the water for crayfish that damage earthen dikes.

"This is my school," Koyanagi says. "I stay junior now, never come senior yet."

Koyanagi has learned a little about *taro* from books, but mostly from other *taro* farmers around the Islands. "In two and a half years I learned real plenty about *taro.* Still yet, when I go see other farmers, I ask all kind questions, and I try listen. This is real stuff. You go school, they no talk about this. The only way to learn is for do 'em."

Koyanagi is not steeped in the mythology that *taro* sprang from the grave of Hāloa-naka, the premature firstborn of Sky Father Wākea and Hoʻohokuʻkalani. The child was either a malformed human or a sickly plant. The best-known Hawaiian creation chant, the Kumulipo, tells how *taro* is therefore older brother to Wākea's second-born, a human also named Hāloa. Yet Koyanagi instinctively speaks of *taro* as human.

"One of the most important things is weather. Too much wind break his leaf and he *make*, he die. No more leaf, he no grow, no more way for absorb sun and atmosphere. The leaf his mouth, the stem his throat, the *taro* his stomach. When you cut him, he bleed. Too much shade, he not going get *keiki*. Plant too deep, he drown. But plenty sun, plenty cold water, whoo, he come big. Each plant he grow different, like humans."

To Koyanagi it's "sad and bad" that now less than 300 acres in Hawaiʻi are *taro* farms. At the time of the first Western contact in 1778, perhaps 20,000 acres were planted in as many as 300 varieties of *taro* for a population estimated between 400,000 and a million.

"I like go back the old ways, but ho! Stay hard," Koyanagi says. He compromises by combining hand tools—shovel, pick, cane knife, machete, sickle—with a gas-powered tiller to turn soil in drained patches, a weed eater for the banks and a chain saw for falling *koa haole* and other heavy brush. With an all-terrain vehicle he hauls 80- to 90-pound gunnysacks of corms to the top of his hill. He uses commercial fertilizer but stands firmly against pesticides or herbicides.

Says wife Toby, who works in Wailuku but helps in the *loʻi* on weekends, "When he started this I said, 'What the hell is *taro*?' Now it's everything."

Koyanagi remains clear about his niche in the world: "You take care the *taro*, it take care of you. The land, he stay observe me, trying to see if I can handle. When I graduate, he help me. I'll go down my high school and say, 'I like my diploma now.'"

Koyanagi rests a moment, stretching his back. "After a while your mind travel to different problems. Land rights. Water rights. I think, 'No more land, no more water—no more *taro*. No more *taro*—no more humans.'"

And he's back to his relationship with the plant that is his brother, Hāloa, the plant that gives life to Hawaiians, gives meaning to Koyanagi's life.

"The leaf look like one heart," says Koyanagi. "If he had one mouth, I would talk story with him." He caresses a velvet leaf. "I stay struggling, but I no care. This one make me happy, this *taro*. He my brother. I no can give up. He stay locked in me already. I got the soul of the *taro*. I'll keep opening *loʻi* and plant and plant, until I die. That's all."

❧

CELEBRATING HULA MOLOKAʻI STYLE

1996

Voices of little girls ring in an early morning chant: "Blessed is the sun that rises from the east and starts our day!" It's 8:15 a.m. at Pāpohaku Beach Park at Kaluakoi, Molokaʻi. The girls from Hula Hālau o Kilohana begin their dance on the grass in front of a singers' stage, the first of a dozen varied groups of dancers and singers to perform this fine and sunny day in a seaside grove of lacy-leafed *kiawe* trees. The gnarly gray limbs are twined for the occasion with sprays of red heleconia set off with the green of monstera, *lauaʻe* fern and palm fronds.

Already, hundreds of spectators have settled themselves on the expansive lawn, anchoring *lau hala* mats and patchwork picnic quilts with coolers and stubby-legged folding lawn chairs.

"*Mākaukau,*" the *kumu* of another *hālau hula* calls out to her dancers: "Make ready!"

The dancers whirl and swoop to the galloping slap of the *kumu*'s palm and fingers against the *ʻumeke,* the gourd.

At the end of the applause for the performance, the MC calls out: "We got lost parents here! Children, please keep an eye on your parents. Make sure they hold your hand."

It's family entertainment time at Pāpohaku Park, the sixth annual Molokaʻi Ka Hula Piko festival's *hoʻolaulea.* It's a day of singing and dancing, capping a week acknowledging the birth of *hula* on Molokaʻi. The 1996 theme of the free festival is "*Molokaʻi Nui a Hina,* Great Molokaʻi, Child of the Goddess Hina."

"The focus of the festival is always on the traditions of pre-Western Molokaʻi," says John Kaʻimikaua, a *kumu hula* and the festival's cultural adviser.. "Hula and chanting were a means and a mode for preserving history and religion. Dance was to give visual expression to words."

This year he concentrates on the Hawaiian mythology that tells of sky father Wākea uniting with Hina to give birth to Molokaʻi.

❧

Although Ka'imikaua lives and works on O'ahu, his father's family is from Ho'olehua, Moloka'i, and his *hula* training was with Kawahine, a *hula* master from Moloka'i who gave him a genealogy of her teachers that went back to the year 900. She tapped Ka'imikaua as her successor in 1972, when he was 14. She was 92. He studied with her until her death in 1975. By 1977, at 19, he had his own *hālau*.

As the years went by, Ka'imikaua "saw a need to preserve Moloka'i. Of all our Islands, except Ni'ihau, it is the most untouched. Many historical and religious sites are on private land under lock and key, so they're preserved. The spirit of the land is strong, and will not yield to the destruction of development.

"If you picture the island chain, it is like a human body. The most important part is the *na'au*, mind, heart and intestines, and the *piko*, the navel. If you destroy that part, you destroy all the islands. Moloka'i is that *piko*."

A man enormous in both spirit and body, Ka'imikaua is as eloquent in English as he is fluent in Hawaiian. "The way to educate people is with awareness and pride in their island, so that when they fight to preserve Moloka'i, they know why the island is sacred to all Hawaiians."

Yet the festival welcomes all people, whether families from other islands or visitors from the Mainland and around the world.

Ka'imikaua believes all Hawaiians must teach the world how to love. Though he does not expound his philosophies to the *ho'olaulea* crowd, the spirit of his words permeates the day.

Moloka'i families sit side by side with mainlanders. A local man offers a visitor an extra lawn chair. People try not to step on each other's picnic blankets. Even little kids leaping between blankets call out, "Excuse me."

Upwards of 2,000 people mass in the park, covering all the available lawn by late morning. Among them, toddlers nap under makeshift umbrellas, and school-children cavort in the beach showers. But not a one does anything to provoke a sharp parental word.

The nonstop entertainment branches from *hula* and Hawaiian songs into variety that delights the crowd: Motown tunes, Patsy Cline numbers, even a do-wop group.

To some, the non-Hawaiian acts come as a surprise. But, Kaʻimikaua says, people come to the festival early in the week for the cultural, spiritual and educational aspects—and to the *hoʻolaulea* for fun and feasting.

The feasting is even more varied than the entertainment. One whole side of the park is lined with two dozen food booths, from which drift the international smells of Korean *kal bi* and *kim chee*, Portuguese *malassadas* and Hawaiian *laulau*. An ostensibly Japanese *bento* box features "rice, mochiko chicken, hot dog, luncheon meat, kim chee, only $4.75." At another booth, you can choose raw fish, raw crab or *ʻopihi* shell-fish. Or Rice Krispie bars, lollipops or pronto pups. Or move on for a prune *mui*, *kūlolo*, or a macadamia nut chocolate chip cookie.

In early afternoon, the MC precedes an introduction with a thank-you from under the stage's makeshift blue tarp roof: "*Mahalo* for the stir-fry," he says. "Hoo, the buggah *ʻono*."

On the other side of the crowd, across from the food booths, Island craftspeople sell shell earrings, *kamani* seed pendants, pig tusk necklaces. Choose a miniature gourd mask, or a hat of coconut fronds or *lau hala*. You can buy *tapa* greeting cards, feather hat bands and fresh *lei* fragrant with the jasmine of *pīkake* or the lemon of *pakalana*.

At one booth, artisans teach children how to pound *wauke*—mulberry bark—with water to make the *tapa* that served as cloth in ancient times. At the back of the crowd, a *lomilomi* practitioner has set up a massage table to demonstrate his healing art to whoever might have an ache or pain.

Behind the stage, dancers wait their turn to perform, eating a bite of sticky *kūlolo*, then licking their fingers clean. Their *ti* leaf *hula* skirts are laid flat on beach towels. From a Mickey Mouse beach bag spills items its dancer-owner will need later: jeans and hair spray.

A vocal dead-ringer for Patsy Cline finishes falling to pieces, and John Kaʻimikaua brings out his male dancers, Hālau Hula o Kukunaokalā, Dancers of the Rays of the Sun. Six of his men march onto the dancers' grass performance area, clad only in the ancient loincloth, the *malo*. The crowd has no trouble shifting from Patsy Cline.

This is the Hula Akua Kiʻi, dance of the temple images, a

dance seldom performed now, done long ago only by the temple priests in ceremony.

"The movements imitate every temple image," Ka'imikaua says. "They have no eyes, their knees are bent, their arms are sticking out. Pāku'i, the *heiau* just above Moloka'i's Kilohana Elementary School, is still in use."

The dance is angular, muscular, defiant. The crowd is rapt while Ka'imikaua relates the history. After the death of Kamehameha I in 1819, the ruler's powerful favorite wife, Ka'ahumanu, broke the ancient prohibitions and ordered her men to destroy the temples.

Moloka'i's people resisted. The priest of the temple Pāku'i hid their artifacts in a cave, and when Ka'ahumanu's army came, they lined up on the *heiau* walls and chanted a prophecy:

"The spirit of Moloka'i is encompassed in the face of death … the day shall fall, the night shall fall, the heavens shall fall, the highborn shall fall …

"When the waves rise and crest, the *maka'āinana* shall rise like the *ali'i*, like a wave into the heavens."

The crowd listens. Ka'imikaua says he believes the first half of the prophecy is fulfilled by the past. "The last part, foretelling the rise of commoners as leaders, is yet to come. As Hawaiians today look forward toward sovereignty, this is the fulfilling of the rest of the prophecy."

The crowd stirs, claps, roars. And Ka'imikaua, with the fine timing of a master showman, launches the men and women of his *hālau* into their finale, a *hula ma'i*, a suggestive love dance to chanted words of double meaning.

Ka'imikaua retreats to a chair under the trees. The MC searches for a segue into the next scheduled performance, but admits, "This is a stretch. To do-wop from *hula kahiko*." He announces $2 raffle tickets for sale while the do-woppers arrange themselves. A few wet spectators straggle up from the beach. The singers open with "My Girl," sounding for all the world like the Temptations. The crowd loves them, too.

Later, the Martin Pahinui Band returns the focus to Hawaiian music, with Martin himself delighting spectators with a rhythmic falsetto rendition of "Nā Ka Pueo." Still later, when the *kiawe* shadows have lengthened and the trash cans are overflowing with the debris of plate lunches, a *hālau hula* from Japan takes the stage.

The four women are graceful in a formal Japanese way, their pale bare feet pointing delicately upon the grass in a modern *hula*.

Hula, says John Ka'imikaua, has everything. Whether watching or dancing, he says, "you cannot help but feel the emotion. To dance connects us to the past, and slowly we understand.

"When we work in the old ways, we make the same motions our ancestors did and they teach us through the *na'au*, not the intellect, and we know how they felt and we become like them."

꒳

TEMPLES OF THE GODS

1998

In predawn darkness, smoking torches flicker on the silhouetted stone ramparts of Puʻukoholā Heiau at Kawaihae on the Big Island of Hawaiʻi.

Warriors stand guard in bristling capes of dry *ti*. Up the stone path to this grand *heiau* on the Hill of the Whale winds a solemn torchlight procession—women dressed in *kīkepa* that drape over the shoulder; men in feather shoulder capes. Again and again the *pū*, the conch trumpet, sounds, and chants echo from the massive walls.

This ceremony occurred not centuries ago, but in 1991, to mark the bicentennial of Kamehameha's victory here over his rival, Keoua Kuahuʻula, and to heal psychic wounds still festering after two centuries. In 1791 Keoua, chief of the districts of Kaʻū and Puna, was killed on the beach as his canoe landed. His body was then sacrificed at Kamehameha's new *heiau luakini*. Two hundred years later, descendants of both chiefs embraced in peace.

In retrospect, that 1991 day at Puʻukoholā, a national historic site since 1972, also marked a turning point. Hawaiians are once again very publicly using their *heiau*, the stone temples that governed the political and spiritual life of *aliʻi* and commoners alike from about A.D. 1200 until 1819. Today Hawaiians are returning to the *heiau* of their forefathers, eager to reclaim their heritage through religious and cultural ceremonies, and visitors have new opportunities to learn about ancient and modern Hawaiian culture.

"Twenty-five years ago some Maori leaders from New Zealand asked us where our meeting houses were," recalls John Keolamakaʻāinana Lake, a professor of Hawaiian language studies at Honolulu's Chaminade University. "We said, 'Well, we have *heiau*, but we don't use them.' Now we're in a period of reawakening that's turned a lot of people to preserving things before they are lost, and to making these things a living experience."

Heiau are traditional Hawaiian temples of worship. For centuries, hundreds, perhaps thousands dotted the Hawaiian Islands. The largest—the equivalent of grand basilica and tabernacles—were in locations thought to possess intrinsic spiritual power and functioned as Westminster Abbey, Parliament and Buckingham Palace rolled into one. Most *heiau*, however, were more humble, like country chapels, and some, such as the few *ko'a* or *kū'ula* fishing shrines, served specific purposes. Major types of *heiau* included centers for healing, *heiau ho'ola*, and for agriculture, *heiau ho'oulu 'ai*, as well as for politics and war, *heiau luakini kaua*. Presiding over the *heiau* were *kāhuna*, who, contrary to the widespread misconception that they were all either sorcerers or mystics, often held positions as priests and governmental ministers.

"We know who the *kāhuna* were, and are, for there are some today," says Lake, who, as *kahuna nui*, high priest, of Pu'ukoholā, conducts ceremonies and gives advice on protocol and spiritual matters. "Now we sometimes call them *kahu*, keeper or guardian."

The first people to arrive in Hawai'i from central Polynesia, in about A.D. 300, built *heiau* as small platforms and altars. With 12th-century migration came Pa'ao, a priest who introduced a more complex religious-political-social system. By 1400 *heiau* became larger and more elaborate as chiefs sought to define sacred areas of power. Builders stacked rocks without mortar to form platforms, terraces, and walled enclosures, making each *heiau* as unique as any of the world's great cathedrals.

As Hawaiian religion evolved, two of the four great gods became paramount: Kū, god of politics and warfare, and Lono, god of agriculture. Some temples honored both, either by alternating during the year or by remodeling and rededicating the *heiau* to both gods. The largest and best-known *heiau* are the state temples called *heiau luakini*, where high chiefs sometimes sacrificed animals and humans to Kū According to Hawaiian artist-historian and architectural designer Herb Kawainui Kāne, however, "Although tour drivers love the idea, it's a fallacy to equate *heiau* with rampant human sacrifice."

By 1810, King Kamehameha had unified the Islands and was ruling a nation with a political and religious system centered in *heiau* and rooted in *kapu*, extensive taboos. But these old ways lasted less than a decade longer. Beginning with Captain James Cook's arrival in 1778, Hawaiians had noticed white men broke *kapu* without retribution from the gods. Some of the women, including Kamehameha's favorite wife, Ka'ahumanu, rankled at *kapu* that restricted their gender. After Kamehameha died Ka'ahumanu and the king's heir Liholiho (Kamehameha II) deliberately violated the *kapu* against men and women eating together, declared the gods dead, and ordered their images and the temples destroyed.

Just months before the first Christian missionaries arrived in 1820, the pole buildings and carved figures of many *heiau* were burned. Some temples, such as Mo'okini Heiau on the Big Island, survived and stood as visible, silent monuments for seven generations before becoming national or state parks or national historic landmarks. But most *heiau* fell into disuse, the rock platforms reduced to rubble. Some were bulldozed to make way for modern construction. Hundreds lay forgotten in tangles of *hau*, Christmas berry or guava.

In 1962, the federal government identified several *heiau* as national historic landmarks. The state took over jurisdiction of others. Funding began to flow in for preservation and, in some cases, reconstruction. The interest in preserving these sites was part of what some have called the Hawaiian Renaissance. In 1970, leaders of the annual Merrie Monarch Festival refocused the festival's goals to celebrate traditional Hawaiian dances, songs and crafts. A few years later, a group interested in re-creating ancient open-ocean canoe voyaging using non-instrument navigation formed the Polynesian Voyaging Society. Islanders were beginning to rediscover Hawaiian culture and to regard it with renewed appreciation.

Fortunately, hundreds of *heiau* still exist. Some were remodeled to suit different needs at different times; others, such as Ulupō Heiau on O'ahu, remain in ruins but have been cleared of brush and stabilized. The Kailua, O'ahu-based Hawaiian Civic Club now serves as *kahu* for this *heiau*. And although half its stonework was carried away before the 1951 rededication, Keaīwa Heiau in 'Aiea, O'ahu, still stands in a forest of eucalyptus and Norfolk pine.

At still other *heiau*, the stone architecture has been rebuilt, and Hawaiians are using the temples for religious ceremonies and cultural workshops. "This is not 'inventing culture,'" says Marion Kelly, cultural anthropologist and professor of ethnic studies at the

University of Hawai'i at Mānoa. "Culture is never static but constantly in motion, responding to the needs of the people in it. Now we're rediscovering *heiau* in another context, and they serve the purposes of people now."

Hale O Keawe at Pu'uhonua O Hōnaunau on the Big Island, for instance, was built as a mausoleum and once housed the bones of 23 chiefs. Today the *heiau* has been restored and is part of a larger National Park Service site called the Place of Refuge. Visitors can tour the site, and rangers lead guided walks. Throughout the year, artisans demonstrate such crafts as wood carving and making *tapa* cloth from bark.

In April, workers at Pi'ilanihale Heiau at Hāna, Maui, completed a 30-year restoration project. The *heiau*'s name means "house of Pi'ilani," the 16th-century chief who united Maui. The national historic landmark is bigger than two football fields and is the largest *heiau* in Hawai'i. During the Great Mahele, the land division of 1848, Pi'ilanihale Heiau was part of land deeded to a chief named Kahanu. For generations the Kahanu family thought the *heiau* was best left overgrown. Younger family members later concluded, however, that the *heiau* was a resource that should be shared with the public, and in 1972, they arranged for it to become part of the educational programs at Kahanu Garden, part of the National Tropical Botanical Garden system.

"The *heiau* in our present times are steppingstones to the past," says Kahanu Garden director Chipper Wichman. "The ancient Hawaiians were such a religious people. They recognized the spirit in everything. *Heiau* were the pinnacle of religious expression. We must always tread carefully in deciding how to use them. And yet, the sites can't be just museums."

A few other *heiau* have been restored with the pole-framed altars, towers and thatched houses of ancient times. In 1975 American Factors, owner of King Kamehameha's Kona Beach Hotel in Kailua-Kona on the Big Island, reconstructed a waterside temple on the hotel grounds: "A proposed expansion of the hotel drew attention to the rock pile that had been Ahu'ena Heiau," says Kāne, who designed an exact re-creation from early drawings and published descriptions. Noted archeologist Yosihiko Sinoto had located the cornerstones, so Kāne was able to rebuild the *heiau* on the exact location of the original. Now the temple images stand again at this *heiau* that was Kamehameha's private chapel and the national capital from 1812 to 1819. Not 50 feet away, hotel guests sunbathe on the beach.

Visitors are welcome at all *heiau*, but the experts remind us that a *heiau* is like a church. People should visit a *heiau* for a *pono*— right—reason. "I use *heiau* for a place of contemplation," says Tamara Moan, a Hawaiian who grew up in Oregon and moved to Hawai'i as an adult in 1986. "It's easier at *heiau* than at some other historical places to imagine the ancient lifestyle. At some *heiau* you can feel the power, the *mana*."

Colleen Allen, a Protestant Christian, has learned of *heiau* since moving to Hawai'i from the East Coast 12 years ago: "I'm not sure of the history of *heiau*," she says, "but the ones I've visited all convey power and stillness, and they make me feel reverent. I am acknowledging a power that is there. Different cultures put different names to it, but it's all one power."

Heiau to Visit

The Big Island

- Hale O Keawe at Pu'uhonua O Hōnaunau (Place of Refuge) National Historic Park. A reconstructed mausoleum and *heiau*.
- Ahu'ena Heiau, King Kamehameha's Kona Beach Hotel, Kailua-Kona. A reconstructed *heiau*.
- Pu'ukoholā National Historic Site. The restored Pu'ukoholā Heiau and the restored ruins of Mailekini Heiau.
- Mo'okini Heiau State Monument, Kohala. A *heiau luakini* near the birthplace of Kamehameha I.

Maui

- Pi'ilanihale Heiau, Hāna. The largest *heiau* in Hawai'i. Visit by guided tour only, daily at 11 a.m. and 1 p.m. Reservations are required.
- Haleki'i and Pihana Heiau, Wailuku. Partly restored ruins of an *ali'i* residence and a *heiau luakini*.

O'ahu

- Keaīwa Heiau State Park, 'Aiea. A healing *heiau* with a medicinal garden.
- Ulupō Heiau, Kailua. An agricultural *heiau*.
- Pu'u o Mahuka Heiau, Waimea. A *heiau luakini* with three walled enclosures.

Kaua'i

- The Wailua River Complex. A national historic landmark that includes the ruins of four *heiau* and a royal birth site.
- Kauluapa'oa Heiau, Hā'ena, adjoins a ceremonial *hula* area.

LIVING AN ANCIENT ART

1997

Voices, guitar and *'ukulele* blend together in a lilting rendition of "Hanohano Wailea" in the Sunday afternoon humidity, Kane'ohe Bay turquoise behind the *pā hula* at King Intermediate School. Seated on the grass, 17 tiny dancers move together to Kīhei de Silva's *mele* about Lanikai, O'ahu, where the girls learn their art from his wife, Māpuana de Silva, at Hālau Mōhala 'Ilima. The *keiki* concentrate with all their four-year-old might, following the moves of their *kumu hula*, Māpuana, and their *'anakē*, "auntie," or *hula* helper.

With the last notes of the song, the crowd of families and friends of these dancers and their older "*hula* sisters" of Hālau Mōhala 'Ilima applauds loud and long, moms and dads smiling as big as the tiny performers.

Today these little girls end their first year of *hula* study by performing at the annual, informal fund-raiser of the Mākālei Foundation that supports special activities of the *hālau*, which Māpuana de Silva founded in 1976. As the afternoon continues, their big sisters, mothers and aunties dance in their turns.

Midway through the program, de Silva presents awards, not for performance excellence, but for number of years as a *hula* student. Four nine-year-olds receive five-year inscribed wood bowls. A 20-year-old in the Merrie Monarch competition group receives a 15-year plaque.

To Māpuana and her husband and *hālau* partner, Kīhei de Silva, the Hawaiian values of longevity and belonging are much more important than individual dance excellence. For them, *hula* has become a road back to cultural roots.

Kīhei quotes a line from a song he wrote based on a proverb from Mary Kawena Pukui's collection, *'Ōlelo No'eau*: "*'Aia ke ola i ka hana.* There is life in work, in partnership." His voice is soft, yet firm. "That's the clarifying line of our lives."

Now 47, Kīhei ponders, "I'm sure we've grown into it. But it's been so gradual, I don't remember when it happened."

He and Māpuana certainly knew nothing of "life in work" in 1963 when they met in the seventh grade at Kamehameha Schools, where Kīhei later spent 12 years as an English teacher. In the eighth grade, Māpuana asked Kīhei for a date, to see the movie version of James Michener's *Hawaii.* "Kīhei's dad drove us there," Māpu says. "I don't remember watching the movie."

Later, after Māpuana had transferred to Punahou for her last two years of high school, she invited Kīhei to the prom. "I was really shy," he says, in his still-shy manner. "If she hadn't been aggressive in a nice way, I would never have become anything but a hermit."

They graduated in 1967, then parted for college, he to Pomona in Southern California, she to Pacific University in Oregon, where she learned some basic *hula* from other Hawai'i students. Eventually, she began choreographing for the group's performances, but she'd still never had "a real teacher."

Māpuana and Kīhei graduated from college in 1971 and married the following year. Māpu went to work for an insurance firm in Honolulu. While waiting for action on applications to teach physical education, she accompanied a college classmate to observe a session of Maiki Aiu Lake's *hālau hula.*

"I was enthralled," Māpu remembers. "I said I wanted to take lessons. That was in December. I started February 4, 1972. I was 23."

The class was in *hula 'auana,* modern *hula.* One day the *hālau* announced a class for anyone interested in *hula kahiko,* ancient dance. Māpuana showed up on the appointed Friday.

"Aunty Maiki didn't expect me. But neither did she give me the feeling I didn't belong," Māpuana says. "I thought it was a new class, but it had been meeting a year and a half. When I came, it was the last time she let anyone new in."

Māpuana attended for months before she figured out the class was for teachers. "I had known from when I was little that I would be a teacher. I just didn't know of what. I never did get a job teaching physical education so maybe this was meant to be. It was like somebody had a plan and it wasn't ours. It wasn't spooky-spooky, it was just that opportunities presented themselves and I took them."

Shortly after she graduated three years later, she formed Hālau Mōhala 'Ilima. Now she teaches some 400 girls and women in 17 weekly sessions. Some jokingly refer to Hālau Mōhala ʻIlima as "Māpu's Army." If it's true, the motherly commanding officer always seems to be in the trenches.

⤸

General de Silva arrives at Kamehameha Schools on a Tuesday evening for the class for nine-year-olds as sunset drops a brilliant orange curtain behind the Waiʻanae Mountains. Under one arm she squeezes two ʻukulele in cases. In the other hand she totes an enormous lau hala bag. On trip two from the parking lot she hauls a ghetto blaster and a big brown grocery bag full of more paper bags. Two teenage girls trot behind, each clutching a gigantic plastic storage box full of brand-new costumes to be tried on this evening and doled out to little girls to take home in the brown packages.

Students wander in, pull practice skirts of calico, gingham and Hawaiian prints over their shorts. Some 60 of them—mostly little ones, but also a dozen teenagers and a few adults—sit on the floor under their voluminous skirts, waiting. Māpuana has surrounded herself on the floor with paperwork, glasses perched on the end of her nose.

Minutes go by. Long, silent Māpu's Army minutes. The general is carefully checking lists of costumes and assignments for the upcoming fund-raiser. At last it's time to take roll by counting off.

"Kāhi!" One!

"Lua!"

"Kolu!"

The count slows at "iwākalua." Twenty. By 32, "kanakolu kūmālua," it bogs down, giggles erupt, and Māpuana coaches on the formation of numbers.

Eventually the last girl says slowly, thinking as she speaks, "Kana-ono-kūmāwalu!"

"How many is that in English?" Māpuana flashes her toothy, ready smile.

"Sixty-eight!"

"Hiki nō!" All right!

And then: "Hoʻomākaukau!" Make ready! Māpuana's ipu, her gourd drum, seems to be an extension of her. Her fingers gallop against it, and her full voice rolls a chant to the far corners of the large room. She gives her gourd not a glance, for her eyes are entirely on her dancers.

A little girl loses her place, and her big *hula* sister smiles at her until she synchronizes her hands and feet again. Another *keiki* can't stop coughing, and an older girl takes her out for a drink of water.

When the dance is finished, the girls are ready to chant themselves. Māpuana coaches: "Chant to somebody. Look at their flowers. Look at their bracelet. They'll think you're chanting right to them."

Māpuana commands her young charges to chant in a round, with the front row beginning. As row after row of young voices join the canon, the 68 girls hear themselves echoing richly from the walls and ceiling of this gym, and they are clearly filled with power.

In the early years of the *hālau*, as Māpuana became more forceful, Kīhei became more poetic, studying the ancient forms of oral literature. He began writing in the old highly metaphoric manner, producing *mele*, songs or chants to be danced. At the root of them all is the natural world, which provides comparisons and lessons instructive to people.

In 1988, the year Kīhei left Kamehameha to become a full-time part of the *hālau*, he wrote a *mele* called "Līhau"—gentle, cool rain—inspired by a wedding at Kamehameha Chapel. One verse says "Now love alights like a soft mist ... a cooling *līhau* rain at the *pali*'s very limits." In his notes about the song, Kīhei says, "Māpu and I pray that all our ladies' courtships will evolve from initial attraction, to gentle requests for more time together, to the soft arrival of love, to marriage, and the growth-through-marriage of 'hilina'i'—the tying of two people in trust and mutual reliance."

The last verse says "Contentment will soon attend us ... Yes, here it is: peaceful love."

Contentment attends the de Silvas, the marriage of Māpuana, self-described as "independent, bull-headed and a scrapper," and Kīhei, the quiet poet and latent hermit.

In growth-through-marriage, they have discovered, as Māpuana puts it, "We do better together than by ourselves." She insists, "He's the boss."

Kīhei says, "I'm not the boss. I'm her brake. In a way, I'm her conscience. She speeds around and I sort of play things back to her. I have to keep her in check or she'll say yes to everything."

He considers computer technology to be a blessing for keeping track of myriad *hālau* details, and jokingly says that when paperwork overruns Māpuana, she simply buys a new desk. "Now tell me," he says, "have you seen her three desks? I just told her again, it's time for another new office. I follow her, cleaning up. She's a taker-outer and I'm a putter-awayer. But she can take out a lot faster. There's just so much life in her. She has not much concept of failure."

Māpuana's drive came as part of Western-style education, for she and Kīhei were born in a time—1949—when Hawaiian heritage was not a matter of pride. For Kīhei, "Hawaiian was the secret language of my mother's family." Only later, academically, did he learn to speak it himself. "But," he says, "it is amazing how much sat in my ear and head waiting for formal learning."

Says Māpuana, "We both grew up hearing Hawaiian, but not speaking it. Our daughters are growing up using it. When Kahikina (now a 20-year-old sophomore at the University of Hawai'i aspiring to a Ph.D. in Hawaiian language) was little, she sang in Hawaiian. Not songs I knew, but songs she was making up."

When Kahikina reached sixth grade, Kīhei organized a language class for *hālau* students that age. Now the class is in its ninth season, and Kahi is one of the assistant teachers. "It's free and completely voluntary," Kīhei says. "If the kids sign up, I expect them to show up. That's all. They're so language-ready at that age, it's duck soup to teach."

Hālau Mōhala 'Ilima teaches far more than *hula* and language. Through its very organization, students can't help getting big, unspoken doses of Hawaiian values—commitment, sense of belonging, spirit of helping, tie to the *'āina*, historical and cultural pride, and its flip side, humility.

When the *hālau* takes the stage at a competition, spectators often remark on two things: the large number of dancers and their noticeable, almost palpable serenity.

Says Māpuana, "Competition is a tool to educate. In our *hālau*, the whole class goes to the competition, not just the best students.

It's more important for them to work together." *Laulima*. Cooperation. A basic Hawaiian value.

Yet Hālau Mōhala 'Ilima often wins awards, including the 1996 second-place *hula kahiko* trophy at the Merrie Monarch Festival. In the early 1980s, Kīhei recalls, "We were wrapped up in competition. We won *hula kahiko* at Merrie Monarch in 1981, 1982 and 1983. In 1984, we won top awards for *'auana, kahiko* and overall performance. And that was the end of the fever. Now the competitions are a chance to work hard, for our dancers to really develop confidence in themselves."

Onstage at Chaminade University, 22 women of Hālau Mōhala 'Ilima file on stage. They wear orange, from feather head *lei* to skirt, the color of the delicate *'ilima* blossom. Merely taking their places looks like a perfect dance, as each woman lays her *lau hala* mat on the floor and sets her *kala'au*—dance sticks—in front of it.

Their fund-raiser performance tonight serves as a dress rehearsal for the ultimate competition, Hilo's Merrie Monarch Hula Festival. As the members of this competition group seat themselves upon their mats, a little voice pipes from the audience: "I see my mama!"

For "Maika'i Kaua'i," a spirited *hula 'auana* for a *mele* Kīhei de Silva composed, the dancers wear black-and-white plaid shirts tucked into white skirts, and orange bandannas around their necks. Together, the four rows of dancers swoop and glide, turning in formation like a darting school of fish or a flock of migrating birds. Beneath the exterior precision lies more—a certain calm, a love of the art, a love of being Hawaiian. And when the dance is done, the women of Hālau Mōhala 'Ilima exit the stage two by two, arm in arm.

"*Hula* helps you to find the person you are," Māpuana says. "My adult students work one life and live another. We try to get them to where their work and their lives aren't so separate, to find values they can apply to home and work and *hula*.

"One of the basics is the self-discipline of choosing what you want to do instead of letting it happen to you. The women who come here like that. I hope being in this *hālau* helps make people thinkers, choosers and communicators.

"That's why, with the fourth graders, we don't even talk about 'competition,' we just say we're going to Keiki Hula (an annual competition for young dancers sponsored by the Kalihi-Pālama Cultural and Arts Society). We work to be the best we can be on that day. Most *hālau* select the best dancers, but we take the whole class. We don't even mention judging. We even tell parents we probably won't place. Our kids look plain and simple—no make-up, no fancy costumes, no fancy *lei*. We don't want them to look like short adults. But sometimes judges like glitz and glitter."

Paint and flash simply have no place in Hālau Mōhala 'Ilima. The *hālau* is not available for entertaining, nor does Māpuana teach crash courses for people who want to do their own one-time performance. The curriculum includes not only dance practice, but the study of history and culture, with serious field trips to the neighbor islands and to sites on O'ahu that include 'Iolani Palace, Bishop Museum and Queen Emma's Summer Palace. It even requires homework.

Kīhei sets the academic pace, going, for instance, way beyond the Merrie Monarch entry specs requiring a fact sheet on each competition dance. "The judges ask for a fact sheet," he says. "One sheet. Not plural. But I write for Māpu and the dancers. Otherwise we don't know what we're doing. It used to be, people were just doing the motions and were never told what they were dancing about."

When he was a young student himself, Kīhei learned Hawaiian songs by rote. But later he learned the language, and now "I run an old rote song through my head, translating. And sometimes I say, 'Oh, we were doing it wrong.' It's the strangest feeling, like getting two parts of your brain to shake hands."

His thirst to get the information right fuels his research so strongly that once his always-thorough Merrie Monarch fact "sheet" ran 150 pages, plus an appendix. He observes, "I think we're the thorn in the judges' sides. I've heard them whisper to each other, 'Did you get "the book" yet?'"

⚬

On a Saturday afternoon, Kīhei sits on the *lānai* on the *makai* side of the de Silva home, designed by Kīhei's father with a large first-floor wing for Hālau Mōhala ʻIlima. Under a *kamani* tree in the yard, younger daughter Kapalai, who is 13 and a natural musician, is having an *ʻukulele* lesson with Uncle David Kaʻio. Through the screen doors, the voices of the sixth-graders ring in song as part of their weekly class.

When they practice a seated dance using *ʻuliʻuli*, the feathered gourd rattle, Kīhei can see one of the *ʻanakē*—the older *hālau* members—behind a young dancer, her hand gently over the child's fingers clutching the rattle's neck, helping the girl turn her wrist and arm just right.

"These kids," Kīhei says, nodding toward the doors, "they become my kids, Māpu's kids. We have 30-year-olds who've been with us since they were freshmen in high school. The one class who will be *kumu*—teachers—they were our little girls. And now they are 30-year-old women. It's so nice to feel that sense of continuity."

That link, generation to generation, is essential to any culture. In *hula* and *mele*, Māpuana and Kīhei grasp the past and hand it to the future.

Explaining his winning entry in the 1995 Polynesian Literary Competition, "Ka Pāʻū o Hiʻiaka," Kīhei wrote that he composed the *mele* on the eve of his daughter's departure for summer school in Italy. He was full of fatherly fears about his first-born being so far away.

"I'm little more than a dabbler in chant fragments—but a memory drifts in, takes hold and binds me up in old-new meaning," Kīhei says. "That memory is this: Each year after Merrie Monarch, we take our *hālau* to the Kaʻauea *hula* mound. As part of our little ceremony of thanks and value-focusing, Māpu presents each first-year dancer with a plain beige skirt. She ties the dancers into their skirts, instructs them in their skirts' significance and has them dance.

"Two months before Kahi left for Italy, she was tied-in at Kaʻauea … In the act of composition, I was 'hit' by the conviction that Kahi was, in fact, tied in, protected and guarded—not necessarily by Māpu's knot, but by the presence there and now of all that has come before us."

◦〜〉

LUA: THE ANCIENT HAWAIIAN FIGHTING ART

1995

Night lies heavy on Kapālama's ridge—moonless, a trace of rain dancing down from the spine of Oʻahu's Koʻolau Mountains. Inside the Pā Kuʻi-a-lua, the place of training in the art of hand-to-hand fighting, a command rings:

"Hoʻomākaukau!" Make ready!

Nearly 20 haumana—pupils, men and women who by day are teachers, lawyers and farmers—poise themselves two by two, knees cocked, drawing huge breaths and releasing them, gathering strength.

"Kāhea!" The chanter commands: Call!

As one, the black-clad haumana chant in a slow, march-like rhythm: "E hea i ke kanaka, e komo māloko!" Call the man to enter!

"Pā!" comes the reply. Commence!

The low, guttural voices punch the close, still air: "Ā-he-hū! ā-he-hū!" Bare feet stamp with each syllable, cocked arms jab alternately with the cadence. The entry chant gathers power in the humid confines of the school. The grunting litany—Ā-he-hū!—grows primeval, more and more like the ferocity of Kamapuaʻa, legendary pig-man demigod, coiling energy like a hurricane spinning around the eye.

Every Thursday evening, this group gathers in a blue-matted wrestling room provided by Kamehameha Schools to practice lua. They are led by four ʻōlohe lua—lua masters—who trained for almost two decades before deciding they needed to pass on their art as a matter of cultural preservation. Each student in Pā Kuʻi-a-lua, the best-known and most visible lua training school in Hawaiʻi, has completed a 48-hour introductory course in this ancient Hawaiian fighting art that is similar in some ways to the martial arts of the Orient. Now these students work to expand their knowledge and their skill. They work not out of curiosity or to entertain, but to understand ancient precepts that form a model for living well.

The sounds of the entry chant give way to individual challenges—genealogies declaring the identity of the warrior, and loud, creative verbal insults and threats hurled at the enemy in Hawaiian, accompanied by gestures of strength. The challenger often uses metaphor, the Hawaiians' favorite form of expression.

A *haumana* shouts, "I am the hawk that hunts in the heavens, devouring your *mana*, for I am hungry! Fearless am I!"

On to the *haka*, a martial dance found in some form throughout Polynesia. The *haka* is essential to *lua* training for grace, agility and muscle memory. In ranks, the dancers lunge forward and back, dodge side to side. Their arm motions are *lua* strikes. Bare shoulders begin to glisten with sweat like the bodies of warriors of old, oiled to deny an enemy a sure grip. The dancers turn, whirl, pivot in unison, the *'ōlohe hula*—hula master—tapping the galloping rhythm on a gourd, calling the cues in chant, throwing in surprise lines to test the dancers' concentration.

It's easy to imagine that this wrestling room, with fluorescent lights and louvered windows, might be an ancient *hālau lua*: stone walls and thatched roof protecting two training areas, a *kapu* space for the masters and an altar to Ku'i-a-lua, the two-headed god of the fighting art. A lamp trimmer tended the flames of wicks soaked in *kukui* oil, for training was held in secret by night. The *kia'i-o-ka-puka*, keeper of the portal, guarded the sole entry. Without the right password and entry chant, a person—perhaps an enemy spy—would meet his end instantly, garroted, or smashed by a boulder suspended above the door with a trip wire.

Kamehameha the Great, who died in 1819, is perhaps the most renowned practitioner of this art of life and death. Called the Warrior King, unifier of all the Islands, he is famed for his ambition, strength, courage, judgment, and for dodging or catching a dozen spears hurled at him at once. He honed his abilities in the study and practice of *lua*.

In times of peace in ancient days, each high chief kept as guards a select group constantly training in *lua*. Practitioners competed in public in sham battles or in *mokomoko*, much the way Asian martial artists or boxers do today. The annual Makahiki ceremonies, which guaranteed peace for three or four months a year, always included such events. In time of war, though, the sham was over, and the *maka'āinana*, commoners who usually fished or farmed, were conscripted and given crash courses in the basics of *lua*.

It's no wonder a warrior went to battle with his hair nearly shorn, his skin oiled and his clothing nothing but a *malo* with front piece tucked. For if an enemy once got a handhold—*auwe*! First the little fingers were broken in simultaneous, split-second snaps. Then, depending on the instinct and creativity of the warrior and his choice of some 300 moves, the elbows, ribs and sternum were all fractured. Nose, jaw, clavicle. Hips, legs, pelvis—the bone-breaking kick between the legs was far worse than smashing the scrotum. Then, in the end, the back.

A warrior proficient in *lua* could do all this damage to the human body without weapons, yet the training encompassed far more than the mastery of blows, strikes, takedowns, holds, dodges and falls. It included *kōnane*, the game similar to checkers, to teach strategic thinking, and *lomilomi*, massage, to keep muscles from binding. A final test of flexibility was to weave one's body, snake-like, through a ladder of horizontal ropes spaced a foot apart. Command of balance required a student to squat barefoot on a half gourd measuring two feet in diameter, distributing his weight so he wouldn't break the fragile shell. To demonstrate strength, a student stood with his arms outstretched to the sides, parallel to the ground, while another person walked over him, from arm to arm. Focus required allegiance to the patron god, Ku'i-a-lua.

Lua. The common interpretation of the word for the past few generations has been "toilet." Indeed, it does mean "pit." It also is the numeral "two"—the important meaning for the fighting art. *Lua* is based on a yin-yang concept embodied by Hawaiians in Kū, the god representing positive male force, and Hina, the negative female. To use the Kū/Hina duality is to know ebb and flow, positive and negative, dark and light, hard and soft. It is to turn an enemy's energy into a force for yourself, to feel the integrated internal power Hawaiians call *mana*. It is to balance physical and spiritual, emotional and intellectual; to marshal the mind, body and spirit into a committed purpose; to know always who you are, where you are from and for what purpose you stand. It is to use *ho'omau*, persistence and perseverance, so *lua* becomes second nature. It is to use *nalu*, the principle of going with the surf, to be in harmony with nature. It is to embrace passion and pain, life and death.

For centuries, *lua*, with its fine Kū/Hina balance, was a prescription for life as well as the mode of warfare. Ironically, Kamehameha set off the demise of the discipline, first with acquisition of the firearms that gave him his most decisive victories at the end of the 18th century, then with his unification of the Islands, which propelled Hawaiians into extended peacetime. Coupled with the breaking of the ancient *kapu*—the prohibitions that ordered Hawaiian society—not long after his death in 1819 and the arrival of Christian missionaries the following year, these forces spelled doom for *lua*. It amounted, many say, to the emasculation of Hawaiian men.

Yet *lua* did not entirely disappear. Says *lua* master Jerry Walker, "When I was in my teens in the 1950s, I heard stories about old Hawaiians being able to tie people in knots, sometimes without touching them. But when I asked about it, I was told, '*huna*'—secret. Or '*kapu*.'"

In 1966, five years after he had started training in *karate*, *judo* and *aikido*, Walker saw an article in *Black Belt* magazine that mentioned *lua*. And it included a name: Charles Kenn.

In 1974, Walker found Kenn, a Hawaiian-German-Chinese scholar in his late 60s. Kenn had trained with Ka-wahine Kaopua, who in turn had been a student under Prince Kūhiō (King Kalākaua's nephew by marriage) and several other turn-of-the-century men of courtly status.

"I went to Kenn's house at nine in the morning and left at 10 at night," Walker remembers. "He talked all that time of Hawaiiana, with about three sentences pertaining to *lua*. But finally he said, 'Get a group of 12—12 was the number in Kamehameha's personal guard. Gather 12 and I will teach you.'"

Soon reduced to five through attrition, the men trained for four years, until Kenn had nothing more to teach. Four of the five kept in touch and practiced—for themselves. Then in 1991, the Native Hawaiian Culture and Arts Program (NHCAP), funded by the National Parks Service through the Bishop Museum, identified *lua* as a dying Hawaiian art. "We had been satisfied, just practicing," says *lua* master Richard Paglinawan, who is also an expert in several Asian martial arts. "The program kicked us in the butt and forced us to reexamine *lua* as a lost tradition."

The group—Walker, Paglinawan, Mitchell Eli and Moses Kalauokalani—agreed with NHCAP to work systematically at saving *lua*. First they researched all available literature, which is now compiled in one of three volumes of their reports kept at the Bishop Museum archives. In September of 1993, they conducted their first introductory class with Hawaiians they knew personally, then followed it with a series of courses on the Big Island, Maui, Kaua'i and Moloka'i with students recommended by their first graduates. In all, they've trained about 150 Hawaiian men and women, some of whom continue their training in Pā Ku'i-a-lua. Word has spread, so that Hawaiian civic clubs on the West Coast of the Mainland are requesting training programs. With NHCAP funding for teaching at an end, the group is now forming a nonprofit school.

Paglinawan winces when he admits to writing a training manual. "It's the *haole* way," he says. "But our age—I'm 59 and Jerry's the youngest, 51—is pushing us. For *lua* to remain viable and accessible, we have to use written methods."

Yet, he says, "We feel it here, in the *na'au*." He touches his belly. "The intellect holds just information. To live and practice this is different. Many people now are proud to be Hawaiian in their heads and their hearts. *Lua* helps them connect all the way to the guts, which Hawaiians believe to be the seat of emotion."

Walker emphasizes *lua* philosophy. "He who throws the first blow and calls upon Ku'i-a-lua for assistance will not receive it," he says. "He who throws the second blow—it doesn't have to be physical—and asks for help will get it."

Bill Laeha spends Thursday nights at Pā Ku'i-a-lua refocusing himself for his daily challenge as a teacher of fourth graders at Sunset Beach Elementary School—kids who would rather have home schooling so they can surf when the waves are up. Laeha's lean body kicks and jabs, practicing for precision. His challenge is quick, forceful. Yet what is most important to him is unseen, unheard.

"*Lua* has given me a spiritual direction," he says. "It's a sense of pride in where we come from and how we relate to others. Kids won't remember a specific math lesson, but years later they will remember attitude. And that's something that comes, not in words, but in my behavior. The essence of *lua* is that we never have to throw a blow. We use this knowledge from the Hina side of us, the discipline side, the spiritual side. *Lua* is the focal point for me that helps me be strong and not lose my cool."

Lua is unlikely to once again become the art of tribal warfare. But it's relevant in the late 20th century. Sam Ka'ai, Maui *kahuna kālai ki'i*—image carver—and an expert on ancient Hawaiian weapons, trained with Pā Ku'i-a-lua on his home island. He notes that *haka*, the dance component of *lua*, means "not only to dance in ranks, but also to perch on a shelf. Not 'discard,' but to not use. For generations, Hawaiian things were *haka*—held and cherished, but not used." *Lua* is one of them.

Ha'a—another form of the word *haka*—"is the old word for *hula*," Ka'ai says. "In world history, dance is locked up in self-defense. Dance (and the accompanying power chants) stops panic and fear going into battle, and propels the warrior into another consciousness." To Ka'ai, the resurgence of *lua* is another "ancient murmur turning into a living song. *Lua* is about how to die well."

As Jerry Walker puts it, "To be ready to die well means to live well. It means always having your life in order."

"We Hawaiians have done too much dying," Ka'ai says. Between the time of first Western contact in 1778 and 1890, the Hawaiian population dwindled by 90 percent. Today's statistics are dismal: Disproportionate numbers of Hawaiians are in prison, on welfare, and ill with cancer, diabetes, obesity and heart disease. And, Ka'ai says, "We die from (overdosing on) drugs; we die from AIDS."

It goes back to spiritual bankruptcy induced eight or nine generations ago. "Hawaiian men lost the ability to have a place with god when they made colonial priests the keepers of our spirits," Ka'ai says. "When the *kapu* were broken, with that went dignity. *Lua* will bring it back. And out of it will return the two-faced god who promises to honor the one who throws the second blow. *Lua* will bring back discipline because the practitioner has to change his life. It comes at a good time, when we're trying for sovereignty in a physical form."

Ka'ai was the force behind the 1991 commemoration of the 200th anniversary of the unification of the island of Hawai'i. It was on an August day that Kamehameha sacrificed his cousin, Keoua

Kuahu'ula, chief of the Puna and Ka'ū districts, at Pu'ukoholā, the *heiau* he had built at Kawaihae. Ka'ai viewed the 1991 occasion as a time to heal old wounds, a time to honor the ancient past and to look to the future.

The ceremonies, now repeated annually, included the concept of *ka'au*, a measure of 40, a full measure. He called for a *ka'au* named Na Koa—40 warriors, 40 men of courage. Some of the volunteers trained with Richard Paglinawan. And when the day came, 40 warriors marched in ceremony, cloaked in 40 *ti* capes, each garment thick with 1,700 hand-tied leaves. They wore 40 *malo* and carried 40 *pololū*, handmade long wood pikes. And these 40 Hawaiian men stood tall; they were a *ka'au*, a full measure.

But that *ka'au* and the Pā Ku'i-a-lua students are just a tenuous, symbolic beginning—the beginning of regaining Hawaiian pride and sovereignty—because Ka'ai knows about the wind, *makani*. He speaks poetically, in the metaphoric language of the ancestors.

"All you have to do is look someplace else and the Lord Makani will blow away the dry leaves of the source. If Hawaiians collect the leaves and make the mat, will it be a new seed, or drop and be dry leaves again, which the Lord Makani blows? Time is moving season by season. What will you keep? Have you picked the flower too early? The fruit too young? Are you the seed from a tree destroyed? Or the living tree? All of these things must be asked.

"For the order of change, Makani is always ready. He blows in the dark times of the night. If you cast my story away, I am blown away as something of no value. To be of value we must have credence; we must beat the story out on the *pahu hula*, the *hula* drum, and on the *pahu heiau*, the drum of the temple. We must sing it in chant—tell it in story."

In his vision of the future, Ka'ai sees the massive lava rock walls of Pu'ukoholā, jutting dark against the pale morning sky. And at this place of destiny, he sees capes bristling in silhouette, *malo* girding strong, healthy bodies, pikes slashing the dawn.

He sees warriors, but not just one *ka'au*, not just one full measure. He sees them regimental, 800 strong. Their chanting voices will ring in the ancient rocks. And they will dance the *haka*.

"Because *lua* is death, it is life," says Ka'ai. "And the dance of *lua*, the *haka*, is the dance of life."

Update: Pā Kuʻi-a-Lua continues under ʻolohe Richard Paglinawan and Moses Kalauokalani. Pā Kuʻi-a-Holo was established in 1996 under ʻolohe Mitchell Eli and Jerry Walker. In 2006 the four ʻolohe authored Lua: Art of the Hawaiian Warrior, *published by Bishop Museum Press.*

5
Resurrection

❧

Canoe voyaging, healing arts,
Hawaiian language and the
joy of putting recovered
knowledge to work

᠅

PŪNANA LEO:
THE QUEST TO SAVE THE HAWAIIAN LANGUAGE

1990

At first glance, Pūnana Leo o Honolulu looks like any other preschool. The children skip through the door wearing *Peanuts* T-shirts and carrying *Ghostbusters* lunch boxes. The day is filled with counting, stories, dancing, singing and playtime.

The only thing out of the ordinary is the language. "We use only Hawaiian," says teacher Lolena Nicolas. "New children, especially, will talk to us in English. We listen, but we answer in Hawaiian."

Pūnana Leo, the "language nest," is an innovative Hawaiian language immersion preschool program that began in 1984 with a single school in Kekaha, Kaua'i. Two others opened the following year—one in Honolulu and one in Hilo—and a fourth was added on Maui in 1987. They now serve about 80 children; 45 others have "graduated." Unlike in most other immersion programs, the children are also serving the language. The tots chattering away on the playground in Hawaiian don't realize it, but they may be the saviors of a language that is virtually on the verge of extinction.

Pūnana Leo is the cornerstone of a dream that began in 1982 when two of the people who had started the highly successful Kohanga Reo Maori language school in New Zealand challenged a group of Hawaiians to do the same in their homeland. The seven Island educators who committed themselves to organizing Pūnana Leo bucked not only financial obstacles, but public opinion.

"People just laughed," says Larry Kimura, who teaches Hawaiian at the University of Hawai'i-Mānoa campus and who, like most of the other founders, remains on the Pūnana Leo board of directors. "And Hawaiians were some of the worst. They said we were just UH professors with our heads in the clouds."

Undaunted, they hurdled obstacle after obstacle, acutely aware that the number of native speakers—now estimated to be only about 1,000, including 200 on Ni'ihau—was rapidly dropping.

They went the extra mile and made sacrifices. From 1985 to 1986, Kauanoe Kamanā, a Hawaiian language instructor at UH-Hilo, took a year's leave to work full-time on organizing Pūnana Leo.

"We realized we couldn't rely on the university, the Office of Hawaiian Affairs or Kamehameha Schools," Kimura says. "At Kamehameha, the highest foreign language enrollment is in Japanese! For about the last 10 years, Kamehameha has had only one Hawaiian language teacher. This year, the Schools finally hired a second one."

Like the others on Pūnana Leo's founding committee, Kimura believes that language is the foundation of a culture, its way of thinking and its mode of expression. Parts of a civilization may survive the death of a language, but such a "relic culture" is an insignificant curiosity.

Kimura faults turn-of-the-20th-century Americans for deliberately trying to stamp out the native Hawaiian language. Under the Hawaiian Kingdom monarchy, 19th-century commerce, politics and education in Hawai'i were conducted in both Hawaiian and English. When Hawai'i became a republic following the overthrow of Queen Lili'uokalani in 1893, the goal of many was for it to become part of the United States. The new Department of Public Instruction furthered the cause by outlawing the Hawaiian language as a medium of teaching in the public schools. English was mandated in classrooms and on the playgrounds; students and teachers were forbidden to speak Hawaiian. Some teachers were even afraid to use Hawaiian geographical names in their classes.

"It was a sure blow," says Kimura. "It took decades of effort and money to wipe out Hawaiian. Now we ought to be putting an equally conscious effort into restoring the language."

The Pūnana Leo organizers researched programs and funding. Immediately, they came into conflict with the old regulations forbidding instruction in Hawaiian—rules that, incredibly, weren't changed until 1986. Government assistance was difficult to find, too. "There's a federal budget for dying species of plants and animals," Kimura says. "It seems ironic that there is none for endangered languages."

But the Pūnana Leo visionaries kept precedents in mind—the Maori, the Navajo, the Breton, the Welsh, the Mohawk in Quebec—whose language schools are today successful realities.

"The younger the child, the faster he picks the language up," says Pūnana Leo teacher Ipo Kanahele. "The older children help a lot. Within a couple of months, the kids are speaking fluently."

Indeed they are.

"*Aloha kakahiaka, Kalena. Pehea mai nei ʻoe i kēia lā?*"

"*Maikaʻi, Kumu* Lolena," Kalena Honda replies, in answer to his teacher.

Later, it's time for calisthenics. Kalena is right in there, shouting along with five-year-old student leader Alohalani Ho. "*ʻEkāhi! ʻElua! ʻEkolu! ʻEhā!*"

"*Hana hou!*" Alohalani calls. The children begin another round counting off jumping jacks.

Inside the classroom, they sit in a circle on the floor. Class helper Kawika Eyre sits with them, telling a story in Hawaiian. Translated, the tale goes:

"Once there was a brother and a sister whose parents died. They were trying to get food at the beach when a giant eel came up and took the sister away to his cave. The brother asked the shark to help him find his sister, but the shark said no. He asked the squid to help him, but the squid said no. None of the big sea creatures would help him. He didn't know what to do. Then he heard a little voice say, 'We'll help!' It was the *ʻopihi*, one of the smallest creatures of all. Two *ʻopihi* went to the cave and covered the eel's eyes with their round shells, and the brother and sister swam to safety."

An elementary schoolteacher for the past eight years, Eyre is studying Hawaiian at the University of Hawaiʻi. "Pūnana Leo parents were suspicious of me at first, this tall *haole* boy," he says. "But I grew up in Honolulu. Hawaiian has always been a part of my life, especially through music. Over the years, I learned some of the language. This year, I decided there couldn't be a better way to spend my sabbatical than to study it intensively.

"The language embodies the total experience of the Hawaiian, and it's in danger of being lost forever. Pūnana Leo is the promise of the future, and the last hope. For me, there's a symbol of Hawaiian-*haole* cooperation—Mary Kawena Pukui and Sam Elbert, who produced the Hawaiian dictionary. Let's join hands like that. This is it—we work together or we lose it."

Eyre's 'opihi story is based on a traditional Hawaiian tale. There's no printed version of it. To provide reading material for the students, Pūnana Leo teachers and parents who serve as volunteers at the school spend countless hours pasting Hawaiian translations over the English words in standard preschool books.

Another major problem is finding teachers. Pūnana Leo has recruited native speakers—many from Ni'ihau—to take courses in early childhood education at local community colleges. Teacher recruitment is such a challenge that parents wanting to start a new Pūnana Leo school in their community—and they do in Hanalei, Kaua'i; Papakōlea, O'ahu; and on Moloka'i—must first find at least one person qualified to teach.

The third problem, predictably, is money. Most of the parents who want to place their children in Pūnana Leo are on the low rungs of the economic ladder, and the $185 monthly tuition is a major sacrifice. For the school, the fees pay only 80 percent of the $50,000 required to run an annual program for 20 youngsters. The rest of the money comes from fund-raising events and benefactors. The Kalihi-Moanalua Protestant Church has never charged Pūnana Leo o Honolulu rent for holding classes in its facilities.

Pūnana Leo is only the first step in the quest to save the Hawaiian language. As soon as it had its preschool nest built, directors, teachers and parents tackled the next obvious question: Where do Pūnana Leo graduates—at the age of five or six—go?

The State Department of Education (DOE) agreed to try a Hawaiian-language immersion program for a combined kindergarten/first grade. In the fall of 1987, the pilot project opened in classrooms at Keaukaha Elementary School in Hilo and at Waiau Elementary School in Pearl City. The following year, the program added a second grade, and third grade is slated for this year. The idea is to provide the immersion alternative through the sixth grade, gradually conducting some lessons in English beginning in fourth grade. Without the program, Kimura says, Pūnana Leo students going on to an English-speaking classroom would lose Hawaiian fluency within two months.

DOE Superintendent Charles Toguchi was one of the earliest supporters of the idea. "I've always believed Hawai'i is made up of people from many backgrounds," he says. "We all should be proud of our roots. It's important for any cultural group to remember its heritage, but Hawaiian is different from any other language. We don't have it anywhere else but here. If there's a way I can help, I will."

Roberta Mayor, the DOE administrator of the languages section, is more specific. "Immersion is one way of teaching," she says. "These children are just learning what every other child learns—but they're doing it in another language. The research suggests they will not suffer in an English-speaking country. Our real aim is that they become bilingual or multi-lingual."

But even some who endorse the immersion idea have doubts. Patrick Seely is the principal at Keaukaha Elementary. It's plain to him that youngsters are learning Hawaiian easily, "Yet," he says, "philosophically, I'm concerned. I don't see any overall goals and objectives, no specifics for each year. The people behind it compare it to a program for the Mohawk Indians in Canada, but this is not a reservation—this is an English-speaking society. My big concern is when do we give them English?"

Waiau Elementary School Principal Diane Oshiro takes a different view. "The program has really opened my eyes to how kids learn. Because the teachers couldn't rely on the printed material, they had the kids start writing first. It was exciting to them to learn by becoming authors. Now other teachers are using the techniques the immersion instructors developed."

Almost all of the Pūnana Leo graduates enroll in the public school language immersion program. Ka'umealani and Kamoa'elehua Walk have two children enrolled at Waiau and one at Pūnana Leo. The Walks live in Hau'ula, more than 40 miles away, but Ka'umealani, like other parents, believes it's worth the time and effort to transport her children to the programs, pay preschool tuition, and fulfill obligations to do volunteer work and attend weekly language classes for parents.

"You have to learn who you are," she says, "or there will be unrest inside. If you go through the regular school system, you learn from a Western point of view. We're giving our children values that will guide them for life. Because of that, these kids will have the edge. We cannot change the past, but we can give them tools for life through language and culture."

The Walks are committed to a program that skeptics say not only won't save Hawaiian, but may later put their children at a disadvantage. Says Kamoa'elehua, however, "If there's one thing of worth we can give our children, it's the language of their ancestors. We will forever be in debt to Pūnana Leo for doing something about a dream instead of sitting around saying, 'Too bad Tūtū isn't here.'"

Update: 2008 marks 30 years of Hawaiian as an official state language, 25 years of the Pūnana Leo programs, and 20 years of Hawaiian language immersion programs in state Department of Education schools. Currently 11 Pūnana Leo preschools operate statewide, enrolling approximately 200 students. Since 1983 about 1,500 pre-schoolers have "graduated." Public school immersion programs now are offered at 19 sites, most within larger "regular" schools. The three with programs through grade 12 awarded their first Hawaiian language high school diplomas in 1999. Currently about 120 students have followed programs through all grades to high school graduation.

LOMILOMI'S LOVING TOUCH

1996

Jimmy Lewis is a *lomilomi* practitioner, but it wasn't always so. It took him years to hear the calling to this ancient holistic healing art of massage practiced by his Hawaiian forebears. Today, glasses sliding down his nose and graying hair tied back at his neck, he is clearly in tune with his true work.

When I'm settled face-down on a massage table, a sheet covering my shorts and my legs, Lewis takes a quick look at my back, touches it with one finger and says, "Hoooo, you work too hard."

He's also read my new-client form, including my nagging problem: TMJ, temporomandibular joint dysfunction. My jaw is so out of whack, I'm dizzy and exhausted most of the time. My neck and shoulders are a study in muscular tension.

In a handout called "A Traditional Procedure," I read, "While the therapist performs the physical work, it is not *from* the therapist that relief and healing come; rather it is *through* him or her that it flows."

Lewis' voice is warm, his touch is warm. He works unhurriedly, firmly but lightly, beginning far from my troublesome jaw. His rubber slippers squeak on the concrete floor, the massage table creaks a little as he attends to my muscles. His big, warm hands, slick with a mix of *kukui* and olive oil, work deeper and deeper. All I can see is the floor, but I know from his hands that Lewis' full attention is on me. From his hands I feel for sure that Lewis has what his teacher, legendary *lomilomi* master Aunty Margaret Machado, calls "the loving touch."

I ask Lewis if the oil is the secret. "No," he says. "The secret is *pule*." Prayer. Before and after a treatment, most practitioners do this either silently or out of the presence of the client, and they practice other purification rituals as well.

Lewis has been in practice only a few years, for *lomilomi* is a spiritually based ancient healing art in which substantial interest has rekindled only recently, along with the companion practices of *la'au lapa'au*, herbal medicine and *ho'oponopono*, elder counseling that "sets right."

Lomilomi shares some physical characteristics with other forms of body work such as Swedish massage, acupressure, physical therapy and even Rolfing. It can work in conjunction with Western medicine, and it can work outside Hawai'i.

Massage therapists come from far-flung places—Sweden, Australia, Germany—to study with Aunty Margaret Machado in intensive courses she gives at her modest beach house at Ke'ei, near Nāpō'opo'o on the Big Island. And sometimes her Hawaiian protégés take the art elsewhere.

Maka'ala Yates, who grew up near Machado's beach house and later trained with her and other *kūpuna*, recently established Mana Ola, a practicing and teaching clinic in Ashland, Oregon. Yates, who's also a chiropractor, has practiced *lomilomi* for 18 years and considers himself always learning. His dual orientation comes through in large, sure hands that are both powerful and gentle, and in his philosophy: "I choose to integrate traditional, ancient ways because the ancients knew the spirit world, and we need to reconnect. If you can communicate with the patient at the soul level, you create trust. And when two souls meet, healing takes place."

Yates departs from the ancient idea of passing down knowledge genealogically. "We don't need lineage," he says. "The spirit world is available to all people. Let's keep an open mind. My role is to link the traditional world with the modern world. The teaching of *lomilomi* shouldn't end with perpetuation of an ancient way, but be integrated into other health care systems."

Like many Hawaiians, Yates did not seek out *lomilomi*. In 1977, he and his friend John Kruse were home in Kona after sailing on *Hōkūle'a*'s first voyage to Tahiti. "We were at Ke'ei Beach," Yates recalls. "At the end of the day, John and I walked out past Aunty Margaret's house. I told John, 'Don't look at the house. There's a *kahuna* lady who has this power to look into your soul. She does miracles.'

"But then this voice came out: '*Hui!*'

"I said to John, 'Pretend you didn't hear.'

"'*Hui*! Maka'ala!'

"'Oh, no,' I thought. I saw John shaking.

"I got on her porch. She was teaching her second class ever, and she wanted to use me as a model to work on. I said, 'No. Use John.'

"She looked me in the eye. I said I was a naughty boy. 'Never mind,' she said. 'I want you.' I had no idea why."

But Yates complied that day. And he signed up for Aunty Margaret's next class.

Some don't heed the call so easily. Jimmy Lewis tended bar for 15 years, then spent nine years as finance manager for a car dealership in Scottsdale, Arizona. But his Hawaiian soul slept restlessly, and sometimes he'd drive all night to San Diego just to see the ocean.

In 1989, Lewis came home. His Aunt Kahau Maunakea Mokiao, who had just started Lomilomi Ola, the Institute of Hawaiian Therapy, in Honolulu, wanted someone in the family to carry on her work, and she introduced him to Margaret Machado. When he started training with her, he was 48.

"Now I make a quarter of the money I used to," Lewis says. "And I'm happy. A lot us had the calling earlier and ignored it. Too *pa'akikī*—stubborn."

Ronnie Dudoit ignored it, too. Practicing on O'ahu through a Saint Francis Medical Center program and on his home island of Moloka'i, Dudoit, now 47, spent the first couple of decades of his adult life as a professional bass player. In 1986, Dudoit's father suffered a slipped disk, for which doctors ordered spinal surgery. Dudoit called Kalua Kaiahua, a Maui and O'ahu healer.

"I went to get him at the airport. We'd never met, but he walked directly to me and shook my hand." Dudoit remembers the handshake—firm, discerning somehow. In retrospect, he knows the handshake was behind Kaiahua's next words: "You should be doing what I'm doing."

Kaiahua's treatment had Dudoit's father exercising in his hospital bed in 45 minutes. He never did have surgery.

Four years later, Dudoit's wife, Francine, a registered nurse who now works with him, injured her back and stomach while caring for her horse. Once again, Dudoit called Kaiahua. Instead of coming to Moloka'i, Kaiahua instructed Dudoit on the phone, talking him through the *lomilomi* steps until Francine was better. And then Kaiahua said, "I told you, boy, you have this gift."

From then on, Dudoit used the gift. He studied with Kaiahua and teamed up with Francine. Now the Dudoits log a thousand miles a week, zipping from house calls in Honolulu to clinics in windward O'ahu. In 1995, their first patients through the Saint Francis program waited at a mobile clinic in silence. The next time they came, they brought *'ukulele* and guitars, and now they sing away the wait.

"Our Hawaiian people are hungry for our methods," says Francine Dudoit. "They have so much distrust of Western medicine. We're saying here's another option—not instead of, but to bridge the gap between two worlds. Ronnie does *ho'oponopono* and *la'au lapa'au*, too. And we take our patients to doctors and the pharmacy, and make sure they understand their medication. We deal with problems, not massage just to make you feel good."

In six months, the Dudoits see a thousand patients. Some lack cash, but they know they can come anyway. "Sometimes they bring fish, bananas, *limu*," Francine Dudoit says. "One man brought a baby pig. They bring what they can, and we accept. We're there for them, no matter what."

For lack of suitable rental space, Dudoit sets up his battered portable massage table once a week in the offices of a Kaka'ako factory. To this odd location come people with Parkinson's disease, lupus, diabetes, high blood pressure, people complaining of killer headaches, sore backs, of "no can walk good."

Many of them also have "'ōpū huli," Dudoit says, the turned stomach he believes must be adjusted before anything else.

Says Francine Dudoit, "We've been doing this for years now. We look at people on the street and we know already whose stomach is *huli*. We watch how you walk, look at your eyes." And then Ronnie Dudoit's long, knowing fingers gently find the trouble. He begins working far from the pain, "so when we get to it, there won't be so much pressure."

A retired psychologist, a *haole* guy, came to Dudoit limping with a pinched sciatic nerve. Face upon the table, fully clothed, as Dudoit always works, the man didn't notice any effect during the few minutes' treatment. "But by the time I got back to my car," he says, "I was dancing. I'm amazed, but not shocked. I know healers can work in wonderful and mysterious ways."

Hawaiian practitioners would use the word "spiritual" rather than "mysterious." Some interpret that in a Christian context. Others characterize "spiritual" more broadly. Part of practicing *lomilomi* now "is reconnecting with the spiritual," says Maka'ala Yates. "Then we keep that link open with meditation, prayer, whatever it takes. There are a lot of misinterpretations of *lomilomi*. Sometimes people learn the technique without the spiritual depth."

It's easy to recognize the spiritual base from the touch of a true *lomilomi* practitioner. The hands radiate energy. They are strong and reverent all at once. Even if you can't see the practitioner's face, you can feel that his or her whole attention is on you. The air warms with trust, and you feel safe. This is what Aunty Margaret Machado calls "the loving touch."

That touch doesn't require special surroundings. Dudoit gives treatments at the Moloka'i Ka Hula Piko Festival on his table set up in the open at the edge of the picnic/concert grounds. Says Francine Dudoit, "We could do *lomilomi* in a parking lot if we had to."

Louella Vidinha's Leeward Therapeutic Massage is a plain, practical two-cubicle office in 'Aiea. Though she is Hawaiian, Vidinha first practiced Swedish massage. But three years ago, when her third pregnancy brought on horrible morning sickness, she sought out Uncle Kalua Kaiahua, knowing one of his specialties is pregnancy and conception problems. She was carrying her baby unusually low, and Kaiahua moved her uterus up. Her nausea abated. And, after delivery, she studied with Kaiahua and added *lomilomi* to her professional services.

Says Vidinha, "My clients like the massage I do now way better."

Sometimes clients even weep during a treatment, in physical and emotional relief. Often they say that finding a *lomilomi* practitioner is an answer to their prayers.

Learning *lomilomi* was the answer to Randy Jones' prayer for meaning in his life. About 20 years ago, he graduated from the University of Georgia with a degree in horticulture. Then he "played music professionally, and had a successful restaurant business that made lots of money. But I abused myself."

He came to Hawaii, to Waipi'o Valley. "I got into yoga and meditation, but still there was something lacking. I wanted purpose, to make sense of my life. I was raised Catholic, but my prayer was not 'Hail Mary.' It was just asking God to help me."

The path led to Margaret Machado's house at Ke'ei Beach. "When I first met Aunty, this place felt like home. She told me, 'I love you.' I was 43. It was the first time in my life that I thought someone meant it.

"Aunty Margaret says that your heart has a door without one of its handles. Love is knocking, but the door only opens from the inside."

When Jones finished Machado's basic *lomilomi* training in 1995, she asked him to apprentice with her. "She's worked a lot of miracles," Jones says. "Even with people who've had strokes. I've watched her. Her loving touch is something the world really needs."

The "loving touch" is outlined on a poster Jimmy Lewis set up at a class he taught. As the words on the poster read, the healing art of *lomilomi* "is a gentle, graceful, rhythmic, light or deep massage to parts of the external body's pressure points, nerve centers, muscle tissues and internal organs. It removes toxic waste, tension, pain and fatigue, and replaces them with positive energy, increases circulation and improves muscle tone.

"*Lomilomi* is an attitude on the part of the therapist, who must be clean and positive in mind, body and spirit ... the (patient) trusts that *lomilomi* can help, and comes from a higher power."

Machado puts it this way: "Hawaiian *lomilomi* is praying work."

In her grandfather's time in the 19th century, *lomilomi* was passed down only in families. "My grandfather was a *kahuna*, a master of secrets," she says. "Secrets not to be taught. Some of my cousins still say don't teach, not even Hawaiians. I say now is the time for education."

Most licensed practitioners trained with Machado, who is now 80. Others, like Dudoit, studied with Kalua Kaiahua. Some, like Jimmy Lewis, use both styles, or, like Yates, carry *lomilomi* beyond its cultural boundaries. Many practitioners, in turn, teach people seeking a little skill to use just in their own families rather than to train more professionals.

Finding a *lomilomi* professional requires more than a search of the phone book's Yellow Pages. Only eight of the 144 licensed massage therapists listed in the O'ahu directory mention *lomilomi*. For a license, the state's Massage Board requires a stringent 150 hours of academic study of anatomy and related sciences, followed by 420 hours of supervised practical work, but it does not test for additional training in specialties such as *lomilomi*, shiatsu or acupressure. Any licensed therapist can legally hang out a "*lomilomi*" shingle.

Whether you seek a licensed therapist or a family-based practitioner, inquire about training. According to Lewis, it should lead back to Machado or Kaiahua, not to a short course intended for personal use. "Twenty hours' training doesn't cut it," he says.

Says Yates, "I applaud the many legitimate forms of *lomilomi*, but people should beware of self-proclaimed *kahuna* and opportunists who exploit Hawaiian culture."

Like other Hawaiian elements that have been revived in recent decades, healing arts resurfacing from oral tradition are subject to change as they rub against modern society. According to Yates, that may not be all bad. "We should not be stifled by tradition. If we stay entirely with ancient ways, we'll lose our abilities to apply ourselves to the present. The value of the ancient ways is in information that is timeless, and in the ability to communicate with the spirit world. It takes time to make that link."

❦

That link became clear to me the day I met Margaret Machado. The memory is still fresh in my mind. It's the first day of her new class, perhaps her 20th or so. This old-style wood beach house, where she spent part of her childhood in the 1920s, creaks with the bustle of students moving in for a month to study, eat and sleep on the big *lānai* that faces the sea pounding a black rocky shore.

Amid the hubbub on this porch, where Maka'ala Yates tried to deny Aunty Margaret's call, this tiny, forceful woman commands me: "Sit."

I take a folding chair facing her. She takes both my hands in hers, and begins the Lord's Prayer in Hawaiian.

Then she says, "Pull your hair back." I am still tying it at my neck when she says, "You're lacking oxygen to the brain on the right. Turn your chair around."

She stands behind me, pressing a spot on the right side of my neck. Sore! Major sore! No wonder I'm dizzy—no oxygen. It's all from the TMJ. It's been two weeks since Jimmy Lewis worked on me.

For five minutes, Aunty Margaret's short, gnarled fingers probe gently but firmly around my jaw, in my right eye socket, across my forehead and over both temples. Then she says, "Breathe. In the nose, out the mouth." Each time I exhale, she leans into the top of my shoulder with her forearm, coaching me to breathe faster, until I am almost panting. Then she goes after my biceps, nearly encircling me from behind. She feels warm, soft and firm.

She releases me, turns me around, seats herself and takes my right foot in her lap. She strokes the top of the second toe three or four times and says, "Oh! You were a nice baby. But as a teenager you knew it all. That's all right, because now you are calm. It's all over."

Yes. I feel cold. I almost cry. She's seen into my soul through the top of my foot, and she's eased my body's pain with her loving touch.

Just above her, on the porch that's older than she is, hangs a faded sign: "If your hands are gentle and loving, your patient will feel the sincerity of your heart. His soul will reach out to yours, and the Lord's healing will flow through you both. By Margaret Kalehuama kanoelulu'uonapali Machado."

Now I understand something Aunty Margaret's apprentice, Randy Jones, told me. "You bring your mind to study the anatomy," he said. "But you learn the loving touch from the heart."

Update: Since 1996, lomilomi *and other Hawaiian healing arts have gained more and more acceptance as viable solutions to today's health problems, and are being integrated into comprehensive treatment programs.*

Setting Things Right

1998

Maile Meyer and three other women leave their store on Merchant Street in downtown Honolulu, and head *mauka* to the YWCA. Afternoon coffee break? No. Instead of relaxing in the courtyard, the four are sitting down to settle a problem.

Meyer, founder and one of the managers of the cooperative retail store, Native Books and Beautiful Things, has spotted *pilikia*—trouble—among these co-op members and she fears distrust and backbiting will spread to the entire 25-member *hui*. Today she's called for *ho'oponopono*, a Hawaiian method of "setting things right" that is written into the *hui's* mission statement.

"People had been talking stink, not even knowing they were doing it," says Meyer, who served as *haku*, the leader who guides the multi-step procedure. "Things festered, and these members undermined each other. In our store, everybody impacts everyone else's business. Many problems are simply miscommunication, and one of the things *ho'oponopono* provides is a way of communicating directly in a group that includes all the parties.

"As *haku*, I kept steering back to what we can do to support one another in the *hui*. *Ho'oponopono* is about solving a problem, not about being right or wrong. In the end, it really worked. When the parties had a chance to speak their feelings to each other, they resumed sharing information instead of hoarding it. It set the *hui* back in balance."

❧

"Setting things right" is how most experts define *ho'oponopono* now. In ancient times it was conducted in the extended family, with an elder, usually the oldest man, as *haku*. Now, unrelated Hawaiian experts sometimes perform the function in their communities.

About 20 years ago, social workers at Queen Lili'uokalani Children's Center began working with *ho'oponopono* under the guidance of the late Mary Kawena Pukui. From that experience (documented in *Nānā I Ke Kumu*, the two-volume collection of Hawaiian cultural traditions), the method has been adapted in social work and related fields. Currently, the state's Unified Family Court uses numerous "alternative dispute resolution" programs, including *ho'oponopono*.

"Conflict resolution," as *ho'oponopono* sometimes is tagged, differs considerably from Western ideas of mediation or counseling.

"In contrast to conflict resolution," says Wai'anae *haku* Kamaki Kanahele, "you begin and end spiritually. The result is a spiritual as well as a physical commitment."

Originally, the opening and closing prayers were addressed to *'aumākua*, family gods. Today, many Hawaiians address the Christian god. Because not everyone is Christian, social worker Richard Paglinawan addresses "Powers That Be."

"The prayer is for wisdom, to let us do the work," says Paglinawan, who was in the original Lili'uokalani Children's Center group. "It sets a serious tone. You have to be *ha'aha'a* and *'oia'i'o*, humble and truthful. For some, the Powers That Be can even be science or logic."

Other major differences between *ho'oponopono* and Western mediation include the Hawaiian view that the self is relational, not autonomous; that the purpose is to restore harmony, not to make agreements; that all parties are connected personally. Additional differences: The leader has special skill and status as an elder rather than authority through credentials; discussion takes place with the entire group rather than partially in private; resolution comes from mutual apology and forgiveness, not from negotiation and written agreement.

It's easy to see how such a procedure came out of an Island culture. "It was a survival tool," says Naleen Andrade, chairperson of the Department of Psychiatry at the University of Hawai'i School of Medicine. "Hawaiians arrived on canoes. On a canoe, you must have true harmony."

Andrade sees *ho'oponopono* as a good process for families to learn. "It's a means to create the ability to live well with your differences," she says "That's the core of *ho'oponopono*."

But it's no panacea. "I use it if it's appropriate, if a family asks for it," says Andrade. "With families without spirituality as a major way of communicating, you shouldn't impose it."

Says Kanahele, "*Ho'oponopono* is a delicate, sensitive healing art. It requires the light of God, and the whole family to put all the cards on the table and make a commitment to settlement item by item. You must deal with anger and hatred, with physical desire to hurt, with depression and disgust. These all need to be healed, and everyone contributes to the healing."

Unlike Western counseling or mediation in sessions of an hour or two, *ho'oponopono* takes as long as it takes—minutes, hours, a whole day, maybe longer.

After the *pule wehe*, opening prayer, the *haku* leads *kūkulu kumuhana* or statement of the problem. The words also mean "pooling of strength," a nuance that reflects the belief that every party has something positive to contribute and that no one will hold a grudge.

The next step is *wehewehe*. "You focus on one problem, without bringing in the kitchen sink, the toilet and everything else," says Paglinawan. "When you work that one through, you go on to another." Rules require a promise to tell the truth, to keep no secrets, and to talk only about yourself, not the other guy.

"You talk to the *haku*," says Paglinawan. "Talk, not act it out. And the others, *pa'a ka waha*—shut the mouth and listen."

The discussion, likely to take up the bulk of *ho'oponopono* time, covers layers of *hihia*, entanglements to be unknotted one at a time, and *hala*, transgressions of commission and omission, until the root of the problems surfaces. Only the *haku* may ask questions, and answers must be couched positively. The *haku* may also call *ho'omalu*, a time out. "During *ho'omalu*, do not talk to others," says Paglinawan. "Clear your mind and do your work."

Three stages usually follow as parts of one procedural unit. In *mihi*, the parties ask forgiveness of each other and the higher powers. If they are *ho'omauhala*, holding a grudge, the *haku* may have to declare *mō ka piko*. Literally it means to sever the umbilical cord. This happens when a person refuses to accept responsibility for himself, says Paglinawan. "*Mō ka piko* cuts the relationship to the *'ohana* and the Powers That Be. It was the ultimate, and hell for a Hawaiian."

But *ho'oponopono* seeks peace and harmony, and the *haku* may repeat portions of the process. At the point of sincere forgiveness, the *haku* proceeds to *kala*, untying the knot of the problem. In *'oki* the parties not only cut the problem from their lives, but promise never to bring it up again.

A closing prayer—*pule ho'opau*—usually includes the summation of the *ho'oponopono* by the *haku. Pani* follows, a closing ritual often involving eating together as spiritually symbolic. Some *haku* include *na hana imua* as a possible final section that outlines future tasks.

Once Meyer used *ho'oponopono* with a problem that involved all 25 *hui* members. They agreed to stay in session in the closed store until they had answers.

"We sat in a tight circle for three hours, looking at each other, talking about the problems one person at a time," she says. "When we had restored internal trust, we found solutions as a group. Nobody was any longer *namunamu*—grumbling, complaining."

She says the session also produced an unexpected benefit. "It put our business group in a family mode and solidified the group."

The session was intense, as *ho'oponopono* usually is. But every member saw it through, and every member stayed with the *hui*.

"I have a business degree and I can come up with a formulized, profit-oriented way of making the *hui* work," says Meyer. "*Ho'oponopono* takes longer, and it's messy, but it gets to the root of the issue. It works, if people have faith in the collaborative process."

Kahoʻolawe in Limbo

1992

Maui. In the cold of a January midnight, the sounds of a lone *ʻukulele* and a young, clear voice drift over a parking lot at Māʻalaea Bay. Intermittently, there is the rip of duct tape and the rustle of plastic garbage bags as members of the Protect Kahoʻolawe ʻOhana waterproof baggage for four days of camping on Kahoʻolawe. The singer, a University of Hawaiʻi student named Kauaʻi, and about half the group of 75 are first-time travelers to Kahoʻolawe, which is accessible only by special federal permit.

At dawn everyone swims with the *ukana* to a fishing boat at Mākena Landing. The bags bob from swimmer to swimmer. "Careful! This one's got *ʻukulele*! This one's got flowers!" Some parcels are *hoʻokupu* for Lono, the great god and sustainer of life to be honored at this January closure of the annual ancient Hawaiian Makahiki season.

At the boat, the group climbs over the stern and soon is underway, crossing the eight-mile ʻAlalākeiki Channel to Hawaiʻi's most controversial island.

For 50 years, the smallest major Hawaiian island, only 11 miles long and seven miles wide, was dominated by one thing—bombs. But since late 1990, destruction has been on hold while the Kahoʻolawe Island Conveyance Commission created by Congress studies how to return the island from federal to state jurisdiction.

The day after the Japanese attack on Pearl Harbor on December 7, 1941, the U.S. Navy commandeered Kahoʻolawe as a practice bomb target. The Navy argues the island is still essential to training operations.

Bomb craters pock much of Kahoʻolawe's highlands. Some gullies are full of debris. Despite a recent massive clean-up, the Navy still cautions that there is "unexploded ordnance," as it calls live bombs, on the island.

The Navy has struck the most recent blows to the tiny island once called Kanaloa, after the great god of the sea. Kahoʻolawe was ranched from the mid-1800s, and by the turn of the century, over-grazing and goats gone wild had denuded the island. From Maui, you can see clouds of red soil swirling in the wind on Kahoʻolawe. During torrential rains, streams bleed with red mud.

Yet it wasn't always so. Some 500 archaeological sites dating back a thousand years attest to the existence of people who once lived more harmoniously with the land. An ancient adze quarry at Puʻumōiwi is second in size only to one on the Big Island's Mauna Kea. Kahoʻolawe's 1,500-foot summit, Puʻu Moaʻula, was the sacred school of ancient Hawaiian astronomer/navigator priests.

In historic times, Kahoʻolawe served as a mission school and as a penitentiary. After over-grazing and diminishing rainfall bared Kahoʻolawe of *pili* grass, the Territory of Hawaiʻi declared it "forest reserve" in 1910, then leased it for ranching again in 1917. Within two decades, Angus MacPhee had established a cattle ranch on the island. Then the U.S. Navy served its notice.

A 1953 executive order issued by President Dwight D. Eisen-hower gave the Navy control of Kahoʻolawe so long as it needed it for training purposes, but specified that it would be returned to the Territory of Hawaiʻi in a condition fit for human habitation. The island was not released with other federally managed lands when Hawaiʻi became a state in 1959. It would be another four decades before political pressure forced the Navy to halt its assaults of the most bombed island in the Pacific.

Hakioawa. A half-finished *hale hālāwai*—a meeting house—stands above the high water mark next to Hakioawa Stream's dry, red bed. The *hale* is the chief feature of the Protect Kahoʻolawe ʻOha-na's permanent camp and testimony to its ongoing commitment to the island. *Makai* from it, people erect tents against the backdrop of Haleakalā across the channel. In a cargo net hammock, Kauaʻi strums his *ʻukulele*. Others join the song, and lilting melodies and laughter float through the camp.

Behind the *hale* on this January morning, ʻOhana workers fire an underground oven, the *imu*, heating rocks to cook food offerings to

Lono. At noon, a procession begins at the beach, 30 marchers dressed in white *malo* and *kīkepa* bearing *ti* leaf bundles containing ceremonial foods that function much as bread and wine in Christian communion—*taro*, red fish, black coconut, banana and sweet potato.

The *pū* proclaims a *kapu* on talking. With white *kapa* banners and fern *lei* flying from the hand-carved staff of Lono in the ocean breeze, the priests begin a chant, slowly wending their way toward the earthy-smelling, smoky *imu*.

At day's end, two additional processions climb the sides of Hakioawa Valley to the ruins of men's and women's *heiau*, special places of worship. Bare feet carefully feel their way over the lava path, white raiment and Lono banners fluttering in the wind. This time, the offerings are laid on platforms hoisted on fragile wooden stilts.

The small group of Hawaiians is silhouetted against the vast and deepening evening sky. A gecko chirps in the lacy leaves of a *kiawe* tree, and the ferns of the Lono staff wave bravely. For a moment, it's not hard to believe that Kahoʻolawe will be green again.

In 1969, when a live 500-pound bomb was found in a Māʻalaea pasture on Maui, the Maui County Council made the first of several fruitless efforts to stop the bombing. Seven years later, a fledgling grassroots organization called the Protect Kahoʻolawe ʻOhana illegally landed nine Hawaiians on the island, the first in a series of incidents that grew increasingly adversarial, provoked headline news coverage and polarized public opinion.

Guerilla tactics peaked in January of 1977 when five Hawaiians "occupied" Kahoʻolawe and forced the Navy to suspend target practice. Three were soon arrested, but two—Walter Ritte, Jr., and Richard Sawyer—remained on Kahoʻolawe for 35 days. Toward the end of their stay, ʻOhana members George Helm and Kimo Mitchell were lost in the ʻAlalākeiki Channel while on a mission to rescue Ritte and Sawyer.

Illegal landings and public demonstrations drew the most press, but the most important ʻOhana action was a lawsuit charging the Navy with failing to comply with laws concerning religious freedom, historic preservation and environmental protection. The name of the plaintiff would become synonymous with the Kaho'olawe movement—Noa Emmett Aluli, a Hawaiian family practice doctor from Moloka'i and a founding member of the 'Ohana.

The court declined to prohibit bombing or to require an Environmental Impact Statement, but the Navy agreed to suspend bombing for 10 days a month, 10 months a year, to allow public access for religious, cultural, educational and scientific activities. It also agreed to clear bombs and shells from the shoreline, to limit bombing to the central third of the island, and to refrain from bombing within 300 yards of archaeological sites. And it officially recognized the 'Ohana as the steward of Kaho'olawe. A year later, the 'Ohana got the whole island listed on the National Register of Historic Places.

Recently, the Navy brought the population of wild goats under control, a major boon to revegetation. Emmett Aluli hopes for the greening of Kaho'olawe in his lifetime, but he also sees the importance of the Protect Kaho'olawe 'Ohana in another way: "Every Hawaiian grassroots organization had its beginnings with PKO, whether it's the Office of Hawaiian Affairs or the protest against desecrating Hawaiian burials at the building site in Mākena on Maui. It all started from people paying attention to what was going on."

The eloquent Aluli insists that he and other PKO members "are just the *maka'āinana*—the common people—working and learning. And one of the things we're learning is to finish what we start."

Pu'u Moa'ula. On the third day of the trip, most of the 'Ohana group hike the length of the island, following the Lono standard all day into the parching sun. This is the first time the Navy has allowed a "free roam" without a military escort.

At mid-island, those in the ceremony change into white again and pad barefoot a half mile to Pu'u Moa'ula. At this promontory, priest-navigator *kahuna* schooled their students to read the stars and the currents to sail 2,500 miles back to Tahiti, the ancestral homeland. From their lava chair, it's possible to see the channel Ke-Ala-i-Kahiki—"The Way to Tahiti."

Now the ritual begins, wind whipping the legs of the altar. The gusts carry away much of the chant. When the final *pū* blows, people resume conversations—but another chant comes from behind. It's Kaua'i, without his 'ukulele. Unaccompanied, his impromptu chant carries clearly and beautifully above the wind. People stop talking as Kaua'i unties a red kīkepa from over his shorts and holds it above his head, outstretched as a sail. His lithe brown body glides toward the shrine. When he reaches it, his chant finishes. The power of his voice lingers and no one moves. Then applause breaks. He smiles and says simply, "I couldn't help it."

In late 1990, President George H.W. Bush halted target practice on Kaho'olawe indefinitely. At the same time, Congress created the Kaho'olawe Island Conveyance Commission "to conduct a study to recommend the terms and conditions for the conveyance of Kaho'olawe by the United States to the state of Hawai'i." The governor and the Navy would each appoint two commissioners, with a fifth nominated by the Office of Hawaiian Affairs.

One of Governor John Waihe'e's choices was former Maui Mayor Hannibal Tavares, who once voyaged across the channel with the 'Ohana to plant Maui's flag at Hakioawa. Asked to recommend his second appointment, PKO chose Emmett Aluli. The Navy appointed Bank of Hawai'i Chief Executive Officer Howard Stephenson and retired Navy officer and international business consultant Jim Kelly. OHA chose trustee Adelaide "Frenchy" DeSoto, who was instrumental in creating OHA more than a decade ago. The executive director of the commission is Roger Betts, one of three Hawaiians who served on the nine-member Native Hawaiian Study Commission in the early 1980s.

Since its formation, the Kaho'olawe Conveyance Commission has conducted public hearings and hired experts to report soil culture, history, biology, botany, archaeology, soil erosion, fresh water and ocean resources, and military use and clearance of remaining ordnance. About a third of the $1.5-million commission budget has been earmarked for these studies.

The public will have a chance in October to comment on the draft of the final commission report, which will be submitted to Congress in mid-December. Some worry that if Congress doesn't act on the report within the 120 days specified by legislation, bombing will resume.

Not so, says Betts. The Department of Defense's moratorium on bombing may end and Congress' time limit will likely run out, but President Bush's administrative order, like President Eisenhower's edict granting the Navy use of Kahoʻolawe, includes no specific time element.

"It's an order from the Commander in Chief," Betts explains. "That still stands."

Lae o Kealaikahiki is the westernmost point of Kahoʻolawe. Off the white sand beach scalloped with shells, a humpback whale breaches. A massive Hawaiian *kahuna* arrives by boat to lead the final ceremony. He seems as large as the ancient chiefs, and it's easy to picture him in a feather cloak and helmet. "We're healing this island and we're healing our people," he says. "No one can do it but ourselves."

On the sand a hundred feet behind him, a four-foot scale model *koa* canoe balances on its outrigger, its *kapa* sail a bright white triangle in the waning light. For the last time in these Makahiki days, Hawaiians hand their offerings to the god Lono. The priests carefully pack the canoe, securing the *hoʻokupu* with a fishnet.

At the ocean's edge, the *kahuna* spanks the waves with a broom of *ti* leaves. When the surf calms, four of the strongest swimmers guide the symbolic miniature canoe toward the channel. The sky fades until only the tiny sail is visible. Just at last light, the canoe catches the current and drifts down Ke-Ala-i-Kahiki—the connection to the ancient homeland.

The future of Kahoʻolawe is perhaps less predictable and more hopeful than ever. A public opinion poll commissioned by the state early this year showed that 77 percent of Hawaiʻi residents favor returning Kahoʻolawe to the state.

The commission will recommend return—but if, how, how soon, and under what conditions are up to Congress. If bombing were to resume, commission Executive Assistant Hardy Spoehr believes there would be "massive civil disobedience in the native Hawaiian community. There would be 500 people on Kahoʻolawe overnight."

Commissioner Kelly cautions against expecting quick Congressional action: "Commissions are not created to solve problems, but to postpone them. There are special places for commission reports and none of them involves activity."

Betts acknowledges that Congress is "famous for doing nothing," but believes Hawaiʻi's delegation will keep up the political pressure.

But when Kahoʻolawe is returned to Hawaiʻi—what then? Some say it should be left entirely alone to heal itself. Others see potential for development. Most advocate limited use of both the island and its surrounding waters.

Emmett Aluli, for one, hopes for "Kahoʻolawe to be green with native species, for the shrines and *heiau* to be used again, for the island to be a school for Hawaiian experience."

Kelly sees "the potential for something useful for the people of the state, and in particular those who are Hawaiian. The military's interest and reaction have changed over time. There's no enthusiasm now for trying to hold on to the island."

Norma Wong of the Office of State Planning says, "We don't often get a chance to take an entire island and do what is right by it. We have to be careful in this transition period that we don't overload the island with activity it can't sustain."

The Navy publicly says it's ready to defer to the commission. "The adversarial days have gone," says Pacific Fleet spokesman Captain Tom Jurkowsky. "We're committed to working with the commission in every possible way. It's time to let the chips fall where they may."

The last night at Hakioawa, everyone should be waterproofing their *ukana*. But Kauaʻi engineers a *hula* performance at the hand-built *hula* mound near the *hale hālāwai*. The dancers are dressed in sweatshirts because of the chilly night air, but as they move to an ancient chant and the driving rhythm of the gourd drum, it's easy to imagine them in *malo* and *kīkepa*, in dog-tooth anklets and feather head *lei*.

It's nearly midnight when the weary campers head to bed.

The full moon gleams over Haleakalā. The sea breeze whispers in the partly thatched *hale hālāwai*. The rafters for the unfinished part of the roof stand strong and stark in the moonlight. It is a portrait of hope, faith, courage and perseverance—mirroring the indomitable spirit of the champions of beleaguered Kahoʻolawe.

Update: In 1994, Kahoʻolawe was returned to the State of Hawaiʻi, with access control transferring from the U.S. Navy to the State in 2003. While still under Navy control, 74 percent of the island's surface was cleared of unexploded ordnance, although only nine percent was cleared to a depth of four feet. Ten percent of the island remains unsafe to access. Today the Kahoʻolawe Island Reserve Commission (KIRC) manages the island while holding it in trust for a future native Hawaiian sovereign entity. KIRC oversees environmental restoration aimed toward a future of healthy forests, shrublands and ocean waters. Protect Kahoʻolawe ʻOhana (PKO) continues cultural practices, coordinating with KIRC a planting ceremony each October and seasonal ceremonies honoring Kāne and Kanaloa.

꒜

FINDING THE WAY

1993

July 14 is launch day. It's mid-summer in Honolulu but it's pouring rain, torrents, curtains and buckets of rain. It puddles deep on the asphalt at Pier 35 and sloshes in sheets from the gray tarps rigged drum-head tight to shelter 300 guests awaiting the ceremony. Many carry *lei* carefully draped over their arms, *lei* they have brought as *ho'okupu*, offerings. Gifts for *Hawai'i Loa*, the first Hawaiian voyaging canoe to be built of traditional materials in hundreds of years.

The conch blower sounds his shell horn, the *pū*, three times. An opening chant tells of one of the four great gods, Kū, as god of canoes. A loincloth-clad Hawaiian priest offers the canoe builders ceremonial coconut, breadfruit and *taro*, rain glistening on his bare shoulders and soaking the red T-shirts of the crew.

Hawaiians pile their special guests from the Haida and Tlingit tribes eye-high with *lei*. Through the flowers and the rain the Alaska natives strain to hear the thump of the fish-skin drum and to see the ancient *hula* danced in their honor. Rain is said to be a Hawaiian blessing, and though the details of continued chants are lost in the din of the downpour, no one in the crowd stirs. A sense of *mana*, spiritual power, pervades.

Fern *lei* run the 60-foot length of the canoe's massive twin hulls. *Lei maile* festoon bow and stern. Then a crane lifts her, swings her over the harbor. Just as she touches the water, the conch sounds again, and the rain lifts.

I first saw this canoe in 1991, when it lay as two logs in the yard of Honolulu's Bishop Museum. I sneaked over an orange plastic fence to touch the behemoth spruce, feel its *mana*. I thought of my cousin, master builder Wright Bowman, Jr., who would make these logs a canoe, of how family is all-important to Hawaiians, even to this day. I thought of the *koa* model canoe in my office and the ceremonial paddle on my wall, gifts years ago from my uncle, Wright Bowman, Sr., an octogenarian canoe builder from whom his son learned his art.

⚯

Almost two years later I stood in a shed at Pier 35 with the same logs, transformed into twin hulls. The tin roof magnified the din of hammers, chainsaws, routers, rotary saws, and sanders. The air stormed with wood chips, curls and sawdust. It would be a scant half year to launching, to the day *Hawai'i Loa* would become a public symbol of Hawaiian people reviving our culture—a Polynesian equivalent of the phoenix rising from its own ashes.

Hawaiians, although never systematically slaughtered, have suffered from cultural genocide as much as any other colonized people. But two centuries after the coming of English explorer James Cook, we started piecing together the shards of our shattered culture.

In the late 1960s while some were rekindling ancient *hula*, Hawaiian painter Herb Kawainui Kāne chose another way. Kāne saw the ancient canoe at the heart of Polynesian culture. "'Without it there would be no culture, no dance, no chants," he says. "I was curious to see if rebuilding the central object would motivate recovery of a culture."

While Kāne pondered, Ben Finney, now chair of the University of Hawai'i's anthropology department, aimed "to challenge the dismissal of Polynesian sailing and navigational abilities, and consequently warped portrayals of Polynesian pre-history," as he says in his new book, *Voyage of Rediscovery*.

Norwegian explorer Thor Heyerdahl, of *Kon-Tiki* fame, contended that Polynesians lacked sufficient nautical skills and vessels to sail eastward against the prevailing winds and currents. He concluded that the settlement of the Pacific must have come from the Americas. New Zealand historian Andrew Sharp conceded that Polynesians migrated from Southeast Asia but maintained that they lacked navigational skill for anything but accidental landfall.

Both theories—Heyerdahl reiterated his as recently as the early 1980s—contradict Polynesian oral tradition. Chants tell of two-way voyaging between Hawai'i and Tahiti and indicate that a one-way trip takes about a month. They record 127 gods of the canoe, list 42 types of canoe lashings, and name 30 kinds of canoe-building adzes.

Finney thought he could prove Heyerdahl and Sharp wrong by reconstructing a Polynesian sailing canoe and navigating it without instruments over the legendary migration route from Tahiti. In 1973, he and Kāne formed the Polynesian Voyaging Society and set their course.

Wood boats unfortunately are highly biodegradable, and only a few pieces of ancient canoes existed, in New Zealand and on Huahine in the Society Islands. Lacking an ancient description in chants, Finney and Kāne turned to the records of Westerners who had explored the region since the early 17th century. They assumed the oldest hull design, sail plan and construction to be those most widely distributed and therefore likely to be from the same geographical center of diffusion. With these guidelines, Kāne and catamaran designer Rudy Choy drew plans, and then fashioned V-shaped hulls of marine plywood and crab-claw sails from canvas. In early 1975 they launched the 60-foot *Hōkūle'a* at Kualoa on windward O'ahu, a site once so sacred that canoes lowered their sails as they passed.

Finney and Kāne had built a voyaging canoe, albeit of modern materials, but they couldn't find a single Polynesian who knew ancient navigation. Then, on Satawal in the central Caroline Islands, they discovered master navigator Mau Piailug. He had been trained from childhood as both canoe builder and navigator and had traversed all of Micronesia for 30 years. But he had never sailed in the Southern Hemisphere and would be without the North Star.

"We try," Piailug said. On May 1, 1976, *Hōkūle'a*, named for the Star of Gladness, or Arcturus, Hawai'i Island's zenith star, sailed for Tahiti.

For the next month Piailug scarcely moved from the stern of the windward hull. A navigator's mind is filled with the rise and set points of at least 120 stars and planets, as well as the sun and the moon on any given day. From the celestial paths he determines latitude and direction. During the day, or if the heavens are obscured, he uses the pitch and roll of the canoe, caused by the dominant swells, as a guide.

For proximity of land, the navigator interprets the subtle signs of the sea: currents and clouds, water color and temperature, sea life. For example, when land is within about 25 miles, the greenish underside of clouds may reflect a lagoon. A darker hue indicates a wooded island. Swell patterns bend around islands; reefs cause water to green; floating debris suggests land to windward; floating seaweed indicates upcurrent reefs. Terns or boobies, birds that fish at sea but sleep on land, range only 20 or 30 miles seaward. The navigator synthesizes this unwritten knowledge of astronomy, marine biology, oceanography and meteorology into a discipline on which he stakes his and his crew's lives.

On the 31st day of its maiden voyage, as the ancient chants foretold, *Hōkūle'a* made landfall at Mataiva, the westernmost atoll in the Tuamotu group. Two days later the crew sailed into Pape'ete, where 20,000 Tahitians sang and danced on the beach in greeting.

Even with such a welcome, no one expected a second voyage. Not Finney, not Kāne, not Piailug. Not even Nainoa Thompson, a young Hawaiian who crewed on *Hōkūle'a*'s return from Tahiti, a kid questing for nothing more than adventure.

But Thompson, now 40, was touched permanently. Being on the crew was not enough. Determined to learn how to navigate, he spent hundreds of hours in the Bishop Museum planetarium imprinting star paths on his memory. Then he apprenticed himself to Mau Piailug. He studied ocean sciences at the University of Hawai'i. In 1980 he sailed again on *Hōkūle'a*, forming his own mental navigation maps under Piailug's tutelage on the 6,000-mile round trip to Tahiti.

He came to know the vagaries of the sea; of skimming so fast as to leave the escort yacht in his wake; of the deck awash in treacherous waves; of starless nights when he feared the canoe might have veered off course; of coming into the doldrums just at sunset, the sky a golden dome and the sea flat and shimmering like a sheet from King Midas' bed. He hoped to stave off hunger by catching fish and prayed for a rain squall to catch fresh water in a sail. He learned to catnap like all navigators, catching 40 winks here and there, perhaps two hours' sleep during the day if he was certain of his course and utterly trusting of his steersman.

Thompson's passion for the sea had deep cultural roots. His ancestors had established what Captain Cook called "the most extensive nation on earth." Polynesians discovered Hawai'i more than a millennium before Cook was born. They systematically sailed 16 million square miles of the Pacific. They settled almost every inhabitable island in an ocean with but one square mile of land for every 500 square miles of water. When their main voyages ended in the 13th century, the Vikings were still hugging the coast of Greenland and the sextant would not be invented for another four centuries.

Herb Kāne had been right: Hawaiians and their cousins from all over Polynesia rallied around *Hōkūle'a*, generating a scale of public interest and commitment of hundreds of volunteers that produced additional voyages (in 1980 to Tahiti; in 1985-87 the Voyage of Rediscovery to Tahiti, the Cook Islands, New Zealand, Tonga, Samoa and the Tuamotu Archipelago; and in 1992 Voyage of Education to French Polynesia and the Cook Islands). It also resulted in the current five-year Explorations Project of the Bishop Museum's Native Hawaiian Culture and Arts Program funded by the U.S. National Park Service. With Thompson as director, the project has built the voyaging canoe *Hawai'i Loa* and the coastal sailing canoe *Mauloa*, and is training a dozen new non-instrument navigators from all over Polynesia.

The lithe, intense Thompson is Polynesia's acknowledged sailmaster. Some compare him with the navigators of Hawaiian legend, and a recent Honolulu newspaper poll named him one of Hawai'i's most popular native leaders. Those who know him well say he remains truly humble. "In the beginning I just wanted to learn," says Thompson. "Now the vision is to instill a sense of pride in the great accomplishments of those early people by recovering and perpetuating traditions. If Hawaiian people are proud of their traditions and themselves, it upgrades society as a whole."

When Thompson's quest for tradition expanded to building *Hawai'i Loa* with ancient materials and *Mauloa* with both ancient materials and tools, he and his colleagues encountered a problem. After nine months they had not found any *koa* trees large enough for a 60-foot double-hull voyaging canoe. *Olonā*, the native plant favored for making cordage, was in short supply. The right kind of pandanus for plaiting *lau hala* sails no longer grew in Hawai'i.

Faced with a lack of native natural resources, they substituted coconut sennit for cordage and imported pandanus from the Cook Islands. Planning for future canoes, they started reforesting *koa*, cultivating *olonā* and nurturing pandanus. In the forests of Mauna Loa builders finally found a *koa* tree large enough for the 24-foot *Mauloa*, which teams wielding stone adzes felled in two days.

But there was still no *koa* for *Hawai'i Loa*. Thompson and Kāne thought of spruce. "Even though spruce doesn't grow in Hawai'i, it would be an acceptable substitute," Thompson says. "The biggest ancient canoes were made of drift logs." Kāne contacted his longtime friend Judson Brown, a Tlingit elder and trustee of the SeAlaska Heritage foundation, the cultural arm of SeAlaska Corporation owned by Alaska's Tlingit, Haida and Tsimpshean tribes.

Brown recalls, "I called SeAlaska's CEO, Byron Malott. Basically he said, 'How many trees do you want? They're yours.'"

The tribes' donation included two 66-foot Sitka spruce logs cut from trees more than 400 years old. Thompson insisted on bringing a party of Hawaiians to the Alaska forest for an inter-cultural blessing ceremony before the felling. In return, Alaskan tribal representatives, including master canoe carvers, participated in ceremonies in Honolulu before Hawaiian master builder Wright Bowman, Jr. began transforming the logs into *Hawai'i Loa* in mid-1990.

Building crew member Harold Ayat remembers when the hull work started. "I saw two huge logs and a whole lot of work. Bow (Bowman) said, 'I see two beautiful hulls.' The drawings weren't ready, but Bow said, 'Now.' He stood at one end of the log. I walked slowly along the side. Periodically he'd say, 'Mark it.' When we put a template on, he was only one-eighth of an inch off in 66 feet. He is truly a *kahuna kālai wa'a*—the canoe-building master."

Ayat and some dozen others—including a retired fire chief, a lawyer, a Hawaiian entertainer, a sculptor, a shipfitter and a high school student—spent every Saturday for almost two years working on *Hawai'i Loa* with no more recompense than lunch.

Bowman seizes the "Mean Machine," a wood-digging monster with which he will hollow a bit more of a *manu*, one of the prow pieces. He moves toward the sawhorses where the *manu* is resting and begins. One of the crew taps him on the shoulder, holds out a metal apron and ties it around him so he looks like James Beard playing the role of the Tin Man. The crew likes to ensure Bowman's health; once, on another project, he cut his stomach with the Mean Machine.

Crew members stay with him because he's an artisan, an even-tempered man of few words who teaches in the same way his father did, hands-on, a step at a time, a man who reveres each individual and his family—blood family, canoe family, family of the heart. But there's more to *Hawai'i Loa* than Bowman's charisma.

"It's not just building a boat," Ayat says. "To build something that hasn't been done in a thousand years brings on a spiritual and ancestral pride. I'm sure when the ancient people built their canoes, it was total involvement. That's what it is here. I have a B.S. in aerospace engineering. I don't use any of it here."

While *Hawai'i Loa* was constructed in Honolulu, *Mauloa* took form at Pu'uhonua O Hōnaunau, the ancient place of refuge and safety that is now a National Historic Park on the Big Island. Mau Piailug, a master builder as well as navigator, led a team fashioning the smaller outrigger using traditional tools.

In the canoe shed Piailug sits, swinging a knife-sharp finishing adze, its black basalt blade hitting its precise mark with every stroke. Fine shavings the width of the two-inch blade curl and fall. A breeze ruffles the thatch on the A-frame canoe shed, and sunlight dances on the water lapping in the cove that was once the Royal Canoe Landing. Birds twittering in the palms accompany the tap-tap of Piailug's adze. Perhaps four times an hour Piailug and his apprentices stop to sharpen an adze, grinding it in rhythmic circles on a basalt whetstone.

The dozen different adzes and the wood itself—*koa* for the hull, prow and gunwales; *hau* for the outriggers and booms—are *kapu*: sacred and consecrated. None but the master and his apprentices may touch them or enter the *hālau wa'a*, the canoe-building school. Visitors may watch and ask questions, so long as they stay behind a sennit rope marking the sacred boundaries.

Plans call for *Hawai'i Loa*'s sea trials this year followed by a 1995 voyage to Nuku Hiva in the Marquesas, where many believe ancient Hawaiians began their colonizing odysseys. As on *Hōkūle'a*, a crew of about a dozen will live for a month under cramped conditions, sleeping in shifts, always on short rations. They will risk hypothermia when sea storms break over the deck and heat stroke when the canoe stalls in the doldrums.

"It says something about Hawaiians, that they could live together on a canoe," says Herb Kāne. "There can be only one star, and that's the canoe. If you take care of it, it will take care of you."

Thompson sees a canoe as a model island, where people work together to use limited resources for the common good.

"Hawaiians learned to live on islands—limited land bounded by a shoreline of ocean," he says. "How were they able to keep their needs balanced with the natural environment? The world is an island bounded by a shoreline of space. Can Hawaii be a model for the world?" He's hopeful that youngsters will take the lessons of the canoes to heart and think seriously how to apply them to all parts of their lives.

Seeing ancient canoes come alive captivates onlookers, but those fortunate enough to be chosen as crew members from hundreds of applicants are affected profoundly. When *Hōkūle'a* returned from the 1987 voyage to sacred Kualoa on windward O'ahu, thousands thronged the beach. Myron "Pinky" Thompson, Nainoa's father, was there and recalls, "We were all on that canoe, whether you strung one *lei* or a thousand, whether you looked after her as so many have throughout the Pacific, or had one thought of *aloha* for her. We voyaged together, and we are changed. *Hōkūle'a* was built to answer questions about our past. We went out as Hawaiians and scientists, and came home as Polynesian brothers and sisters."

Explorations Project manager Ben Acma says, "This is all part of a traditional culture that is fast disappearing. The canoe building and the sailing and the reforesting all connect into capturing what was yesterday so we'll have it for tomorrow."

Chad Baybayan, ready for his first solo navigation after years studying with Nainoa Thompson, agrees. "This is much more than just sailing on a boat. A lot of it is about feelings. It shows how our culture began. Our ancestors saw the ocean as a means for travel, not as an obstacle. And they became by far the world's best sailors." For Baybayan, voyaging symbolizes all Hawaiian culture, and he's acutely aware that the culture remains endangered. "Unless we are committed to regaining it," he says, "we'll end up where we were before, a nation without navigators."

On a Sunday afternoon I sail from Pier 7, bare feet planted apart on *Hōkūle'a*'s afterdeck. The orange crab-claw sail catches the wind, and the canoe eases into ink-blue waters, dancing on the ocean highway she has sailed for the better part of two decades.

Her center sweep creaks in its lashing as the steersman rhythmically works the massive paddle. The canoe rides the waves and the wind, alive as the ocean beneath her. Her deck seems thin as split bamboo, her length hardly matching a harbor tug. With three other first-time sailors, I help hoist the rear sail. The rope tingles in my hand with the power of the wind.

Nainoa Thompson kneels, drawing invisibly with his finger on the deck, explaining the complicated scientific principles of wind dynamics. I try to soak up his words with my brain, but my head seems the least important part of me.

I am overcome with the feeling that the strangers on board are my family, that the canoe itself cradles us as a mother. Maybe Herb Kāne is right, the canoe is the cultural symbol that links us all, the ancestral bond. So is my Uncle Wright, who told me 10 years ago, when I was barely over 40 and too young to understand, "The only important things in life are health and love." With the deck and the ocean under me, I realize he meant not just individuals, but all of us, together.

The sun begins to drop and the air grows chilly. But beneath my bare feet I feel *Hōkūleʻa* breathe warm, and into my body rushes the intangible power Hawaiians call *mana*. We are finding our way.

Update: By the year 2000, Hōkūleʻa had sailed more than 100,000 miles, visiting every corner of the Polynesian Triangle. In 1995 two additional Hawaiian voyaging canoes, two canoes from the Cook Islands and one from Aotearoa (New Zealand) sailed together from the Marquesas Islands to Hawaiʻi. Today Hawaiʻi has nine navigators, with more in training. Experienced deep-sea sailors now number about 135. Some 525,000 men, women and children are part of the voyaging canoe family through participating in the Polynesian Voyaging Society's programs of education, training, research and dialogue.

6
Coming Home

❦

Loving a prison,
circling Oʻahu on foot,
returning pulled-up stakes
and learning the meaning of roots

⌁

KALAUPAPA: HOME OF THE HEART

1995

This July day was insufferably hot in Honolulu. Henry Nalaielua sat perspiring at the grounds of 'Iolani Palace, even though his chair was in the shade. He and some 500 others had listened all morning to prayers and hymns and speeches.

And then, near the end of the long ceremonies and ecumenical service, it was Nalaielua's turn. The notes for his speech were under his ginger *lei*, in the pocket of his *aloha* shirt—his best blue one. He shuffled the few steps to the *lei*-draped lectern on hobbly feet that reminded him of his mission of honor. He had come to the palace from his home at Kalaupapa on Moloka'i, where he was sent as a Hansen's disease (leprosy) patient before World War II, and where he has lived most of his 70 years.

Up to that point, Nalaielua was sure he was going to use the notes. But all of a sudden something else came up in his mind. He couldn't deliver his talk by looking at a piece of paper.

He rested his hands on the podium and looked up through his sunglasses. His resonant Hawaiian voice rang rich and warm as spontaneous words flowed out of his mouth from his heart, as if from a freshwater spring.

He spoke of a man long dead, a man he never knew, a man who nevertheless is his friend and neighbor and part of his daily consciousness—a Catholic priest who was beatified in Brussels just a month earlier, while Nalaielua watched in a chilling Belgian rain. Nalaielua spoke of Father Damien de Veuster, a man honored on this hot July day in Honolulu before his relic was to be returned to the remote peninsula of Kalaupapa, where he volunteered to serve leprosy patients who had been exiled there, and where he died in 1889.

Father Damien, Nalaielua said, "came, saw and conquered, not shrinking from what no one else wanted to do. Yes, he came, and yes, he delivered." His message rolled through the crowd surrounding the palace bandstand. "And yes, he brought out the best in his fellow ladies and gentlemen of that time."

The noise of the crowd rising from its folding chairs rippled in the still, hot air. It took Nalaielua a moment to realize that the standing ovation was for his words. Words from his heart.

Blessed Damien. This Catholic priest of the Order of the Sacred Hearts is so much the hero of all Hawai'i that his statue stands as one of the state's two choices for Statuary Hall in the U.S. Capitol. Beatified by Pope John Paul and titled "Blessed," Damien is now but a single step from sainthood in the Catholic scheme of things. His feast day is May 10, the day in 1873 that he arrived at Kalawao, the village on the windward side of the Kalaupapa peninsula to which the kingdom of Hawai'i condemned people with leprosy beginning in 1866 in a futile effort to stem an epidemic.

To the world at large, the 33-year-old Belgian priest soon became a celebrity. To Hawai'i health authorities and his Catholic superiors in Honolulu, Damien became somewhat of a nuisance, badgering them for supplies and support. To the 600 residents at Kalawao, he became doctor, nurse, carpenter, engineer, farmer, legal advocate, plumber. And priest. In his first year at Kalawao, Damien dug 100 graves.

To the patients—the vast majority of them Hawaiian men—Damien was simply "Kamiano." Though he contracted leprosy after 12 years at Kalawao and died of its complications, he triumphed over his chosen adversity by love and spirit and bigness of heart. That spirit pervades Kalaupapa today, in the very air whistling in from the sea, in a kind of *mana* that emanates from the land shadowed by the world's tallest sea cliffs. Some of the five dozen patients remaining at Kalaupapa settlement freely give of their stories with the same bigness of heart as Kamiano.

One day in May 1936, a school nurse inspecting fourth graders in Nīnole on the Big Island's Hāmākua Coast dismissed the class—except for Henry Nalaielua. She asked if he knew his home phone number.

"Yes," said the boy. "Three longs and two shorts."

She called the plantation house and talked to his mother.

Recalls Nalaielua, "That nurse gave me one look, and boom! I'd never heard of leprosy or knew I was sick. She told my mother they had three days to get me to the hospital in Honolulu. By the time I got home, my parents were crying."

His father could go only as far as Kawaihae Harbor because of his duties as a sugar plantation *luna*. But his mother accompanied him to Honolulu's Kalihi Hospital, a quarantined leprosy treatment station. The three of them left Nīnole—"a two-horse town with a post office the size of a two-hole outhouse"—at one in the morning to reach the harbor by 5:30 a.m. There they had to wait to board the steamer while ranch hands from Waimea loaded cattle on the deck.

Nalaielua had had some fevers and pain, but now he didn't feel sick. He looked in a mirror. He didn't look sick. His mother wept, but he didn't understand why—that he was embarking on a one-way trip, condemned for having an infectious disease for which there was no cure. Nalaielua was 10, and he was having an adventure. He still remembers the thrill of watching mounted men reining and spurring their horses this way and that, herding hundreds of cattle bawling and pawing and snorting in that dawn at Kawaihae. The scene was a boy's dream come true. He recalls, "I'd never seen real cowboys before."

Damien spent his first several weeks at Kalawao sleeping near Saint Philomena's Church under a *pū hala*, a pandanus tree, ignoring the scorpions, centipedes and other creatures living in the aerial roots at its base. He took his meals on a nearby flat rock, ignoring the insatiable wind and the cold shadows of the 3,000-foot cliffs rising a few hundred yards to *mauka*. In his book *Holy Man: Father Damien of Molokai*, historian Gavan Daws describes Damien's ministry as one "of ghastly sights and suffocating smells, of the most awful physical and spiritual misery." Damien took up pipe smoking to combat the obnoxious odor of infected sores caused by the disease.

The four-square-mile peninsula of Kalaupapa, Daws wrote, was "an unlikely place for people to live ... hard to get to, hard to get away from ... a natural prison ... in which a watcher could see what he wanted, beauty or desolation or both." For his first decade on

Moloka'i, the courageous priest was the only non-patient in permanent residence.

Damien lost his repugnance for Hansen's disease within two weeks. And he hardly had time to ponder either beauty or desolation in Kalaupapa, or ancient relics like abandoned *taro* terraces, rock windbreaks for sweet potatoes, or the rock boundary walls of the three *ahupua'a*, the promontory's land divisions. He simply plunged into his ministry in Kalaupapa with his hands, his carpenter hands, his farmer hands—for he had grown up a peasant on his family farm in Belgium. Kalawao's tiny churches, the Catholic Saint Philomena's and the Protestant Siloama, had drawn in some of the patients. But more had turned to drinking and crime.

Shelter for all of them was makeshift, and food, clothing and medicine scarce. They would pick up the little available medicine on fence posts, where visiting doctors would leave it to avoid physical contact with the patients, some of whom ridiculed the treatment as "medicine that doesn't cure." Some patients called the kingdom's Board of Health, which oversaw the settlement, the "Board of Death."

To Hawaiians, family and physical proximity are paramount. Patients—many turned in to authorities by bounty hunters who were paid $10 a head—often came with a *kōkua*, a healthy family member electing lifetime exile as a companion and nurse. After 1873, those condemned noticed they had another friend—Damien, the priest who learned immediately to wash sores and change dressings. This priest, this *haole*, was the only one who would touch them.

For Henry Nalaielua, five years at Kalihi Hospital led exactly where it had for many: Kalaupapa. In many cases, the transfer was not so much for medical reasons, but to control troublemakers and runaways.

Yet Nalaielua, then 15, wanted to go. "A lot of my friends in Kalihi had gone," he says. "At Kalihi, everything was black and white. A chain-link fence and a hedge separated us from visitors by the width of a truck—we could pass things, but no touching. If we passed money, it had to be soaked in alcohol."

In Honolulu, in September of 1941, Nalaielua made a trip to another wharf. This time it began at 4:30 a.m., in the back of an

Army truck with a heavy canvas curtain drawn across the back. At 6:00 a.m. he sailed on the steamer *S.S. Hawaii*.

By 2:00 p.m., it reached Kalaupapa landing, where Nalaielua was met by familiar faces—and something he hadn't expected: cowboys. Quite a few cowboys, with red bandannas tied around their necks. Soon he learned the kerchiefs covered tracheotomy tubes that substituted for collapsed nasal passages.

Along with about forty other young men, Nalaielua lived at the new Kalaupapa Baldwin Home, built in the early 1930s to replace the original 1886 home at Kalawao. "When I came there, it was still the time of separation," he remembers. Patients were not permitted to touch anyone who did not have Hansen's disease. "The visiting house had a chain fence in the middle, from the floor to the ceiling. If a baby was born, it was put in the administration building and the parents could look at it through three-inch-thick glass." Such children were then removed from the settlement to be raised by relatives or in "homes" akin to orphanages. Life at Kalaupapa was a mass of prohibitions.

But the Baldwin boys—three-fourths of them able-bodied—simply bypassed many of the myriad regulations. So did some of the young Catholic brothers serving at the home.

"Brother Patrick was right in there with us," Nalaielua says. "He'd get sick of cooking, and we'd go fishing for *ulua* behind the lighthouse. Kenso Seki was the oldest of us, a small runt of a guy but a natural leader, and he had a truck. Brother Patrick and us, we'd just jump on the truck—even on the running boards—and go. Whenever the Catholic holidays came around, we did things together, like make ice cream, or kill a pig or some ducks for a feast. People in other housing areas would ask us to fish for them, or to *kālua* a pig." Other times, Brother Patrick would give Nalaielua pointers in oil painting.

At the settlement school, Nalaielua took issue with his teacher. "'Where am I going with a diploma over here?' I said to her. 'Drive a rubbish truck?' She said, 'Someday you might be able to get out.'"

But Nalaielua quit school. So did other students. "I didn't think I'd ever leave Kalaupapa," he says. "But you know, that teacher, she was right."

✧

For almost a century, the "shipments" of those afflicted with Hansen's disease kept coming. By 1887, the graves numbered 3,000. By 1888, 15 years after Damien's arrival, the village of Kalawao had 400 structures. Twice Damien had enlarged Saint Philomena's Church. By then, he himself had contracted leprosy, and Brother Joseph Dutton, Mother Marianne Cope and two Catholic Sisters had arrived to take up permanent service.

A photo made of Damien two months before his death on April 15, 1889, shows the ravages of disease in his face and hands, the toll of toil in his battered hat and in his eyes straining through thick glasses. It's the Damien of the statue, the one in Congress, the one at the State Capitol. It's the Damien of the people of the settlement. Kamiano.

In 1949, Nalaielua had been taking the new sulfone drugs for a year in the "parole process," submitting to monthly skin scrapings and snippings for lab analysis. At last he was declared "clean," fit for "TR"—temporary release.

The parole notice provoked panic. "I had not a suitcase to my name," he remembers. "I threw my things in a sheet and tied the four corners in a knot. I've got to admit, I was scared as hell. I'd be going to the outside. I thought people would look down on me, and I would be wondering 'What are they thinking?'"

Nalaielua remained in Honolulu for eight years, living with his oldest brother and working for the electric company. When his disease flared up again, he moved back to Kalaupapa for treatment, and later underwent corrective surgery at the national Hansen's Disease Center at Carville, Louisiana, where he stayed from 1972 to 1982. And then he came home for good. To Kalaupapa.

By his own request, Father Damien was buried in the churchyard at Saint Philomena's, not far from the *hala* tree where he had first slept. As Brother Dutton and Mother Marianne carried on in his stead, the patient population climbed, peaking in 1890 at 1,213. Damien's world fame, considerable during his lifetime, increased.

In 1895, a mortally ill French nun prayed in his name for her life. She regained her health—and thereby provided the miracle for which the Catholic Church beatified Damien exactly a century later.

By 1900, the last of the Hawaiian families who had farmed the Kalaupapa *ahupuaʻa* for generations left, and settlement residents slowly moved to that drier side of the peninsula. Brother Dutton stubbornly remained at the Baldwin Home in Kalawao, but within a year of his death in 1931, a new Baldwin Home was constructed at the *mauka* edge of Kalaupapa. All that remains of the original home is a few overgrown stone walls. All that is left of Kalawao are Saint Philomena's and Siloama, where the historic toilets outside are still marked, not for men and women, but for "Patients" and "Kokua."

Just a few months before Henry Nalaielua's school nurse started him on the road to Kalaupapa, the king of Belgium decided he wanted Damien interred at home. In January 1936, the body of the peasant buried in the shade of the *hala* tree was exhumed.

"King Gustaf just took it," Nalaielua says. "He didn't ask us. Or the Catholic Church. He just took it."

After sulfone began to work its miracles in the 1940s, more and more patients left Kalaupapa. Some chose to stay, and, until 1957, a few new cases were still referred to Kalaupapa for treatment. Today, only about five dozen patients remain, along with about 70 State Department of Health and National Park Service personnel.

In 1984, Kalaupapa became a National Historical Park, a status for which some patients lobbied, fearing the story of the settlement would otherwise be lost. As yet, the park aspect of Kalaupapa remains in the developing stages, with the Park Service sharing administration with the Department of Health and dealing with other landowners, including the Department of Hawaiian Homelands, which holds title to about 1,200 acres of the Kalaupapa town site. The Park Service mandate includes preserving, protecting and interpreting not only the history of the settlement, but also prehistory and natural history.

Unless sponsored as guests of private residents, visitors are limited to guided day trips. The tour van bounces along the rutted road from Kalaupapa toward Kalawao. It takes just a few minutes to travel backward into the last century. The tour driver stops at Siloama, then at Saint Philomena's. Some days, the guide is Henry Nalaielua.

Henry Nalaielua stands before Damien's altar, reverently but casually, as if he is making a daily call on an old friend. The twitter of birds comes through the open windows, along with the breeze. The church is nearly bare, except for candles and some statuary. Damien's vestments, his tools, and a collection of Hawaiian artifacts are under lock and key in Belgium. Nalaielua, once sorrowful, even bitter, about Belgium exhuming Damien's body, now takes comfort in the reburial last July at Saint Philomena's of Damien's right hand—the "relic," as Catholics call it.

"It's just his hand," Nalaielua says. "But it's part of him." At Siloama, he shows a guest the bell pull, a rope curiously tied with eyelets. "People with good hands can grip this part," he says, taking the knotted end in hands gnarled by the disease. "People with hands like mine can pull in the loops."

Nalaielua drives to the park beyond Kalawao, where, when he was young, all of Kalaupapa gathered on the Fourth of July for a picnic, ball games and tug-of-war along the cliffs tumbling into a surging ocean. He names the offshore *moku*—O'okala, Mōkapu and Huelo—and tells of Kalawao's ancient birthing stone. He shows visitors the Hawaiian fishing shrine not far from Saint Philomena's. Out along the oceanside road, he points out the *ahupua'a* walls marching from sea to cliff, unbroken but for the *makai* and *mauka* road tracks. He knows which rocks are the foundation of the *hale wa'a*, the canoe house, and how the canoe slide worked to launch fishing outriggers. Out near the lighthouse, on the peninsula's jutting point, he sits on a rock in the incessant salt wind. Over the rough ground, where the gray-green beach plant *pōhinahina* creeps low, come Big Red and Angel, aging horses now out to pasture, retired from days when cowboys rode upon their backs.

Damien's presence pervades Kalaupapa, though Saint Philomena's is the only tangible evidence of the stocky, stubborn priest whose Catholic superior called him "tempestuous and ill-bred."

But from the land itself, and from the sea, and from its stark natural beauty, the peninsula breathes with a peace and serenity all too scarce at the end of the 20th century. Perhaps the *mana* has transformed the horror of Damien's time, softened the sadness of only a thousand gravestones standing where perhaps 8,000 souls are laid to rest.

Henry Nalaielua has lived 55 of his 70 years here. Kalawao was gone before he arrived. And now most of Kalaupapa is gone, too. The "new" Baldwin Home where he first stayed was torn down in 1951. At the Bishop Home for Girls, all that remains is Saint Elizabeth's Convent, occupied by a few aging nuns. The 1930s hospital burned down in 1989.

"The houses have just rotted away," Nalaielua says. "And there's so much emptiness."

Yet the windows of the remaining homes glow yellow in the evenings, the smell of plumeria drifts on the night breeze, and from the Visitors' Quarters comes the strum of a single 'ukulele.

And Henry Nalaielua, who travels now as he pleases, like anyone else, chooses to live at Kalaupapa. "There ain't no Big Macs," he says, sitting in the shade of a tamarind tree, "but the things we have here are quiet, peace, serenity. These are my people. This is my home."

Update: The number of patients at Kalaupapa has dwindled to fewer than 30, but Henry Nalaielua remains among them. In 2003 he had a one-man show of his paintings in Honolulu. In 2006 Watermark Publishing published No Footprints in the Sand: A Memoir of Kalaupapa *by Henry Kalalahilimoku Nalaielua and Sally-Jo Keala-o-Ānuenue Bowman.*

E Hoʻi Mai: Coming Home

1998

As a child growing up in Lahaina, Maui, during the 1940s and '50s, Leinaʻala Robinson Seeger heard about her mother's *ʻaumakua*, the owl. In those years, however, the ancestor spirit was merely a myth to the Chinese-Hawaiian-*haole* girl, not a presence.

Leinaʻala grew up, went to Washington state to attend college, law school and library school. Then she carved out a successful, satisfying career as a law librarian at several Mainland universities. By 1989, she was director of the law library at the University of Idaho.

In late February 1995, she got news from Maui that her mother was gravely ill. Outside her snowy Idaho window, an owl appeared. It came each night for two weeks, until she left for Hawaiʻi.

"When I got home, I went immediately to see my mother," she remembers. "I felt that she had been waiting for me. When I left the hospital, a fine rain was falling. I tried to remember what the rain meant. Within an hour, a nurse called to say my mother had passed away. Then someone told me the rain was her, saying goodbye."

Leinaʻala returned to Idaho. "The owl came one more night," she says. "And then no more."

She knew then, after more than three decades away from home, "It was my turn to be the keeper of the family." Two years later, she moved back to Hawaiʻi.

E hoʻi mai. It means "come home." The message comes in whispers and cries, and in songs in the heads of Hawaiians living away from the Islands. Seeger heard it clearly from an owl. Elementary school teacher Bill Laeha heard it first in France. Artist Herb Kawainui Kāne, who spent most of his first 40 years in the Midwest, knew when he was 10 that someday he would take his permanent place in his father's homeland.

Like most Hawaiians, Herb Kāne is a wondrous ethnic mix. He was born in Minnesota in 1928 to a Danish mother and a Chinese-Hawaiian adventurer from the Big Island's Waipiʻo Valley. His father, born in 1895, had worked on the Honokaʻa Sugar Plantation in the early days of the Territory of Hawaiʻi. Deciding he wanted to see all of America, Herbert Mock Akioka Kāne and a friend enrolled in an auto mechanics school in Kansas City. Then he roamed around on his quest, never lacking work, for cars were rolling off assembly lines but mechanics were few. He planned to return home when his itchy feet cooled off.

But while working for Ford in Marshfield, Wisconsin, the car company made him an offer he couldn't refuse: partnership in a Ford dealership. He married Dorothy Christina Hansen, and they had Herb and a younger son.

His parents' marriage "did cause some talk," Kāne says today. "But my father didn't encounter prejudice. He was so different that no stereotypes applied. But he told me and my brother that we would have to do twice as well as the *haole* kids in school. He really pushed us. B's were not satisfactory."

Kāne's father maintained a second home in Hilo, where young Herb spent part of his elementary school years. The family often spent the summer months in Waipiʻo, with Dorothy gamely doing the family laundry in the river.

In 1936, Kāne recalls, "My dad knew war was coming. Everybody thought he was crazy, but he'd been in the Far East, and was afraid Hawaiʻi would be attacked. He moved us to Wisconsin."

Two years later, Kāne's Danish grandfather died. His last words to his young grandson were, "Always remember you are a Viking." He pronounced it "Vikking."

But in his heart, Kāne knew that someday he would go home. To Hawaiʻi.

The elder Kāne's prediction, of course, came true. Pearl Harbor was attacked by Japanese war planes on December 7, 1941. Within two weeks, he enlisted in the Navy at age 46.

After the war, "When my father came out (of the military), I went in," Herb recalls. 'The emergency was still on, although the shooting was over. I only had a glimpse of Hawaiʻi from Pearl Harbor, on my way to the western Pacific."

Later, Kāne used his GI bill funds to study at the Art Institute of Chicago and the University of Chicago, where he earned a Master of Art Education degree in 1952. At the last minute, he turned down a teaching position because "I decided I should keep the brush moving. So I apprenticed at a commercial art studio for $60 a week. My dad was furious!"

But within five years, Kāne went into business for himself, building an advertising client base in Chicago, Milwaukee, New York and Toronto. Chicago was "comfortable," he says, "and an exciting challenge for a kid to survive. Still, I never felt I belonged."

In the early 1960s, Kāne finally made a return trip to Hawai'i. Those were the days of disembarking on the runway of the old John Rodgers airport, back when personal greeters did more than hold up signs to round up dazed tourists on a package vacation. "I got off the plane and smelled the flowers in the air. A girl wearing a hat with a feather *lei* looked at my name on the passenger list and said, 'Welcome back to Hawai'i, Mister Ka-ne.' She didn't pronounce it 'Cane.' I knew I was home."

Nonetheless, Kāne returned to Chicago to continue his career.

Several years later, in 1970, he and his father were planning to come back together. "He was going to introduce me to his old friends in Waimea and Kohala," Herb recalls. "He even told me I should move back for good to 'make a contribution.'

"He died just before the trip."

But Herb came anyway, driven by regret, looking up his dad's friends on his own.

Herb was also driven by researching ancient-style Polynesian voyaging canoes for a series of large-scale paintings. Although he learned how the canoes were built, no one knew how they performed. "The best experiment would be to build an actual canoe," Kāne says. "I had in my mind the idea that the canoe was the central cultural object in all of Polynesia. I wanted to see if bringing it back as a living thing would stimulate the growth of the cultural renaissance."

In late 1970, he moved to Hawai'i, began working as an architectural consultant and bought a cottage near Maunalua Bay at Kuli'ou'ou—banyan tree in the back, *hau* terrace in the front.

A youngster named Nainoa Thompson—destined to become today's Hawaiian master navigator—belonged to a paddling club that kept canoes across the canal. Some of the paddlers began modeling for Kāne. A few, including Thompson, sailed with him.

Kāne and several friends founded the Polynesian Voyaging Society to build his visionary canoe. Kāne served as primary designer, construction supervisor and first captain of the *Hōkūleʻa*, which was launched in 1975.

As soon as *Hōkūleʻa* finished her maiden long-distance voyage—to Tahiti and back—Kāne moved to Kona. It was here he discovered perhaps his finest treasure. Among memorabilia in a long-forgotten wooden box lay a manuscript. The 150 typed pages told a story that began at the turn of the century: Herbert Mock Akioka Kāne's memoir of his youth in Waipiʻo Valley.

Such a home place—and a longing to connect with his father—formed the core of Bill Laeha's quest.

He graduated from Radford High School on Oʻahu in 1972, floundered at Leeward Community College, and traveled to Switzerland in 1974 as part of a one-year student overseas program. Laeha also visited France, where he was impressed by the culture because it was not governed by, in his words, "the almighty dollar." He returned to Hawaiʻi after the summer when his father's cancer took a turn for the worse. His dad died that October.

In earlier times, the elder Laeha, a teacher at ʻAiea High School, had taken his three sons and daughter to his childhood home in Laupāhoehoe on the Big Island each summer. "The ocean was his tool for teaching us," Laeha says. "But it was a unique form of learning, without language. We had to pay attention. If you weren't alert, the water would slap you around, and you'd get nailed. I learned all my motor skills by climbing coconut trees, swimming, just being with the land."

But as a Chinese-Hawaiian-Japanese teenager in a high school populated by kids from U.S. military families, Bill says, "I needed a Western explanation of life. Dad wouldn't give those answers. I felt shortchanged. And angry."

After his father died, Laeha floundered for several more years, working in a lunch wagon and at Kuilima Golf Course. In 1979, he enrolled in an architectural drafting program at San Diego's Palomar College. There, he met Nancy Ellen Widfeldt from Nebraska, an English-German girl who thought Hawaiʻi was a dream place. "She had a solid, centered heartbeat about her, a certain honesty and warmth," Laeha says. "It was the heartbeat of my dad."

He and Nancy moved to Anchorage, Alaska in 1981 Laeha went to work as a draftsman, they married, and Nancy bore him two sons—Jason in 1984 and Evan in 1986. Laeha looked at his sons bundled in Alaskan snow-suits, unable to play outside for more than 10 minutes because of the cold, and his mind filled with visions of Laupāhoehoe summers wearing nothing but shorts, of scampering up coconut trees and of walking barefoot over surf-sprayed lava. The visions also included spending time with aunts, uncles, cousins and grandparents.

In 1987, Laeha moved his family home. "Home is where I wanted my boys to spend the most impressionable part of their lives," he explains.

He then set his feet firmly on the path of his father, mother and grandfather, and enrolled at the University of Hawai'i-Mānoa to become a teacher. Life felt better.

But a piece was still missing.

In the summer of 1994, a lifeguard on Kaua'i told Laeha about the nearly lost Hawaiian martial art, *lua*. A weekend class would be held in October on Moloka'i. Bill called the lifeguard later for the dates. "I put you on the class list," the lifeguard said. "Go. Eight o'clock Saturday."

Laeha recounts the story: "I couldn't find any more information. It was the weekend of the Moloka'i-to-O'ahu canoe race, and all the flights were booked. I woke up at 5:00 a.m. to try stand-by and waited in line with people carrying paddles. I got on the first flight out, landing at 6:00.

"But now what? Who am I looking for? And where? I hitched a ride. The guy asked, 'Where you going?' I said, 'I don't know.' I explained as much as I could, and he took me to a gym in Kaunakakai. But there was no one there. I walked to the fire station. '*Lua*?' a guy said. 'Bathroom?'"

Laeha smiles. "I stopped in a mom-and-pop store, and a short guy walked in. I knew him from somewhere. It turned out he used to teach with my dad. I told him my story, and he gave me a ride to an elementary school. I saw people dressed in black, and I shouted, 'That's them!' It was 7:55. I signed in."

Immediately, Laeha heard a chorus of guttural Hawaiian

voices punching the air: *Ā-he-hū! Ā-he-hū!*

He watched a procession of 20 *lua* practitioners chant themselves into a state of power.

Recalls Laeha, "The entry chant might as well have said, 'You're here for a reason. Pay attention.' I felt like I came off the ground. I cried. It seemed like my ancestors were singing, 'This is the gift. This is where you are supposed to be.'"

Laeha took the weekend class, then joined an ongoing *lua* school in Honolulu. In practicing the art, he's learned Hawaiian language, chant, protocol, cultural foundation and the dual nature of humans that Hawaiians characterize through the war god Kū and his consort, Hina.

"*Lua* has given me a spiritual direction," Laeha says. "It's a sense of pride in where we come from and how we relate to others. It's everything I looked for from my dad for 20 years."

Last summer *lua* and Laeha's father melded at the Laeha family reunion in Laupāhoehoe. Laeha devised ceremonies: paying respect to the ocean, touching the sea water; lighting *kukui* nut candles, a nut for each ancestor on a coconut leaf midrib; teaching 25 Laeha cousins to walk barefoot on lava and to chant the sun up in the morning.

"E ala e! Ka lā ka hikina!
I ka moana, ka moana hohonu
Pi'i ka lewa, ka lewa nu'u
I ka hikina, aia ka lā
E ala e!"

"Arise, the sun rises from the east, from the deep, deep ocean, climbing to its highest peak. From the east the sun rises."

But the *kaona*, the underlying meaning, is about Bill Laeha coming home: "Look up to the elders, teachers, ancestors. May they enlighten us … so that we may one day climb to our highest point and share our knowledge with others."

He didn't translate the *kaona* into English, for he is home. He has found his father, and so he teaches his children without words.

❦

Though Leina'ala Seeger's yearning to come home intensified after her mother's death, the voice of her father, dead for 20 years then, called perhaps the strongest.

When Seeger was a girl, the family lived beyond Lahaina, at the edge of cane fields. People thought her father was her granddad. He'd been born in 1884 and was 59 when Leina'ala was born.

Before she was of school age, Seeger tagged along with her father everywhere he went. Each day, they fed the rabbits and chickens, pigeons and ducks. She picked hibiscus and strung them on coconut leaf ribs.

"Among other things, my father had the contract to deliver mail from the wharf to the Lahaina Post Office," she recalls. "He had built a crank-engine flatbed truck we'd take to Mala Wharf to meet the mail boat captain. Then we'd make the rounds, talking story with all the different merchants. I got to meet everyone in town.

"During World War II, my dad went out of his way to take care of personal keepsakes belonging to local Japanese families. That's the kind of man he was."

She was just starting law school in Seattle, at age 30, when her father died in 1974. Later, she moved to Boston, then on to Idaho. "But no matter where I settled, whenever I said 'home,' I meant Hawai'i," says Seeger. "I longed to come back, to find a way to contribute to the home that had given me so much. I'm grateful to have a position now—director of the library at the University of Hawai'i Richardson Law School—where I can both do that and practice my profession.

"This has been a personal journey on lots of levels. Sometimes it's been a conflict of heart, mind and spirit. At times, my brain made me deny parts of myself. But my brain got logical when I listened to my heart and gut."

And then she—like Herb Kawainui Kāne, Bill Laeha and countless other Hawaiians—answered the call. *E ho'i mai.* Come home.

⸙

PRINCESS KAʻIULANI AND THE OLD GRAY MARE

2004

The email said: "I asked all my cousins who had lived at Kaʻiulani Home if they remembered the song about Kaʻiulani. They all said no, they don't think the song even exists. I think you and Jackie are both having big, fat brain farts."

The message was from my classmate Nanette—"Titi" to intimates, which is to say, everybody except the IRS. She, Jackie, myself and maybe a dozen of our slightly older or younger sisters and cousins had spent our first boarding year at Kamehameha Schools in the early 1950s at Kaʻiulani Home in downtown Honolulu. It was a desperate measure on the part of the Girls School, which had too many boarders to house on the Kapālama Heights campus.

A couple of weeks before the email, Titi, Jackie and I had celebrated the golden anniversary of our friendship. To mark it, we visited the site of Kaʻiulani Home at 567 South King St. and tried to sing songs we'd learned when we were 12.

The old board-and-batten house named for the tragic princess who died in 1899 had long since been replaced with the concrete and glass of Kawaiahaʻo Plaza.

When we lived there in 1952-53, an enormous full-length oil portrait of the beautiful Kaʻiulani loomed over us in the parlor. Rubber-treaded steps formed a central interior staircase that split left and right, leading to two wings of a dozen or so rooms. Each was spartanly equipped with a set of bunk beds, two desks, two chairs and two dressers, the surface of which we each were expected to cover with one of the two dresser scarves from the precise list of items we were to bring with us.

Outside, the yard was bounded in front by a waist-high, wrought iron, picket fence and a hedge running along King Street. Behind a high wooden fence in the back was the Mission Homes complex.

Every day, 40 of us little girls commuted by private school bus to the campus. I mean every day, weekends included. On Sundays, we attended church in the school auditorium, stiff as soldiers in the starched white dresses required for the Sabbath and other special occasions. Saturday evenings, the school bus also transported us upward for the weekly supervised social event with students from the Boys School. Often it was a movie; sometimes it was a "play night" featuring various outdoor games.

Our housemothers, Mrs. Chang and Mrs. Vincent, regimented our hours at Ka'iulani Home. Mrs. Chang was a tiny Chinese-Hawaiian grandmother in sling-back high heels. She dyed her hair black and swept it up to gain some height, the better to be supremely effective when she bored her black eyes right through a little girl's spine. Mrs. Vincent was her assistant, hardly any bigger, an ancient paper-skinned *haole* with violet-blue eyes and white hair done flawlessly in the same stylish upsweep. Many of the girls took to Mrs. Vincent, but some of them hummed "The Old Gray Mare" behind her back. Mrs. V's white hair was the inspiration, but Mrs. Chang shared equally in the dedication of the song.

It may have been our housemothers' joint hope that the after-school schedule for us—scrubbing our laundry with our knuckles against tin washboards, raking the curling red *kamani* leaves that fell daily from the tree in the side yard, polishing the dark and dreary *koa* furniture beneath the princess' portrait—would keep all 40 little girls too busy, as they say, to make humbug.

It worked for us wimps. But Jackie was much tougher.

We had not been at Ka'iulani Home more than a couple of weeks when Jackie climbed out her second-story window into the limbs of the *kamani* tree. About the moment she settled herself in the branches, Mrs. Chang happened to stroll out of her office near the front door onto the walkway that circled the house. And she looked up.

"Jac - que - line! You get inside!"

The rules didn't specify "no climbing out windows" or "no perching in trees," but there seemed to be one big blanket unspoken rule that prohibited everything a 12-year-old tomboy might naturally do. The 687 specific rules that outlined what we were expected to do struck us as ridiculous: Make your bed with hospital corners. Bedspread must have no wrinkles. Always break your piece of bread in quarters before buttering it. Wash your hairbrush and comb every Thursday and check them in with the Old Gray Mare on duty. Certainly you were not to leave the grounds.

All this goes to say that at Kaʻiulani Home, Jackie was doomed.

One afternoon, her after-school job was to squirt dirt and leaves off King Street's public sidewalk, which was outside the iron fence. While she wielded the hose and nozzle, teenage boys cruised by in a convertible, cat-calling and wolf-whistling at Jackie in her shorts. She hollered back.

Still, she might have escaped the notice of Mrs. Chang, except the boys decided that getting a rise out of Jackie was worth repeating. When they came slowly along King Street again, Jackie was ready. They hooted at her, and she doused them all—just as Mrs. Chang came out the front door.

"Jac - que - line!"

On Saturdays, most of us—Titi and I included—put on one of our two perfectly starched and ironed "outing dresses" and went to the matinee movies downtown at the Princess or Hawaii theaters. Jackie always had so many hours of detention to serve on Saturdays that she didn't get out of Kaʻiulani Home until Thanksgiving vacation.

One Saturday, Mrs. Chang assigned her and another sinner to scrub the concrete floor of the wash house. Jackie the tree climber was not only athletic, but also creative. Before long, she and her partner had a game of hockey going, with scrub brooms for sticks and a cake of soap for the puck. Inevitably, Jackie hit the puck, sending it sailing soapily out the door onto the walkway, just as Mrs. Vincent came to check on the girls' progress.

The episode may have been a first—getting detention while serving detention.

Fifty years later, surviving the whole year at Kaʻiulani Home seemed like something to celebrate.

The three of us bought *lei* and took them to 567 S. King St. Although no trace of the old house remained, the iron fence was still there. A park bench and a public restroom occupied the spot where the wash house had stood. In the ʻEwa side yard, the old *kamani* tree shaded coarse grass. Someone had encased the base in a concrete planter in which a thicket of *lauaʻe* ferns grew.

We leaned our *ʻokole* against the rim of the planter, looking at our shadowy images in the glass walls of the new building as if they were rotund gray ghosts of little girls.

After we left our *lei* for Princess Kaʻiulani in the tree, Jackie said, "OK, we have to sing."

"What?"

"The song to Kaʻiulani."

But none of us could remember it. Titi didn't think it had ever existed.

"OK, we'll sing something else," Jackie said, and then launched right into:

"The old gray mare
She ain't what she used to be!"

The song seemed as pertinent as it had been 50 years before. We all laughed. And on the next downbeat, Titi and I joined in, belting out the rest of the words under the old *kamani* tree:

"Ain't what she used to be,
Ain't what she used to be.
The old gray mare
She ain't what she used to be,
Many long years ago."

༄

THE LONG WALK HOME

2004

Three a.m. Kailua, O'ahu, in mid-November, winter rains began two weeks ago.

Kapono Aluli Souza sets out in the stormy dark from Ulupō Heiau on the second leg of his annual *huaka'i*, or voyage, that will snake around the entire island of O'ahu. His journey is modeled on the ancient annual observance of Makahiki, the Hawaiian new year and season of peace, a time long gone when chiefs and priests representing Lono made four-month walking circuits of their islands.

This night, as Kapono walks, he carries an 18-foot staff topped with a carved stone image of the ancient god Lono. White banners, symbol of Lono, hang from the cross piece.

A man appears from nowhere and starts walking beside him.

"He was a practitioner of *lua*, the Hawaiian martial art," remembers Kapono months later. "At Waimānalo, the strong Kona winds blew out our camp, but he stayed. He found a piece of turtle shell there, and that was his *ho'okupu*, his offering, to Lono. Then he disappeared. I never knew his name."

For Kapono, such occurrences—less and less unusual—are pieces in the puzzle as he seeks his true purpose in life and a solid identity as a Hawaiian. Makahiki is the frame he is using to put the pieces together.

As a child Kapono knew little of Makahiki, and in that he was like most people in the Islands: It had been too many generations since anyone had celebrated the season for it to be known. Instead, in the huge family of Kapono's maternal *tūtū*, or grandmother, famed Hawaiian composer Irmgard Farden Aluli, the emphasis was on music. Yet Kapono never learned to play an instrument, and he grew up marked by asthma, a sickly child unable to play sports. When he couldn't breathe—at times he thought he was dying—his *tūtū* would calm him with *lomilomi*, the Hawaiian healing art of massage.

"There was this feeling that came from her," he says. "It was *aloha*! That's what helped me, her healing touch. My grandma's *kuleana*, responsibility you are born with, was to perpetuate *aloha* through music. She spoke to me, even scolded me, about my *kuleana*."

Even as a youngster, Kapono knew his *kuleana* lay in the healing arts, and when he graduated from Kamehameha Schools in 1991, he became a *lomilomi* practitioner. But his mind and heart continued questing. When he studied the works of 19th-century Hawaiian historians, he read about Makahiki.

"Hey!" he thought. "We have Chinese New Year. We have Western New Year... But this is Hawai'i! Why don't we have Hawaiian New Year? It's a whole season!"

He first took action in 2001 when he was 28.

"I was raised Hawaiian, and yet I knew something was missing," he says. "I needed to find a way to reconnect with what's important. Our ancestors had a period of time specifically for peace, a four-month time for harvest, celebration, competition, sharing, checking the conditions of the *'āina*, the land and the nation. Lono is a symbol representing food, harmony and sustenance. The social classes equalized in harmony. I'm thinking: 'Why was this so successful before? Why are we not doing it today? How can we find the best of then and apply it now?' To discover the answer, you have to do it. There is no book."

So he put his *lomilomi* practice on hold and set off around O'ahu, alone, wearing only a *malo* and *kāma'a*, loincloth and sandals. He carried a Lono *po'o*—a stone head carved by artist 'Imaikalani Kalahele—in his backpack, along with his cell phone. His neighbor, a distributor for a seed company, gave him outdated packets of seeds. He planted them in wet spots along the way, imagining watermelons and tomatoes sprouting in the wake of Lono, god of agriculture.

"I needed a walkabout to start to understand," he says. "At first, in the course of walking, I sort of went through 'withdrawal.' My body was sore and my mind full of clashing thoughts. But after the first moon, my mind began to quiet and my thoughts became clearer."

Not knowing the original trail around the island, he walked 137 miles, choosing his route by coupling maps and historical/archeological references with his own intuition, walking beaches and roads, highway shoulders and sometimes even drainage ditches. People stared, pointed, honked. He camped, stopping at about 15 of O'ahu's 50-some *ahupua'a*, or traditional land divisions, and at a few historical sites, organizing Makahiki games at receptive schools, occasionally giving talks about the season, planting seeds. When the Lihu'e-Kahanu-Paoa-Kea-Lono *'ohana*, a Hawaiian family from the *ahupua'a* of He'eia on the windward side, found out about Kapono's walk, they invited him to join them in opening and closing Makahiki at Mōkapu, the stunning peninsula that most people know as the home of Hawai'i's largest Marine Corps base.

"He has a vision that is practical and crazy," says *'ohana* spokesperson Donna Ann Kameha'ihu Camvel. "He's got energy, youth, vigor, charm. He's so good with people, with children. When he conducts our games with kids, he brings out the competitive spirit, but flavored with respect and honor."

Childhood asthma long gone, Souza today is the picture of an athlete, a warrior of old, his body even resembling the muscular carved temple images of ancient times. He's also charmingly eloquent—passionate convictions tumble from his mouth in the King's English or in Pidgin, as the occasion requires.

"We cannot go completely back in time," Souza says. "But the challenges we have today are the same as those our ancestors faced: land, power, resources and the politics that go with those. We can use the principles of Makahiki now."

Makahiki prevailed in the Islands each winter for hundreds of years. Traditionally, it began when Makali'i, or the constellation of the Pleiades, first appeared in the Eastern evening sky, anytime between mid-October and late November. During the *huaka'i* that followed, the Lono entourage, including champion athletes, called at each *ahupua'a*, where they conducted ceremonies and collected offerings of food, *kapa*, woven mats, feathers and other valuables. Then the officials released the *kapu*, the elaborate taboo system of the god Kū, who prevailed during the other two-thirds of the year. With the lifting of the rules and protocols, chiefs and commoners could mingle freely, resting from work, exchanging news, feasting, dancing and enjoying exhibition boxing and other athletic competitions. Kapono likens the festival to an extended version of Thanksgiving, Christmas and New Year's celebrations.

Makahiki was in progress when Captain James Cook arrived in Kealakekua Bay on January 14, 1779. Some say the sails of the *Resolution* and *Discovery* so resembled the flying banners of Lono that the captain was mistaken for an incarnation of the god.

Makahiki continued annually for another four decades. Then, Kapono says, it stopped abruptly with the destruction of *heiau* following the death of Kamehameha I in 1819. His heir, Liholiho (Kamehameha II), was in his early 20s and no match for two exceedingly strong women: his mother, high chiefess Keopuolani, and the late Kamehameha's favorite wife, Ka'ahumanu. The two women provoked the breaking of the *kapu* and abrogated the ancient gods. By the 20th century, Makahiki celebrations were reduced to a few games, played as a curiosity by school children on a single day in November.

Since the Hawaiian Renaissance began in the 1970s, more and more Hawaiian groups have resurrected Makahiki—in various forms, because no one knows exactly how it was conducted. Some incorporate a short march into a weekend of ceremony and games. The Protect Kaho'olawe 'Ohana has conducted Makahiki opening and closing ceremonies on Kaho'olawe for some two decades, including a one-day, cross-island version of the *huaka'i*. Pā Ku'i-a-Lua, a cultural and educational group, has observed Makahiki in Punalu'u on O'ahu since 1997. Sometimes as many as 300 people come, including children from a number of schools.

"Originally, Makahiki was more of a sharing of resources with the *ali'i*, the ruling chiefs," says group founder and *kupuna* Richard Paglinawan. Games included foot races, fencing, several kinds of wrestling, boxing, throwing and sliding of darts and spears, oratory and the checkers-like game of strategy, *kōnane*. Because competitions showcased combat skills, strength and endurance, Paglinawan believes the *ali'i* also used Makahiki to recruit warriors.

"But when Kamehameha I united the Islands in 1795, there was no more need for standing armies," he says. "The games became exercises. Kū disappeared. Then, in 1819, the *kapu* system went belly-up and Makahiki fell into disuse. I'm glad it's coming back in a new form. It develops pride and deals with rootedness. It raises people from the intellectual level to that of practitioner. You can get in touch for real."

Kapono agrees with Paglinawan. "Makahiki is a season when there is no *pilikia*, no trouble. No *hewahewa*, no errors," he says. "It's *noa*, freedom from protocol, freedom of information. It's time to *kūkākūkā*, talk to each other. Makahiki made the *ali'i* approachable to the *maka'āinana*, the commoners. If today's politicians were smart, they would come with me on the *huaka'i* to connect with the people."

Since the first year, a few others—although no politicians—have joined him for portions of his walk, including the mysterious *lua* practitioner. Now Souza covers his *malo* with a *pareu*—a wraparound cloth—to minimize the attention he draws. And he walks mostly at night when there is little traffic, wearing a light jacket against the chill.

"At night, everyone is sleeping but you and the ancestors. Everything smells different, the *maile lau li'i*, the wind, the sea, the rain. I hear the ocean, the wind, the mongoose in the bush. These are the sounds the ancestors heard. They smelled the *maile*, the *pili* grass in Nānākuli. It's a time when you can pick up on *hō'ailona*, signs, interpreting them in ways that make sense. It's a time of insight."

It came to him on one of these nights that Makahiki is a societal healing. "It was unity—*lokahi*—and balance—*pono*—all conscious during those four moons, a way of immersion in peace. It seems like practicing Makahiki can help us find our *kuleana* as individuals, families, communities, a nation, a country.

"Walking is a universal act, a symbolic act to move people," he says. "Notice Moses, Gandhi, Martin Luther King, Jr. Our Hawaiian ancestors showed us you can change the paradigm by the act of walking. It's a detox, physically, mentally and spiritually."

Yet even Kapono is subject to the pressures of modern life. Near the end of his *huaka'i* in March 2003, when he'd been "power walking" through mud and floods for two weeks, trying to be at certain places at certain times, he pulled a muscle so badly it crippled him completely.

He had forgotten one of the big lessons he'd learned: After some days, or even weeks, of walking, the *'aumākua*, spirits will talk. "But this has to be at their pace, not yours," he says. "Slow, to receive revelation, understanding, insight. Eventually you begin to see your relationship with everything and with yourself."

The injury, he believes, "was my body and the universe telling me to slow down." But he had another firm date: to close Makahiki at Mōkapu with the Lihu'e-Kahanu-Paoa-Kea-Lono *'ohana*. The universe provided for him. Most people sympathized with Souza's plight. But only one, elder Makanani Atwood, a *kōnane* master he'd met earlier in the year during Makahiki ceremonies on Kaho'olawe, said, "I'll walk for you."

Kapono drove the support van and Atwood walked the last 30 miles, from Kahuku to Kualoa, in a storm. On March 6, Souza, in keeping with ancient ceremony, was ferried by canoe from Kualoa, across Kāneohe Bay, to the closing ceremonies at Mōkapu, where he had begun the pilgrimage the previous October.

On that day, Makahiki ended under a bright sky. The ʻohana, their guests and a few families waited on the sand for the canoes bearing Kapono and the image of Lono. The entire image was now completely wrapped, to mark the end of the Lono season and the beginning of Kū time.

A pū, conch shell trumpet, was blown from one of the canoes; another answered from shore. Thirty or so fifth- and sixth-graders, who had been studying Makahiki and Mōkapu with ʻohana members Manu Suganuma and Donnie Camvel, did an ʻoli aloha and haka, a chant and a dance.

"Totally excellent!" Camvel beamed after the students performed. "You guys were awesome!"

Makahiki was officially over. The airy tones of a nose flute drifted in the air as the canoes were hauled ashore and people shared a casual lunch. Then it was Kū time again. Back to work.

In the fall, when it's time for Makahiki again, Kapono Souza will walk once more, and he invites everyone to walk with him. To him, everyone means all local people, regardless of ethnicity, and Island visitors, too.

"Come. Join us," he says. "Bring whatever you have lots of: time, energy, money. Participate, celebrate or donate. This is broadband, direct from the ʻaumākua. Express aloha and get it back! This is the time of peace, and Hawaiʻi is the Geneva of the Pacific! Give it life! E ola!"

7

Looking through Mirrors

❧

A speaking gourd, the old school,
connections far afield and
finding you're not alone after all

VOICE OF THE BELOVED

2002

The morning Kū and Hina joined, I knelt in the low-tide, reef-protected shallows of Mokulēʻia, sandals cast onto the dry sand and skirt hiked up around my hips. My inappropriate dress testified that I had not expected an encounter with the ocean—or with a gourd, or with "Mama," *kupuna* Betty Jenkins' 90-year-old mother, Elizabeth Ellis.

Nor was I thinking of the progenitor Hawaiian gods, the archetypal male and female. My purpose was to learn more about the *kupuna* role at the Office of Hawaiian Affairs. Aunty Betty had invited me to a cultural workshop for OHA staff members she was holding at her beachside home. I expected motivation and morale building. You know, a pep talk about the good of the organization, the glory of being a corporate cog.

I had met the gracious Aunty Betty once before, so I should have known there would be a twist. Should have known my status as observer would last barely minutes.

The first clue was her home's name: Kai Hāwanawana. Whispering sea. Then I spotted 30 or so dry-but-dirty gourds sitting on her rain-washed lawn.

"*Nanā ka maka*," Aunty Betty said to 20 assembled employees and me. "Look at these *ipu*. They have had a hard life. They've been exposed to rain and sun, and they are covered with dirt and mold. But listen to them. One will call to you. Do not pick one up and put it down to choose another. Let one call. *Hoʻolohe*. Obey."

When nearly everyone else had taken one, I walked slowly to the band of gourds. Of the remaining eight, one with a fat neck seemed like a child in need of love. I picked it up.

"*Hoʻomaʻemaʻe ma ke kai*," Aunty Betty said. Time for cleansing in the sea.

We walked our gray and dismal gourds down a slope of coarse coral sand. I strapped my watch to my tank top, hitched up my skirt and knelt at the water's edge, following instructions with the others, scouring the scum from my *ipu* with *limu* and sand.

All the *ipu* began to shine, hidden beauty of gold and brown coming out as if it were the *kaona*, the veiled meaning, of a Hawaiian chant or song. Women called to each other, holding their gourds up and turning them. "Look! Nice, yeah?"

I worked and worked in the oblique morning sun, the quiet water lapping, whispering. *Kai hāwanawana.* I scrubbed away at the bottom, the rounded sides, the neck, around the stem as withered as a baby's umbilical cord ready to fall off.

When we finished, we walked back to the house.

"How beautifully we shine when someone cares for us," Aunty Betty said. "Keep listening to your *ipu*. It will tell you its name."

I listened as I took my *ipu* through the next steps. *Ka 'oki ana.* Cut the neck. *Ho'oma'ema'e na'au.* Clean the inside, the guts. But save the seeds.

The neck was big enough that I could get my hand inside the gourd. I pulled at its dusty, dried fibers. I think I heard a small whisper, like the whisper of the sea, perhaps the rattle of seeds still bound in stringy membrane within. The voice said, "*Pilialoha.*" Beloved.

I thumped the gourd's bottom to loosen the last seeds. The sound was firm, mellow.

"Nice sound," another woman said. "*Ka Leo,*" I thought. The Voice. The next step was *Hā'awi inoa i ka ipu.* Naming the gourd.

With a formal title for the process, I knew this wasn't the time to casually write a word on the bottom of the gourd with a Magic Marker. The name would bring *mana*, the life force, living power.

"I'm ready," I said to Aunty Betty.

"Talk to Mama," she said.

Mama sat in the house, a tiny wisp of a Chinese-Hawaiian woman in a soft *mu'umu'u.* I knelt at her side with the shining, golden gourd, fearing my paltry knowledge of Hawaiian language might be so inadequate I would accidentally give my gourd a name with a hidden meaning of darkness.

"What name do you think?" Mama said.

"*Pilialoha.* It is from the name of my home, *Hale Pilialoha.*"

"Beloved," Mama said. "A good name."

"I think there's more. More came to me." I paused. I wasn't sure of my Hawaiian grammar. Maybe the rest was too stupid, or simple, or presumptuous. "*Ka Leo,*" I said. "May I call it Kaleopilialoha?" Had I really heard these words or were they wishful thinking? My heart thumped beneath my ribs as if it were inside the gourd. I did not want to be dubbed a fool.

"Yes," Mama said, her gentle, milky old eyes looking right into mine. "Yes, that is good. The Voice of the Beloved."

Aunty Betty had said the ancient people used gourds for dozens of purposes, to store things, to carry water, to keep the cadence. Are we not like gourds, to serve many purposes? Must we not cleanse ourselves inside and out to be able to do our work? When we have done all this in the right order, must we not be beautiful? The corporate pep talk was over.

The next morning I took Kaleopilialoha to the beach of my own babyhood, to the morning surf of Kailua. We sang together, Kaleo and I, knee-deep in the chop and backwash of the incoming tide, chanting what Aunty Betty had taught:

E hō mai
E hō mai
E hō mai ka ʻike mai ē
O na mea huna noʻeau o na mele ē
E hō mai
E hō mai
E hō mai ka ʻike mai ē.

Guide us from above. Help us to know the hidden meaning of the chant. Thump-thump, thump thump thump, Kaleo kept the cadence. I splashed the gourd with water. The sea, or the sky, or the spirits compelled me to talk to it.

You were born in salt water, as was I. You seem to be male, for I am female. We are all both male and female, Kū and Hina. I am the Path of the Rainbow, Keala-o-Ānuenue. But I must also be you, a voice. You were born yesterday, Kaleopilialoha, at Mokulēʻia. Today I honor you at my own beloved Kailua. You shall give full voice to *E Hō Mai.* Guide us from above. Show us the hidden meaning of the chant.

Here I was, talking to a gourd, but I didn't care if people

taking their morning beach walk thought I was *lōlō*.

I remembered *kai hāwanawana*, the whispering sea. At the end of the morning at Mokulē'ia, Aunty Betty had hugged me. "I see that you got it," she said. She held me at arm's length, smiling. And she whispered, like the sea, "The gourd is you."

༄

ALOHA, OJIBWA

1997

It's a Sunday, the Kaministikwia River drifting wide and gentle past the front gate of Ontario's Old Fort William. Inside the palisades, on a dampish patch of lawn, 15 men and women sit cross-legged on a circle of Hudson's Bay blankets. They have just begun the Ojibwa purification ceremony at Keeshigun, the annual Ojibwa weekend celebration at this living history fur trade-era fort in Canada.

I had come the day before, a writer on vacation, peeking 200 years into the past. I live in Oregon, thousands of miles from Ontario, equally far from my Hawaiian ancestors' Pacific homeland, where I was born and schooled. Today I have returned to Old Fort William, thinking to catch the canoe-building demonstration, to converse with voyageurs and clarks.

The dance ground of the day before, where I had seen a regal man in purple and a younger Ojibwa in striking black and white, lies quiet in the early morning. On the nearby lawn, slightly inside the blanket circle, a small woman intones something too softly for me to hear. I step closer. A man beckons me to the one remaining seat on the grass. I sit, remove my sandals. What to do now? I had meant to be an observer. To my left sits the purple warrior from the dance, now wearing jeans and a crumpled white shirt. Before him on the ground, grasses smolder in an abalone shell. He whooshes the smoke over his head, around his body. Then he whispers to me: "Remove your jewelry to smudge."

My insides churn like the volcanic middle earth, reminding me how I hate well-meaning but ignorant strangers appropriating my people's ceremonies, how I despise arrogant tourists denigrating our ancient gods. What to do? Clearly the warrior expects me to "smudge."

My rings stick. I lick my finger, force the first ring over my knuckle. The bowl of smoke passes around the entire circle clockwise, back to me. I don't know what to do. I look to my new friend. He just nods. I lean over, inhaling cautiously. To my surprise, the smoke is calming. I turn my hands over it, as if drying them. I waft the smoke toward my face. I hand the bowl to my friend. It feels like a chalice.

The bowl passes back to the elder leading the group. She smudges last, "as a sign that no one is better than any other." Those who are Christian, she says, may recite the Lord's Prayer in Ojibwa. A few people do. She opens the circle to other prayers, exhorts us to include all people in our supplications, tells us that's why Indians refer to four colors, for all the people of the Earth. She says it is up to us to set things right.

In the silence, an ax splitting firewood rings out from across the fort's main square. To my right, a white man prays for the black birch dying from acid rain. A woman across the circle confesses how embarrassed she is to be white, how she carries the sins of the fathers. My friend on my left prays: "I thank the Great Spirit for the gift of sight to see the beauty of the Earth, for the gift of smell ... the gift of hearing ... I thank the Great Spirit for the privilege of having a family to care for."

To me his English words from his Ojibwa heart are like new fire under a full kettle. I think of how I renounced Christianity long ago, of meeting an old Mohawk chief some years later. He looked at me carefully and said, "What are you? I see in your eyes that you must go back to your people." Now, at words from another Indian, the reservoir that is my heart bursts. My eyes fill with tears. My nose begins to drip, but I dare not wipe it. And then, almost choking, I do something I have not done since I was a Sunday school child: I pray by myself out loud. "I pray for my people," I begin, choking, "who are Hawaiian. I pray for my people, who are the people of all the Earth. I pray that we let the Earth heal us, that we in turn might heal the Earth." I have finished. I try not to sniffle.

The elder looks up. "Thank you," she says. "Thank you." She and two young Indian men flanking her take up rattles, and sing in Ojibwa. The ceremony is over.

My new friend, the purple warrior, speaks. Vernon Kimball, a name as Indian as mine is Hawaiian, a name because our grandmothers or our grandmothers' grandmothers married the white men who came to their lands. Vernon wants to know about Hawaiians. I tell him how I go home twice a year to learn, to write about my people. He asks if I would speak a few words at the dancing in the afternoon. I am a writer, not a speaker. I sweat fear, thinking about how large the crowd was yesterday. Hundreds, maybe a thousand. I swallow hard, and I think, "No." And then I hear myself say, "Of course."

In the afternoon the sun beats down and the drums begin. Six singers wail in a center shade pavilion. Dancers of America's first nations wind around the circle in waving ranks, moccasined toes keeping the rhythm, point-step, point-step. I am squeezed among the spectators. Around the curve comes the young man I saw yesterday in the dance with Vernon. Three-fourths of his face is painted white. His long black hair flows over his white bone breastplate. Eagle feathers on his head and back fan with power, black leggings striped with white.

Vernon steps out of the dance, leans toward me and says, "Come." I follow. He introduces me to the announcer, who says, "In five minutes, at the end of this song."

Vernon takes my hand and lays it open. "I have the traditional gift for you." He lays a large pinch of tobacco in my palm, and slides back into the dance. The tobacco is a light rusty brown, fine in texture. I close my hand over it and with my fist I press a little writing tablet against my leg. With my other hand I write some notes. My pen struggles. What will I say? My handwriting careens nervously over the small page. I hear my name on the speakers. My heart thumps like the drums, my perspiring hand clutches the tobacco.

"*Aloha.* I am native Hawaiian." My voice comes from the speakers slowly, clearly. I feel like I have unwrapped in front of the whole world a secret I should never have kept. People listen. "I bring greetings to all of you and especially the Ojibwa and other nations, from the aboriginal people of our Islands in the middle of the Pacific Ocean. We share a similar history of losing our traditional lands. We also share a similar commitment to regaining and perpetuating our culture."

My scrawly notes look to me like someone else wrote them. But I know the voice I hear is mine. "One hundred years ago our king gave us the words that are now the state motto: *Ua mau ke ea o ka 'āina i ka pono.* The life of the land shall flourish when all is set to rights."

I hand back the microphone and stand beside the emcee. The drums resume. And out of the dancers comes the young man in black and white. He takes my hand, holds on to it, locks his eyes into mine. "I shall always remember your words," he says. "Thank you."

The announcer thanks me, the elder from the purification

ceremony thanks me. Vernon thanks me. I walk away, sit on a wooden box to recover. Again, I fight tears. I am proud of myself, a native person standing among other native people, standing to be counted.

But I must do something with Vernon's tobacco, now sculpted by sweat and shaped by the life line of my hand. I sit on the box, my tobacco hand as useless as if it were in a sling. I cannot throw this gift away. I must honor its sacred meaning. In a few moments it comes to me: I'll wrap the tobacco and take it home, to offer it to Pele, our goddess of the volcano. I'll offer it for all of us trying to keep our heritage alive as we face the turn of another century. To Hawaiians, Pele is the literal, fiery force that destroys the old land and builds the new. To me she also is the symbol of my people's rebirth, and of mine, as we rise from the shards of our shattered culture. From Pele's ever-dynamic work is formed the Earth.

I fetch a paper towel from the ladies' room, carefully wrap the tobacco in it and walk down the path that leads out of Fort William along the wide and gentle Kaministikwia River, down the path that leads from this land of strong and gentle warriors to my homeland in the middle of the Western sea.

༄

BACK TO THE BASTION

1999

The year: 1957. Age: 16. We were junior boarders, about 20 girls hoofing it down the hill to KSB—Kamehameha School for Boys—for Exchange Dinner. The dinner happened but once a year, so we ardently desired to be our most attractive.

In eighth grade, on the sleeping porch in Dorm M at the fortress school on Kapālama Heights, we had pushed all our beds to the window, the better to partake of moonbeams to make us beautiful. As we got older, we taught each other to shave legs, pluck eyebrows and bobby-pin perfect pin curls. For Exchange Dinner, we encased our waists in three-yard skirts and our feet in flats. Some girls even had pink or blue flats.

Anyone knows socks with flats is like wearing a sweatshirt under your prom gown. But just before we left for KSB, the decree came down: It's drizzling. You must wear socks.

Halfway down the switchback walk to Exchange Dinner, we peeled our socks off and stuffed them in the crannies of a stone wall. We showed off our ankles to the boys, then, on our way back up the hill, re-dressed our feet. But for a fink of a chaperone, we would have eluded doom.

Instead, Pink Slips—the paperwork of Detention—and the rolling thunder god-voice of the KSG—Kamehameha School for Girls—principal propelled key phrases into posterity: Painted Hussies! Primordial Skin Sensations!

May detention save our souls.

After four decades, last year I returned to the Victorian bastion for Alumni Week and, a few months later, as writer-in-residence. I trod again upon the very stairs that figured in the crime. In the concrete halls and behind rock walls, phantoms jostled, ghosts of old maid Mainland schoolteachers and widowed housemothers clucked at the new teen girls in their jeans and crop tops peopling the halls as latter-day hussies.

༄

Kamehameha went co-ed in 1965. Now, at *my girls' school*, boys clog the halls and sprawl in the classrooms. The student handbook forbids "displays of affection," but girls twine themselves into the arms of boys sitting on railings. In the name of Old Maid Saints, where are their socks?

I start teaching the first Monday of April in Haleakalā 102, where I had marred my GPA with a C in typing for being fast but rottenly inaccurate. On the *lānai* outside I wrote my first *haiku*, a ditty about a *puka* in sunset clouds, while I, as dining hall *luna*, waited to ring the chimes calling captive students and teachers to their dinner tables set for eight with knife-fork-spoon and butter spreader.

At each round table sat hostess, waitress, faculty member, and *kua'āina* plebes learning to be ladies. The greatest challenge to a hostess: If one person was absent on pie night, she had to cut seven equal pieces.

When the pie was gone and we had placed our napkins to the left of the plate, we sang *a cappella* three-part harmony in that high-ceilinged echo chamber. Often it was "'Imi Au I Au 'Oe." I Am Searching for Thee. Without socks.

Now the dining hall is the art department and the kids eat in a mayhem cafeteria.

The kids in Haleakalā 102 look so young. Which means I must appear as old as the Pleistocene alumnae who occasionally came as dinner guests to eat an eighth of a pie and listen to "'Imi Au I Au 'Oe."

Despite today's bare *piko* between crop top and jeans, the kids in Haleakalā were shy. Until the day of the stink fut bridge.

Those foul words—titter, titter, then blatant giggling—came in a recording I played of storyteller Mākia Malo recounting his 1930s O'ahu childhood. The featured bridge, where Kamehameha Highway plunges through the mangrove swamp near He'eia Kea, still stinks.

I uttered "stink fut" myself, thus positioning myself in the same admirable category as writer Rodney Morales, who recently had read on campus the unexpurgated version of his own work and subsequently drew to the English Department a slew of irate phone calls from Mormon mothers.

The day after my stink fut episode, Lois-Ann Yamanaka read to another class from her most recent novel, *Blu's Hanging*. Having been warned of the Morales morality incident, she pointedly censured herself: "'Oh—ah—heck with you,' she said. "'You can just—ah—buzz off.'"

After I brought up the stink fut bridge, the word "crap" escaped my lips once or twice, especially in answer to inquiries about first drafts and writer's block. And, after that, my young charges, their boy hands on girl bodies, their girl socks nowhere to be seen, began to write like real people.

Listen to your Hawaiian heart, I told them. Listen to the *'āina*. Life is made up of relationships, of dualities. Our ancestors composed chants about all this, in layers of metaphor. Write, now, in English, about your name, your home, about being Hawaiian. Write a gift for someone. Talk to an older person and get him or her to tell you a story. Every day, sit outdoors and be quiet, and make an entry in your *'Aina* Journal.

> *4/8/99 as I sit on the damp porch I carefully listen to the music of the rain. I hear the rhythm of the rainfall … Nature's percussion beating down on the earth, leaving pieces of heaven here to remain. I glance at my neighbor's shingled roof and see the rainwater cascade in deliberate successions. A single raindrop comes to the end of its journey as it falls from the heavens, rolls down the roof and nestles in the yearning land.*
> —Jordan Lee

At the end of nine class sessions, 93 students turned in 24 pounds of writing. I read my way through the stacks for more than a week.

Some of the writing came computer-printed, some scrawled in pink tinsel ink. Ekona Ravey wrote about his Hawaiian name entirely in Hawaiian. I stared. I marveled.

Some of these kids have taken Hawaiian language for five years. In my dad's day, the school forbade students to speak Hawaiian. In my day, we studied Hawaiian for six weeks of seventh and eighth grade.

Even in Abraham Pi'ianaia's eighth grade class, we never got past parts of the body. *Maka, pepeiao, papalina*. Eye, ear, cheek. *Ihu, waha, pu'uwai*. Nose, mouth, heart.

One day Mr. Pi'ianaia gave an oral quiz.

"The word for toe?" He pointed at Marcella Choy.

Marcella was both ignorant and impish: "To'e," she piped.

I studied Ekona's upright black calligraphic letters forming a perfect square block on a lined notebook page, like a tablet of runes made of vowels and diacritical marks. I marveled again. And wept, for I could not read it.

I discovered that some students staunchly favor sovereignty. Others are flatly opposed.

One wrote that "Hawai'i was an independent nation a long time ago, the 1940s to be exact," but it was overthrown in the 1950s and became a U.S. state.

I started to chuckle, but the kid was more informed than I at the same age. In the mid-'50s, just before Hawai'i became a state, we knew mainly that our buildings were named for dead chiefs of a dead kingdom. Except the KSG library. William O. Smith was an original Bishop Estate trustee.

Twenty years later, I discovered that he also was Lorrin Thurston's right-hand man in overthrowing the Kingdom of Hawai'i.

In Dorm L at the alumni reunion—I mean Kina'u Hale, because the school likes being Hawaiian now—I take comfort in familiarity. Yeah, there's a smoke detector in my room, and carpet on the floor. But a desk still stands in front of three-paned brass-framed windows that crank outward over the half-round Spanish tiles of the *lānai* roof below. How many times did we shine these windows by pasting them with Bon Ami and wiping it off with newspaper?

I'm thinking: These dorms—built about 1930 of stuccoed lava rock—are designed for ventilation. Unceasing wind blows into the *mauka* rooms, through the hallway via screened transoms, and out the windows of the *makai* rooms. It's June, but so cool I crank the windows shut. And for the first time—it wasn't allowed in ancient days—I pull up the sliding wood panel to cover the screen on my door to the hallway. Suddenly the truth comes to me: Ventilation, my butt. These dorms were designed for housemother surveillance.

My neighbor sharing the room-connecting sink—What? You went to class and left a spot of water on the faucet? Detention!—whispers, lest her secret float over the transom, that a "girl" from the Class of '53 has come to board for Alumni Week with her boyfriend even though she has a husband. Shh. She's only one floor beneath us.

At the opening Alumni Reception, the Reunion Gestapo chastises me for cutting off my Reunion ID Bracelet, the kind you get in a hospital. I'm too old for detention.

In seventh grade, my friend Jackie never got to go home to Pearl City one single Saturday from Labor Day to Thanksgiving because of detention. Wastepaper in the wastebasket. Wrinkle in the bedspread. Towels folded without name tag showing. Worst of all, lipping off to the housemother. Dorm advisors, they call them now.

The regimental days are gone. Nobody cares if you stay up late, or if you don't wash your comb and hairbrush on Thursday, or if the seven school dresses in your closet face the same way. Actually, girls now don't even wear dresses.

But boarding kids today—now a much smaller proportion of the whole student body—still long for home.

> *Tangible*
> *A long road up the mountain*
> *A tedious journey indeed,*
> *A reward awaits my soul.*
> *The closer I get*
> *The more steps I take*
> *The journey to recleanse my soul.*
> *Home provides mana*
> *Home instills tranquility*
> *Home is where I belong.*
> *Makawao.*
> *—Gina Kekiwi*

Affluence—some kids live in condos with swimming pools instead of plantation huts, many travel across the United States and even overseas instead of over the Koʻolau Mountains—can't change the eternal: contending with parents, wishing for a prom date, being thrilled with seeing your breath the first time you go to a cold place.

Or racism.

*One time I was in California and these guys thought
I was Mexican and they called me names. I didn't like that. They
couldn't tell that I was part white and part Hawaiian. There is
nothing wrong with Mexicans but if they were going to call me
something I rather have them call me something that I was.*
—Melanie Park

from "A Gift"
To my parents I'll give this
for thanks long overdue.
Through all the pain and trouble
You're always there to help.
Let's not forget cash.

I may think I know all
but daily I need your help
Problems with life and school
Questions about my future
And how to get to the theater.

You give me so much freedom
I often take advantage of it
I'm lucky that I'm last
You don't let me forget that
Thanks for giving me the car tonight.

You've always trusted me
and believed I'd do good
and I usually do, as much as I can
because you give me that trust
I don't have a curfew, do I?
—Jess Kaneshiro

Where are all the other K names? Kahapea, Kaialoa,
Kamaunu? Kaupiko, Kaupu, Keanu? The rolls have gone to Fujita,
Castro, Todorovich. Where once a quarter Hawaiian was the mini-
mum blood requirement, these kids rattle lists of a dozen bloods in
their veins. For many, Hawaiian is the last microscopic ingredient,
like "natural vitamin E to preserve freshness."

I ask my students to gather stories from *kūpuna*. Many of them talk with grandparents who are Chinese, Filipino or Japanese. Kevin Fong's grandfather fought in Europe in World War II with the famous AJAs of the 442nd Regimental Combat Team and the 100th Battalion.

> *My elder*
>
> *He and a bunch of his buddies went out to a restaurant to eat. They had this steak meal for $1.75, a dollar seventy-five. Then it comes time to tip. Most people are leaving tips like 25 cents so they're throwing down $2. But my grandpa folks throw down $5. That makes a $3.25 tip, almost enough for two more steak meals. The waitress' eyes got as wide as saucers. She swore my grandpa folks were mad and threatened to call the police. But they were sober and sane.*
>
> *They were stationed there for two weeks and they ate out quite often. At all the restaurants they ate, had a good time and left a 300 percent tip. Everywhere they went people thought they were mad, insane, crazy, loony, this band of Nisei Japanese men. But word of their generosity got out and they were met with great hospitality and care. My grandpa and his band had changed New Yorkers' feelings toward Japanese.*
> —Kevin Fong

Ikaika Enos took to heart my ranting about looking for dualities, and metaphorical meaning in names.

> *My name is Lanikeha. I am everything people fear. I am everything people love. I am a changeling. I am 16 years old. I am 4 years old. I am 80 years old. My name is Ikaika. I am strong. I am weak. I am outspoken, yet meek. I am a fading blossom. I am a budding rose. Maybe I'm the thorns also. Yes, I'm the thorns too.*
>
> *I am the root of many. I am the branch of many trees. I nourish. I eradicate. I am fertilizer, I am poison.*
>
> *My name is Kūkaʻilimoku. I am what you fear. I am what you need. I sustain, I destroy. I create, I obliterate. I am shelter. I am your baby blanket, your teddy bear. I am the boogeyman. The monster underneath your bed is my cousin.*

My name is Lebraun. It's French for gentle power. No one besides my daddy calls me Lebraun. I am protective. It is my solace. I am secretive. I have to be. I am resilient. I am thick-skinned. I am dark and cold.

I am predictable. I am unpredictable. My name is Kalani'ana'ole. No, I'm not named after that damn highway. I am rich. I am poor. I am evasive. I'm the best liar you've ever known. I am a master of manipulation. I am evocative. I am precious.

I am Hawaiian. I am Portuguese and German and Irish. I am proud. Damn proud. I will never back away. I will never stray away. I will never run away.

I am invincible. I am fragile. I love. I hate. I cry. I laugh, I enjoy, I covet. I breathe. I bleed. I envy. I am what you have seen, what you hope to see, what you hate to feel, what you need to survive. I am who I am.

—Ikaika Enos

I hear stories, I tell stories. I steal stories, I deal stories. I am a pipeline. I am a gossip. I find out what's happened in 40 years to my own classmates.

Ti flies stand-by, with no itinerary. She's prone to get lost, which she especially likes in England, where "some kind young person" takes her by the shoulders to turn her in the right direction and calls her "Love." She wants to make three more trips to England so she can be lost in the whole country.

Toomey travels to the Mediterranean and Europe with a minute-by-minute itinerary she thinks will prevent her being mugged, robbed, accosted, kidnapped, raped or hijacked.

She is husband-hunting for her kid sister, Carol, who is only 56 or so. At our hen party, Toomey learns the six-second stare technique from Wendy. Look into a stranger's eyes for six seconds and SMILE. He'll come and ask you something. Toomey plans to do this, but she'll duck so the guy will go for Carol.

One evening Rosemary busts out of our seated-only *hula* training. The more she dances—on her feet, using, gasp, her hips—

the more dollar bills flutter at her feet. A one-time football player throws all his credit cards. Then he flings his whole wallet. A measly former tennis player—who's been monitoring snoring in the dorms and so is awake at night anyway—pitches his room key. Ha-ha, we're too old for detention.

Lū'au the last night. We're told it's not "lū'au," it's "'aha'āina," a new old word. The school likes being Old Hawaiian now.

Getting ready is a reprise of graduation afternoon, too excited to rest, gathering in the room that has the most contraband crackseed and sushi, wearing robes and pj's and *pareu*. Worrying that a *lei* is not the right color for a *mu'umu'u*. Worrying that we'll sweat and smell stink. Worrying that we won't take our glasses and then we'll have to read something.

'Āina journal 4/11/99

It's still all right here. I guess there's too much buildings here. But at least you can still see the beauty of the land sometime. It's like our people. We're a minority in our own land. We're the mountains in the back behind of all the buildings. We're here but no one notices us. We're here that's all. I'm telling you, the mountains the ocean they are forever. The buildings will fall.
—Ekona Ravey

One student writes that "darkness is an interesting devil." Another calls the North Star the "Star of Wisdom."

Perhaps wisdom will come from some of these young hussies and their boyfriends.

My last day with my 93 kids—they are my kids, after two weeks—I answer questions and tell writer stories. And then I walk alone on the covered sidewalk where I was busted once for kissing at Sunday afternoon "calling." Today, in the same spot, a boy nuzzles a girl's neck. Kiss-kiss. Kiss some more.

I walk by them to the parking lot, and then motor down the hill. The bastion of Kapālama reels by in the rearview mirror like 40 years of movie. In a freeze-frame, the painted hussies paint themselves into the scene. *Déjà vu.*

⤳

TRUE GRATITUDE

1995

February, midsummer on Aitutaki. At 6:30 a.m. I sweat just from brushing my teeth. The atoll, nearly central in the 15 Cook Islands strung through 770,000 square miles of ink-blue ocean, swelters in its turquoise lagoon 1,200 miles south of the equator. On a map of the Pacific these specks of land might be a printing error.

This morning my daughter, Tamara, and I have hired a fisherman named Ma Tai to ferry us to Maina, a little-visited islet. Ma is gray-haired, lean and leather-brown, lacking one front tooth and the two middle fingers of his left hand.

Ma reminds me of an old family friend. My ancestors were native Hawaiian, and in addition to relaxation I have come here hoping to discover my roots in larger Polynesia. Some connections are obvious: the volcanic mountains of Rarotonga, the main island, look like a miniature of my home island of O'ahu almost 3,000 miles north. And as once was the case in Hawai'i, brown faces are everywhere—more than 90 percent of the population here are Cook Island Maori.

Maori means "the true people." In Hawaiian the same meaning belongs to the word *māoli*, but hardly anyone uses the term. The number of full-blooded Hawaiians, perhaps 8,000, is now officially "statistically insignificant." Few people speak the native language, and fewer still have so much as a house-lot of ancestral land.

In the Cook Islands we hear Maori spoken as often as New Zealand-accented English. The Maori have their language, their blood, their land. Island real estate is all ancestral: People use it, but it cannot be bought or sold.

Ma searches for English words the way he sorts through his bait bucket for the right lure. He hands us each a 300-yard spool of 40-pound-test nylon monofilament, hook and plastic squid on the end. We immediately strike two fish. Tamara hauls in her line in a neat pile; I build a 60-foot snarl in the bottom of the boat. Ma just smiles, takes my tackle, and patiently rewinds.

Midmorning we disembark in Maina's sandbar shallows.

"Barbecue," Ma says. Beyond the pale gold beach, between pandanus and palms, he balances a cast-iron griddle on a log and two coconuts. Wielding a French knife as a cleaver, he whacks each fish in thirds and flops the pieces on the grill with sliced breadfruit. Then he clutches the knife by the back of the huge, heavy blade and delicately peels a papaya.

"You eat. Please." Ma lays the food out on a rickety driftwood table. "Here. Plates." He hands us large, round leaves. Although I haven't felt hungry—it's still not much past 10:30 a.m.—with the first bite of fish I'm suddenly famished.

After snorkeling, we walk entirely around Maina, maybe half a mile, the texture of the sand underfoot and the coral patterns in the water changing every few steps. We pick up dozens of shells, every one occupied by a hermit crab. Ma sits in the shade of a pandanus checking over his fishlines and rolling stumpy cigarettes.

We head back in the mid-afternoon. The tide is so low that Ma cuts the motor and poles the last 80 yards. We step from the boat into bathtub-warm, foot-deep water. Salt mottles my thighs, and I can feel on my shoulders that my sunscreen didn't do much good.

"It's been a wonderful day, Ma," I say. "Thank you." I shake his five-fingered hand. His smile is as broad as his hat brim. He has spoken perhaps a dozen sentences all day. Now one more, seven words in eloquent order. "In my language," Ma says, "Thank you means *meitaki*."

꒳

Inescapably Hawaiian

2003

It's been 10 years, but almost everyone in Hawai'i remembers the day: January 17, 1993, a windless Sunday morning promising oppressive afternoon heat. Ten thousand Hawaiians on foot clogged all the lanes of Halekauwila Street, marching from Aloha Tower to 'Iolani Palace. It was the last day of Onipa'a, the five-day centennial observance of the overthrow of the Hawaiian Kingdom.

No drums beat, but I felt a slow, deliberate cadence in the middle of the shoulder-to-shoulder sea of Hawaiians.

"*Ea!*" A single voice rang out ahead.

"*Ea!*" A chorus answered.

Like many who do not speak Hawaiian, I did not know this word.

"*Ea!*" The chorus grew. Arms punched the air with power salutes. I asked the meaning of the word. *Sovereignty!*

"*Ea!*" I joined in as we turned up Mililani Street. Across King Street, the wrought iron gates of 'Iolani Palace were swung wide. Beyond, in ranks of *kumu hula*, the masters of dance, in full regalia on the palace steps, stood Robert Cazimero. I don't know him well. Robert helped me once with a writing project. We are both Kamehameha graduates, a decade apart. Leina'ala Kalama Heine, also a *kumu hula* and featured dancer with the Brothers Cazimero, is my classmate. That was the sum of our relationship. Or was it? For when our eyes met, we both burst into weeping, then embraced, sobbing.

"*Ea*" means "sovereignty." A few months ago—almost a decade since I shouted it on Mililani Street—I learned it also means life, breath and spirit.

Over the past decade, the press has covered the sovereignty part of "*ea*" so often that the names of leaders of Hawaiian groups seeking some form of self-governance have become household words. The press also has given much attention to certain Hawaiian cultural icons, especially *hula* and *Hōkūle'a*. But beyond, or beneath the daily news lie other questions: Why is being Hawaiian so important? We've intermarried so much no one can tell a Hawaiian just by surname or looks, or the lilt of the voice. I am a case in point, yet I am aware every day of being Hawaiian. Why are we still carrying the torch even though most of us are *hapa*—of mixed blood—in the extreme?

I sidestepped oft-quoted leaders and instead put these questions to Hawaiians practicing Western professions—psychiatrists and psychologists, pastors, a lawyer, academics outside Hawaiian Studies. They are among America's intellectual elite. Yet their stories and convictions refused to march neatly in Western fashion. Instead, their thoughts undulated in the Hawaiian way, like an incoming tide at sunrise, ideas washing over and under one another, some clear and calm, some more like breaking surf.

They would lead me to the other definitions of *"ea"*—life, breath and spirit—into the Jungian world of dreams, intuition and the collective unconscious, to bones and blood, to the despair and darkness of disconnected souls. Three of them would share especially powerful and poignant personal stories. They told how they discovered that, for them at least, being Hawaiian was utterly fundamental to their identity. In the end I would understand why I wept that day with Robert, and why we were not alone in weeping.

A psychologist and a man of the cloth laid the solid-yet-shifting sands under the sea of *"ea."*

Tom Van Culin is the vicar of St. Matthew's Episcopal Church in Waimānalo, ordained in 1990 at age 52, after some 25 years in the business world. "The identity challenge is for everybody," he said. "For me the major fight has been to integrate being Hawaiian and Christian. I was taught that *aloha* is to come face to face with the breath of God in the other person. God was with us before the missionaries came."

He floated easily to intuition, a commodity common, he said, among indigenous peoples, at least as valuable as the "Western mantra," Aristotelian reason. Then a changing tide swept him through politics—and beyond.

"In 1893, we had a fully mature and developed nation. The symbol of unity was the monarch," Van Culin said. "Then, with the overthrow, the monarch disappeared."

Van Culin comprehends the cultural effects of the overthrow by using Elisabeth Kübler-Ross' theories of grief, and other recent psychiatric work. He thinks the overthrow propelled Hawaiians into a national sorrow that has lasted more than a century. Hawaiians are stuck in anger and denial, the early stages of grief, suffering from a societal version of post-traumatic stress disorder. It is expressed externally in family violence or internally in alcoholism, drug abuse, sex abuse, overeating. The crucial connection of mind, body and spirit has ruptured.

"Unless we deal with these issues, they hold us captive," he said.

Some years ago I explained the overthrow to a West Coast *haole* friend. She said, "Forget it. It happened a hundred years ago."

But Hawaiians cannot forget. Psychologist Bill Rezentes argues that the memory of who we are and what happened to us is crucial for Hawaiians. "We not only don't want to forget who we are," he said. "We don't know how. We are influenced by East and West. But under our feet the *'āina* beckons the spirit and the soul."

In Rezentes' view, "You tap into the *na'au*—the heart and guts. Then the *koko*, the blood, the *'āina*—the land—and cultural upbringing. And then the wisdom of the ancients talks to you.

"For us, being Hawaiian matters. We used to know what canoe we came on, which *wa'a*. We still yearn to know. Knowing your *wa'a* and having your genealogy made your connection to *ākua*, *'āina*, *'ohana* and your own *na'au*."

He'd laid out the direct line from god to the individual heart via the land and family. This triangle of humanity, spirit and nature is the ultimate unity, "*lōkahi*."

"Without it," Rezentes said, "you die."

Some years before Onipa'a, I was on the verge of that kind of death. I had felt the signs since college days in Minnesota, gut-stirrings I called "aboriginal twinges." I didn't know what they meant. I thought, or perhaps wished, they would go away, but instead, over two decades, they magnified. I could not escape being Hawaiian.

I had no one like Rezentes to help me understand. I watched my father die too young from too much alcohol, a fate I wished for no one, especially myself. I didn't have violence in me either, as another classic way out. By happenstance—or divine design—I had become a journalist. Writing offered me a way to understand those twinges. I began to write about Hawaiian culture, learning as I went.

Recently I discovered I am not alone. There are many whose Hawaiian identity has pushed its way into the open air like a long-smoldering fire bursting into flame, despite blood mingled with that of other races, despite long times in faraway geography, despite years of education in the refinements of the Western world.

One of these people is Noenoe Silva. Her immediate family moved to California when she was nine. She remembers passing for white then, although her mother couldn't. After high school, in 1972 she joined the U.S. Army, a petite young feminist clerk in a combat airborne unit in Germany. When her hitch was up, she married, moved to Minnesota, divorced, moved back to California.

Then, at age 30, she came to Hawai'i to a family reunion. The cousin she stayed with danced in a *hālau hula*, a *hula* school.

"That was it," Silva said. "That December I moved home." She lived with two great aunts and some cousins.

"In May, Aunty says, 'Come put flowers for Memorial Day.' She has buckets and buckets of flowers. We divide them, so many for each grave. We go to Nu'uanu, Punchbowl, the Chinese cemetery in Mānoa Valley. We have lunch. We go to Diamond Head to the Portuguese Cemetery, eight or 10 graveyards in all. Then we go home and have a beer. I have done this every year since. Man, I am so connected. My bones are here! From time immemorial."

Soon after, in an adult education class, Silva discovered that Hawaiian language came to her easily. It led her to the world of academics, where she earned a Ph.D. in political science at the University of Hawai'i in 1999 at age 45.

In 1996, as part of her graduate work, she researched the anti-annexation and pro-Lili'uokalani activities of the Hui Aloha 'Āina (Hawaiian Patriotic League) in 1895 Hawaiian-language newspapers.

At the Hawai'i State Archives, an archivist showed her an exhibit booklet from the U.S. National Archives. It contained a photo of a single page from "PETITION AGAINST ANNEXATION." At the top of the page was a name she recognized as president of the women's patriotic league, Mrs. Kuaihelani Campbell.

A few months later, while on a personal visit to Washington, D.C., Silva went to the National Archives and asked to see the petition. She expected a few sheets of paper with a few hundred signatures. But in a tidy archival box was filed more than a ream of paper—556 pages signed in 1897 by 21,269 Hawaiians opposing U.S. annexation of Hawai'i. With the signatures on a separate petition, the total came to nearly 40,000—more than 80 percent of the kingdom's citizens.

The edges of some of the yellowed sheets crumbled in her hands, the bottom signatures falling to dust. On one page of the women's petition she recognized a name: Kauhi Lehuloa, age 58. She was Silva's great-great-great-grandmother, from Kalapana on the Big Island, where 101 women of the tiny village belonged to the Hui Aloha 'Āina, the patriotic league that circulated the petition.

"I come from some serious women," Silva said. "Why would I want to forget them?"

Silva suggested the well-echoed theory that most American immigrants came from elsewhere to start a better life. It's important for them—and their descendants—to forget where they came from.

"But we Hawaiians didn't leave our homeland," Silva said. "America came and got us. We have no reason to forget ourselves. We have a continuity of relationship with this place."

Why are so many Hawaiians so passionate about their native identity when it means living with the pain of the past? I asked two psychiatrists, trained in Western medicine, but Hawaiian by blood and heritage.

The first, Benjamin Young, who sailed from Tahiti to Hawai'i on *Hōkūle'a*'s first voyage in 1976, said, "The inclination to hang onto heritage is found in nearly every culture that experiences loss, whether through being conquered, through disease or hegemony. Hawaiians have had so much loss, it's no wonder we cling. If we don't have a sense of Hawaiianness in Hawai'i, where else will we find it? If it's not passed on, how will we retrieve it?"

The second, George Makini, focused on the Hawaiian inclination to value relationships above all else. He pointed out that in the United States the emphasis is on individuality, and "family" is defined as father, mother and children. For Hawaiians, though, family means keiki, ʻōpio, mākua wahine and mākua kāne—children, youth, adult caregivers (not just mom and dad.) And then kūkū and kūpuna—grandparents, elders. Beyond that, he said, "A drop of Hawaiian blood and we can be cousins. Which is like brother or sister. People who grow up in Hawaiian culture get their sense of identity from ʻohana. They're very connected."

In his view, the connection links individuals with community, the metaphysical and the spiritual. "It all happens in the same breath," Makini said. "Illness is an imbalance of these." And one of those illnesses is the post-traumatic stress disorder from which Van Culin feels all Hawaiians suffer.

"When the ancestors were traumatized, it was a wound to the soul," Makini said. "If you don't take care of it, you pass it to the next generation. If you do take care of it, it will heal, and you are empowered as a survivor."

The agony of it is that the trauma lasts indefinitely, for generation after generation. The beauty is that it's never too late to heal, both collectively and individually.

Historically speaking, it may be the right time for Hawaiians to start healing. For instance, attorney Keoni Agard thinks Hawaiians collectively are coming back from a century-long time-out.

"You can disconnect for 100 years, but in the spirit world it's a second," he said. "Three generations have come and gone and we've had a chance to calm overall. Some people are getting mad again, but we're better equipped to handle it emotionally and spiritually. At the time, in the 1890s, it was an awful lot to swallow. Now we're past denial and anger. It's time to resolve and correct it."

Then he volunteered part of his personal story, aware that it might sound off the wall. For him, "correcting" manifests partly in his solo law practice representing Hawaiians with land problems. In court, he stands alone, facing a phalanx of Hawaiʻi's best real estate lawyers. His own team is invisible—his ancestors and those of his clients, and the spirits of all the people who lived on the land in question.

"I believe our ancestors are still here," he says. "All we have to do is call upon them in prayer." He consults them daily—and he feels their presence in court.

It didn't sound nuts to me, which put me in an open frame of mind to meet Leilani Holmes. Her connection to that spirit world of ancestors began in Ohio.

Born to a Hawaiian-*haole* family in 1952, she was adopted as an infant by a *haole* couple living in Hawai'i. When Holmes was four, they moved from Honolulu to Cleveland.

"In Cleveland I was marked by race in an all-white neighborhood," she said. "I didn't even know what 'Hawaiian' was. I was somebody who existed only in books."

She tried to scrub away her brown skin in the bathtub. But she had dreams, of a man she now describes as "Ancestor Man," and of a woman who appeared only when she was sick.

"Ancestor Man" was old, dressed in white, no longer living. Sometimes he sat on her bed and told her everything would be all right. She used this counsel when other children called her "nigger."

"No," she told them. "I am a Hawaiian princess."

She didn't always remember his words, especially when they seemed like riddles. But she never forgot his eyes.

In high school, her parents arranged for her to attend a concert by the Kamehameha Schools Glee Club. "My parents thought they were connecting me to Hawai'i, but I was a spectator to Hawaiianness. It made me feel I belonged to neither place. I was shattered. I threw away the program, then picked it out of the trash. I looked at the names. Any of them could be my family."

In her late 20s, she moved to Southern California, where she involved herself in a *hālau hula* and a Hawaiian *hui*, in which *kūpuna*, elders, assured her she would find her blood family.

Dreams of Ancestor Man came whenever she needed courage—to face cancer and a divorce. The last dream came in 1994, while she was on leave from teaching college sociology and about to go to Hawai'i for field research.

"He told me to go up a hill to a place of sacrifice where I would look down on a confluence of tides. 'The road is easy going up,' he said. 'This is where you will meet your ancestors.' And then he said, 'What is the ancestry of experience?'"

It was a last riddle.

In Hawai'i, Holmes met a genealogist who eventually led her to a cousin, who invited Holmes to visit. The cousin's home was near an upland *heiau*, a place of worship, on O'ahu. The house was full of family photographs.

"It was like being surrounded by a forest of eyes," Holmes said. "It felt like a homecoming even though the people were almost all long dead."

In the forest of photos she saw that pair of eyes she'd known her whole life. "My God, it was him," she said. The face was young, the garb dark. But the eyes were those of Ancestor Man. He was her great-great grandfather.

During the visit, the genealogist phoned, saying that Holmes and her cousin should bathe in salt water together. In the sea below the hill Ancestor Man had described, her cousin cradled Holmes in her arms while she wept for her lifelong loss and for having her family back. While they floated in the healing water, above the hill appeared two rainbows.

In the five years since then, Holmes has never dreamed again of Ancestor Man. She feels his presence, but thinks he has finished the task that required dreams.

"The earth speaks to us," Holmes said. "Sometimes it's through bloodlines, or through the *'āina*, the land. Others don't have the ancestral roots, but they still hear the voices. People do what's righteous and what speaks to them. These issues of 'blood' and ancestry have so much deep meaning for us, so much deeper than the worlds of rhetoric and scholarship are willing to go."

Joe Chang has spent his whole adult life in that world of Western scholarship. I first met him about 1990, seeking him out after I'd read his academic paper, "Pele on Trial in the Christian Court: Western Culture as Manifest Destiny." I was surprised to find him not in Hawai'i, but in Wisconsin.

He is the youngest child in a Chinese immigrant family that ignored the fact that one of his grandmothers was half Hawaiian. Neither of his parents spoke English. His mother's attitude was, "You're Chinese and that's it."

At Catholic School, though—where his parents sent their

children because they believed the public schools were inferior—all the siblings excelled.

In the late 1960s, Chang became a professor of Shakespeare at the University of Wisconsin-Milwaukee. After teaching there for two decades, he took a year's sabbatical leave in Hawai'i.

During that year, one of Chang's nephews introduced him to Hawaiian politics and he volunteered with the Native Hawaiian Advisory Council, a group concerned with water rights. Most of all, he met Hawaiians and his sense of being one himself boomed exponentially.

He started "Return of the Native," a passionate column he wrote for years for the advisory council newsletter.

"Hawaiianness," he discovered, "is a lot more than *pā'ū* riders in a parade and Merrie Monarch *hula*, more than just blood and *mele*. It is so contrary to Western culture in its communal spirit. How do you preserve that spirit in a capitalist system?"

The core of Hawaiian society, he believes, was the *ahupua'a*, the land division that usually was wedge-shaped to include all natural resources a group of people would need, from the shore to the mountaintops. It was a geographical and political concept that promoted sharing and cooperation.

"The problem with the sovereignty movement is that the focus falls, naturally, on the political. It should be more than a movement to free us from American hegemony. If we cannot return to the *ahupua'a*, then we must, in the context of the modern world, at least learn how to reconstruct the social fabric of *aloha* and *lōkahi*."

He sees *lōkahi* as unity and agreement. "It's primarily in human relationships, but it also means cosmic harmony. And then there's *ho'oponopono*, reconciliation, as opposed to 'justice,' in which I win and you lose.

"These are not blood issues, but how people relate to each other. They are ideals that should survive. I don't disown being Chinese, but with one billion Chinese people, I don't have to protect the culture. Hawaiians are an endangered species, not just racially, but culturally. I had to discover Hawaiianness by reading or association. It was a wonderful antidote to the worst features of Western culture that breed selfishness and indifference to your neighbors."

❧

Why is the call of Hawaiian blood and heritage so strong? My quest ended with Kaleo Patterson, associate pastor at Kaumakapili Church, historically the church of the *maka'āinana*—Hawaiian commoners—and scene of many political meetings in the turbulent 1890s. Patterson is a chip off that Hawaiian block, standing often in what he calls the "front lines" of peaceful demonstrations for Hawaiian rights. And he's another guy with a Ph.D.

He echoed much of what I had already learned, that everyone wants to be connected, to be rooted, to have a home, to belong to a place. Then he added: "The *uwē* is what Hawaiians feel when they see *hula* or hear chanting."

Later I looked up *uwē* in the dictionary. "*Uwē*: To cry, weep, lament, mourn." I realized that *uwē* is what I had done with Robert Cazimero. I read the definition again. At the end of the litany of sorrow was one more meaning: To salute.

Uwē welled in me again. But this time I understood it. From all I had talked to, I had collected insights. And these insights were parts of *ea*, like gifts of peace left by a receding tide.

A few days later, I attended a public lecture. UH Hawaiian Studies professor Jon Osorio was speaking on "What Kind of Hawaiian Are You?"

He opened the session with a chant. And then he said, "*Ea.* It is sovereignty, life, spirit and breath. They cannot be separated."

In a dozen words he completed what I had discovered in the Jungian world of dreams and the unconscious, in the haunts of a hundred years, in the unexplained weeping that wells from a dark and unplumbed depth. I was not to choose among these meanings of *ea*, but to carry them together, before high tide washed them to sea again.

Works in *The Heart of Being Hawaiian* appeared previously in the following magazines and anthologies.

Aloha, Anuhea, *Aloha*, November/December 1997

Aloha,Ojibwa, *HONOLULU*, March 1997, and the native peoples' anthology *Gatherings*, Volume VI, 1995

Back to the Bastion, *HONOLULU*, November 1999

Bird in Hand, *Aloha*, September/October 1996, and the anthology *Travelers' Tales Hawaii*, 1999

Celebrating Hula Molokaʻi-Style, *Hawaii*, June 1996

Conviction, *HONOLULU*, November 1998

E Hoʻi Mai: Coming Home, *Aloha*, June/July 1998

Father of Waters, *HONOLULU*, December 1998

Finding the Way, *Pacific Discovery*, January 1994

House of Stories, *Hana Hou!* February/March 2003

Inescapably Hawaiian, *HONOLULU*, December 2002

Kahoʻolawe in Limbo, *Aloha*, September/October 1992

Kalaupapa: Home of the Heart, *Aloha*, May/June 1996

Living an Ancient Art, *Aloha*, March/April 1997

Lomilomi's Loving Touch, *Aloha*, November/December 1996

The Long Walk Home, *Hana Hou!* November/December 2004

Lua: The Ancient Hawaiian Fighting Art, *Aloha*, May/June 1995

A Night at Washington Place, *HONOLULU*, November 2001

Out for Blood, *HONOLULU*, November 1999

Perfect Balance, *Hawaii*, March 2004

Princess Kaiʻulani and the Old Gray Mare, *Island Scene*, Winter 2004

Pūnana Leo: Saving the Hawaiian Language, *Aloha*, January/February 1990

Rage, Bones and Hope, *HONOLULU*, December 1995

Reluctant Kahuna, *HONOLULU*, November 2000

Remembering Mr. Bowman, *Pacific Paddler*, February 1999

Roots, *Island Scene*, Summer 1995

Setting Things Right, *Island Scene*, Winter 1998

Tellers of Tales, *Aloha*, July/August 1997

Temples of the Gods, *Hawaiʻi Westways*, October/November 1999

True Gratitude, *Sierra*, January/February 1995

Voice of the Beloved, *HONOLULU*, August 2002 and the native women writers' anthology *Sky Woman*, 2005

The Way Back, *Sierra*, September/October 1992

Index

About the Author

Sally-Jo Keala-o-Ānuenue Bowman's articles and essays have won several Paʻi Awards from the Hawaii Publishers' Association, and her prize-winning poetry and fiction have been published in a number of literary journals. She is the co-author, with Henry Nalaielua, of the best-selling *No Footprints in the Sand: A Memoir of Kalaupapa* (Watermark Publishing, 2006). A 1958 graduate of Kamehameha Schools who holds BA and MS degrees in journalism, Ms. Bowman is a member of the Pā family from Puna and Hilo. She grew up in Kailua, Oʻahu, and now lives in Springfield, Oregon, with her husband, David Walp, and their Australian shepherd, Cap.